# SECURWARE 2021

The Fifteenth International Conference on Emerging Security Information, Systems and Technologies

November 14 - 18, 2021

Athens, Greece

**SECURWARE 2021 Editors**

Hans-Joachim Hof, INSicherheit - Ingolstadt Research Group Applied IT Security, CARISSMA – Center of Automotive Research on Integrated Safety Systems, Germany

Manuela Popescu, IARIA, USA/EU

Anders Fongen, Norwegian Defence University College, Norway

**Printed from e-media with permission by:**

Curran Associates, Inc.
57 Morehouse Lane
Red Hook, NY 12571

**Some format issues inherent in the e-media version may also appear in this print version.**



Printed with permission by Curran Associates, Inc. (2023)

International Academy, Research, and Industry Association (IARIA)
412 Derby Way
Wilmington, DE 19810

Phone: (408) 893-6407
Fax: (408) 527-6351

petre@iaria.org

**Additional copies of this publication are available from:**

Curran Associates, Inc.
57 Morehouse Lane
Red Hook, NY 12571 USA
Phone: 845-758-0400
Fax: 845-758-2633
Email: curran@proceedings.com
Web: www.proceedings.com

**Table of Contents**

# SECURWARE 2021

# Forward

The Fifteenth International Conference on Emerging Security Information, Systems and Technologies (SECURWARE 2021), held on November 14-18, 2021, continued a series of events covering related topics on theory and practice on security, cryptography, secure protocols, trust, privacy, confidentiality, vulnerability, intrusion detection and other areas related to low enforcement, security data mining, malware models, etc.

Security, defined for ensuring protected communication among terminals and user applications across public and private networks, is the core for guaranteeing confidentiality, privacy, and data protection. Security affects business and individuals, raises the business risk, and requires a corporate and individual culture. In the open business space offered by Internet, it is a need to improve defenses against hackers, disgruntled employees, and commercial rivals. There is a required balance between the effort and resources spent on security versus security achievements. Some vulnerability can be addressed using the rule of 80:20, meaning 80% of the vulnerabilities can be addressed for 20% of the costs. Other technical aspects are related to the communication speed versus complex and time consuming cryptography/security mechanisms and protocols.

Digital Ecosystem is defined as an open decentralized information infrastructure where different networked agents, such as enterprises (especially SMEs), intermediate actors, public bodies and end users, cooperate and compete enabling the creation of new complex structures. In digital ecosystems, the actors, their products and services can be seen as different organisms and species that are able to evolve and adapt dynamically to changing market conditions.

Digital Ecosystems lie at the intersection between different disciplines and fields: industry, business, social sciences, biology, and cutting edge ICT and its application driven research. They are supported by several underlying technologies such as semantic web and ontology-based knowledge sharing, self-organizing intelligent agents, peer-to-peer overlay networks, web services-based information platforms, and recommender systems.

To enable safe digital ecosystem functioning, security and trust mechanisms become essential components across all the technological layers. The aim is to bring together multidisciplinary research that ranges from technical aspects to socio-economic models.

We take here the opportunity to warmly thank all the members of the SECURWARE 2021 technical program committee, as well as all the reviewers. The creation of such a high quality conference program would not have been possible without their involvement. We also kindly thank all the authors who dedicated much of their time and effort to contribute to SECURWARE 2021. We truly believe that, thanks to all these efforts, the final conference program consisted of top quality contributions.

We also thank the members of the SECURWARE 2021 organizing committee for their help in handling the logistics and for their work that made this professional meeting a success.

We hope that SECURWARE 2021 was a successful international forum for the exchange of ideas and results between academia and industry and to promote further progress in the area of security information, systems and technologies.

**SECURWARE 2021 Chairs**

**SECURWARE 2021 Steering Committee**

Steffen Fries, Siemens, Germany
George O. M. Yee, Aptusinnova Inc. / Carleton University, Ottawa, Canada
Rainer Falk, Siemens AG, Corporate Technology, Germany
Hans-Joachim Hof, INSicherheit - Ingolstadt Research Group Applied IT Security, CARISSMA – Center of Automotive Research on Integrated Safety Syst, Germany

**SECURWARE 2021 Publicity Chair**

Mar Parra Boronat, Universitat Politecnica de Valencia, Spain
Sandra Viciano Tudela, Universitat Politecnica de Valencia, Spain

## SECURWARE 2021

## Committee

**SECURWARE 2021 Steering Committee**
Steffen Fries, Siemens, Germany
George O. M. Yee, Aptusinnova Inc. / Carleton University, Ottawa, Canada
Rainer Falk, Siemens AG, Corporate Technology, Germany
Hans-Joachim Hof, INSicherheit - Ingolstadt Research Group Applied IT Security, CARISSMA – Center of Automotive Research on Integrated Safety Syst, Germany

**SECURWARE 2021 Publicity Chair**
Mar Parra Boronat, Universitat Politecnica de Valencia, Spain
Sandra Viciano Tudela, Universitat Politecnica de Valencia, Spain

**SECURWARE 2021 Technical Program Committee**

Aysajan Abidin, imec-COSIC KU Leuven, Belgium
Abbas Acar, Florida International University, Miami, USA
Afrand Agah, West Chester University of Pennsylvania, USA
Chuadhry Mujeeb Ahmed, University of Strathclyde Scotland, UK
Sedat Akleylek, Ondokuz Mayis University, Samsun, Turkey
Oum-El-Kheir Aktouf, Greboble INP | LCIS Lab, France
Mamoun Alazab, Charles Darwin University, Australia
Ashwag Albakri, University of Missouri-Kansas City, USA / Jazan University, Saudi Arabia
Asif Ali laghari, SMIU, Karachi, Pakistan
Luca Allodi, Eindhoven University of Technology, Netherlands
Mohammed Alshehri, University of Arkansas, USA
Eric Amankwa, Presbyterian University College, Ghana
Sébastien Bardin, CEA LIST, France
Antonio Barili, Università degli Studi di Pavia, Italy
Ilija Basicevic, University of Novi Sad, Serbia
Luke A. Bauer, University of Florida, USA
Malek Ben Salem, Accenture, USA
Catalin Bîrjoveanu, "Al. I. Cuza" University of Iasi, Romania
Robert Brotzman, Pennsylvania State University, USA
Francesco Buccafurri, University Mediterranea of Reggio Calabria, Italy
Enrico Cambiaso, Consiglio Nazionale delle Ricerche (CNR) - IEIIT Institute, Italy
Paolo Campegiani, Bit4id, Italy
Juan-Vicente Capella-Hernández, Universitat Politècnica de València, Spain
Roberto Carbone, Fondazione Bruno Kessler, Trento, Italy
Juan Carlos Ruiz, Universidad Politécnica de Valencia, Spain
Andrea Ceccarelli, University of Florence, Italy
Christophe Charrier, Nomandie Univ. | UNICAEN | ENSICAEN | CNRS GREYC UMR 6072, France
Bo Chen, Michigan Technological University, Houghton, USA
Liquan Chen, Southeast University, China

Tan Saw Chin, Multimedia University, Malaysia
Jin-Hee Cho, Virginia Tech, USA
Stelvio Cimato, University of Milan, Italy
Marijke Coetzee, Academy of Computer Science and Software Engineering | University of Johannesburg, South Africa
Jun Dai, California State University at Sacramento, USA
Alexandre Debant , Université de Lorraine | CNRS | Inria | LORIA, Nancy, France
Raffaele Della Corte, "Federico II" University of Naples, Italy
Jean-Christophe Deneuville, ENAC | University of Toulouse, France
Jintai Ding, Tsinghua University, Beijing
George Drosatos, Athena Research Center, Greece
Jean-Guillaume Dumas, Univ. Grenoble Alpes | Laboratoire Jean Kuntzmann, France
Navid Emamdoost, University of Minnesota, USA
Alessandro Erba, CISPA Helmholtz Center for Information Security, Germany
Rainer Falk, Siemens AG, Corporate Technology, Germany
Yebo Feng, University of Oregon, USA
Eduardo B. Fernandez, Florida Atlantic University, USA
Steffen Fries, Siemens Corporate Technologies, Germany
Amparo Fúster-Sabater, Institute of Physical and Information Technologies (CSIC), Spain
Olga Gadyatskaya, LIACS - Leiden University, The Netherlands
Clemente Galdi, University of Salerno, Italy
Rafa Gálvez, KU Leuven, Belgium
Hector Marco Gisbert, University of the West of Scotland, UK
Nils Gruschka, University of Oslo, Norway
Jiaping Gui, NEC Laboratories America, USA
Chun Guo, Shandong University, China
Bidyut Gupta, Southern Illinois University, Carbondale, USA
Saurabh Gupta, IIIT-Delhi, India
Amir Mohammad Hajisadeghi, Amirkabir University of Technology (Tehran Polytechnic), Iran
Mohammad Hamad, Technical University of Munich, Germany
Jinguang Han, Nanjing University of Finance and Economics, China
Dan Harkins, Hewlett-Packard Enterprise, USA
Mohamed Hawedi, École de Technologie Supérieure Montreal, Canada
Zecheng He, Princeton University, USA
Hans-Joachim Hof, INSicherheit - Ingolstadt Research Group Applied IT Security, CARISSMA – Center of Automotive Research on Integrated Safety Syst, Germany
Gahangir Hossain, West Texas A&M University, Canyon, USA
Fu-Hau Hsu, National Central University, Taiwan
Fatima Hussain, Royal Bank of Canada, Toronto, Canada
Ibifubara Iganibo, George Mason University, USA
Sergio Ilarri, University of Zaragoza, Spain
Mariusz Jakubowski, Microsoft Research, USA
Prasad M. Jayaweera, University of Sri Jayewardenepura, Sri Lanka
Kun Jin, Ohio State University, USA
Kaushal Kafle, William & Mary, USA
Sarang Kahvazadeh, Centre Tecnològic de Telecomunicacions de Catalunya (CTTC), Spain
Harsha K. Kalutarage, Robert Gordon University, UK
Georgios Kambourakis, University of the Aegean, Greece

Mehdi Karimi, The University of British Columbia, Vancouver, Canada
Georgios Karopoulos, European Commission JRC, Italy
Sokratis K. Katsikas, Norwegian University of Science and Technology, Norway
Basel Katt, Norwegian University of Science and Technology, Norway
Ferdous Wahid Khan, Airbus Digital Trust Solutions, Munich, Germany
Nadir Khan, FZI Forschungszentrum Informatik, Karlsruhe, Germany
Hyunsung Kim, Kyungil University, Korea
Paris Kitsos, University of the Peloponnese, Greece
Harsha Kumara, Robert Gordon University, UK
Hiroki Kuzuno, SECOM Co. Ltd., Japan
Hyun Kwon, Korea Military Academy, Korea
Romain Laborde, University Paul Sabatier Toulouse III, France
Cecilia Labrini, University of Reggio Calabria, Italy
Vianney Lapôtre, Université Bretagne Sud, France
Martin Latzenhofer, AIT Austrian Institute of Technology | Center for Digital Safety and Security, Vienna, Austria
Ferenc Leitold, University of Dunaújváros, Hungary
Albert Levi, Sabanci University, Istanbul, Turkey
Shimin Li, Winona State University, USA
Wenjuan Li, The Hong Kong Polytechnic University, China
Zhihao Li, Facebook Inc., USA
Stefan Lindskog, SINTEF Digital, Norway / Karlstad University, Sweden
Guojun Liu, University of South Florida, Tampa, USA
Shaohui Liu, School of Computer Science and Technology | Harbin Institute of Technology, China
Shen Liu, NVIDIA, USA
Giovanni Livraga, Universita' degli Studi di Milano, Italy
Flaminia Luccio, University Ca' Foscari of Venice, Italy
Duohe Ma, Institute of Information Engineering | Chinese Academy of Sciences, China
Bernardo Magri, Aarhus University, Denmark
Rabi N. Mahapatra, Texas A&M University, USA
Mahdi Manavi, Mirdamad Institute of Higher Education, Iran
Antonio Matencio Escolar, University of the West of Scotland, UK
Wojciech Mazurczyk, Warsaw University of Technology, Poland
Weizhi Meng, Technical University of Denmark, Denmark
Aleksandra Mileva, University "Goce Delcev" in Stip, Republic of N. Macedonia
Alan Mills, University of the West of England (UWE), Bristol, UK
Paolo Modesti, Teesside University, UK
Haralambos Mouratidis, University of Brighton, UK
Adwait Nadkarni, William & Mary, USA
Vasudevan Nagendra, Plume Design Inc., USA
Priyadarsi Nanda, University of Technology Sydney, Australia
Chan Nam Ngo, University of Trento, Italy
Nicola Nostro, Resiltech, Italy
Jason R. C. Nurse, University of Kent, UK
Livinus Obiora Nweke, Norwegian University of Science and Technology, Norway
Catuscia Palamidessi, INRIA, France
Carlos Enrique Palau Salvador, Universitat Politècnica de València, Spain
Lanlan Pan, Guangdong OPPO Mobile Telecommunications Corp. Ltd., China

Brajendra Panda, University of Arkansas, USA
Balázs Pejó, CrySyS Lab - BME, Budapest, Hungary
Wei Peng, University of Oulu, Finland
Travis Peters, Montana State University, USA
Josef Pieprzyk, Data61 | CSIRO, Sydney, Australia / Institute of Computer Science | Polish Academy of Sciences, Warsaw, Poland
Nikolaos Pitropakis, Edinburgh Napier University, UK
Thomas Plantard, University of Wollongong, Australia
Tassilo Pellegrini, St. Pölten University of Applied Sciences, Austria
Tran Viet Xuan Phuong, University of Wollongong, Australia / Old Dominion University, USA
Bernardo Portela, University of Porto, Portugal
Mila Dalla Preda, University of Verona, Italy
Maxime Puys, Univ. Grenoble Alpes | CEA | LETI | DSYS, Grenoble, France
Alvise Rabitti, Università Ca'Foscari - Venezia, Italy
Khandaker "Abir" Rahman, Saginaw Valley State University, USA
Mohammad Saidur Rahman, Rochester Institute of Technology, USA
Mohammad A. Rashid, Massey University, New Zealand
Danda B. Rawat, Howard University, USA
Leon Reznik, Rochester Institute of Technology, USA
Ruben Ricart-Sanchez, University of the West of Scotland, UK
Martin Ring, Bosch Engineering GmbH, Germany
Heiko Roßnagel, Fraunhofer IAO, Germany
Salah Sadou, IRISA - Universite de Bretagne Sud, France
Simona Samardjiska, Radboud University, The Netherlands
Rodrigo Sanches Miani, Universidade Federal de Uberlândia, Brazil
Stefan Schauer, AIT Austrian Institute of Technology | Center for Digital Safety and Security, Vienna, Austria
Stefan Schiffner, University of Münster, Germany
Savio Sciancalepore, Hamad Bin Khalifa University (HBKU), Doha, Qatar
Giada Sciarretta, Fondazione Bruno Kessler (FBK), Trento, Italy
Liwei Song, Princeton University, USA
Christoph Stach, University of Stuttgart, Germany
Sheng Tan, Trinity University, USA
Yifan Tian, Agari Data Inc., USA
Nils Ole Tippenhauer, CISPA Helmholtz Center for Cybersecurity, Germany
Scott Trent, IBM Research - Tokyo, Japan
Vincent Urias, Sandia National Labs, USA
Emmanouil Vasilomanolakis, Aalborg University, Denmark
Andrea Visconti, Università degli Studi di Milano, Italy
Wenqi Wei, Georgia Institute of Technology, USA
Ian Welch, Victoria University of Wellington, New Zealand
Zhonghao Wu, Shanghai Jiao Tong University, China
Nian Xue, New York University (NYU), USA
Ehsan Yaghoubi, University of Beira Interior, Portugal
Geng Yang, Nanjing University of Posts & Telecommunications (NUPT), China
Ping Yang, Binghamton University, USA
Wun-She Yap, Universiti Tunku Abdul Rahman, Malaysia
Qussai M. Yaseen, Jordan University of Science and Technology, Irbid, Jordan

George O. M. Yee, Aptusinnova Inc. / Carleton University, Ottawa, Canada
Kailiang Ying, Google, USA
Amr Youssef, Concordia University, Montreal, Canada
Chia-Mu Yu, National Yang Ming Chiao Tung University, Taiwan
Wei Yu, Institute of Information Engineering | Chinese Academy of Sciences, China
Apostolis Zarras, Delft University of Technology, The Netherlands
Thomas Zefferer, Secure Information Technology Center Austria (A-SIT), Austria
Dongrui Zeng, Pennsylvania State University, University Park, USA
Linghan Zhang, Florida State University, USA
Tianwei Zhang, Nanyang Technological University, Singapore
Yubao Zhang, Palo Alto Networks, USA
Yue Zheng, Nanyang Technological University, Singapore

**Copyright Information**

# IT-Security Compliance for Home Offices

Christoph Haar
Hochschule für Telekommunikation Leipzig
Leipzig, Germany
email: haar@hft-leipzig.de

Erik Buchmann
Hochschule für Telekommunikation Leipzig
Leipzig, Germany
email: buchmann@hft-leipzig.de

***Abstract*—The ongoing COVID-19 pandemic increases the need to transfer employees into home offices. Securing a home office is challenging. Approaches, such as BSI Grundschutz, ISO 2700x, NIST 800-53 or ISIS12 focus on company premises, and the data carried outside must be strongly restricted. The focus of such approaches is to secure the IT-infrastructure on company premises but not on the employee's private network. In this paper, we explore how the IT-Grundschutz Compendium, a standardized IT-security framework from the German Federal Office for Information Security, can be carried into a home office. Our objective is to extend the scope of protection of the BSI Grundschutz from company premises into the private areas of an employee in a home office. To this end, we apply the BSI Basic Protection to a basic home-office scenario. For each security requirement, we investigate whether it can be implemented by the employee, or by the employer.**

***Keywords – IT-Grundschutz; Home Office Security; Compliance; Basic Protection***

## I. INTRODUCTION

The IT-Grundschutz Compendium [1] maintained by the German Federal Office for Information Security (BSI) allows companies to approach pre-defined levels of IT-security in a standardized way. The security level can be audited and certified, and it is compatible with the International Organization for Standardization (ISO) 2700x series of standards [2] or the National Institute of Standards and Technology (NIST) Cybersecurity Framework [3]. Such approaches ease the definition of a security strategy, the execution of risk analyses on company assets and the implementation of a security management that considers organization, personnel, business processes, the IT-architecture, IT-operations, IT-systems and devices, networks, applications and data. Approaches for specific domains exist, e.g., the Payment Card Industry Data Security Standard (PCI DSS), the International Electrotechnical Commission (IEC) standard 62443, or the Federal Information Processing Standards (FIPS) 199 and 200. In many sectors, a certified level of IT-security is mandatory for any major enterprise. The certification confirms, that the company has achieved a reasonable level of IT-security, i.e., it is not only protected against certain attack vectors.

However, such security approaches focus on company premises. Only two of approx. 100 modules in the IT-Grundschutz Compendium directly address home offices ("INF.8 Working from Home" and "OPS.1.2.4 Teleworking"). Other modules explain how, say, IT-operations on company grounds can be organized without security risks. In consequence, home offices are either considered insecure, or securing them requires elaborate, individual risk analyses and protection mechanisms, as required by INF.8 and OPS.1.2.4.

This is problematic. The Coronavirus-2019 pandemic increases the urge for enterprises allow working from home [4]. Work-life-balance concepts, issues, such as the reconcilability of family and working life, and flexible working-time models also foster this development. However, having obtained a certified level of IT-security means that sensible data must not leave secure areas. But today's homes are filled with networked smart-home devices that do not have security clearance from an enterprise expert, Wireless Local Area Network (WLAN) network connections can be eavesdropped from public spaces, and family members can be expected to enter the work place at home at any time. A recent (meta-)study [5] illustrates the scope of this issue.

Many existing guidelines promise to secure private networks [6]–[8]. Even the BSI has published a checklist for employees in the home office due to the ongoing Coronavirus-2019 pandemic [9]. This checklist covers some basic rules of conduct in a home office. However, none of the guidelines we are aware of reach the completeness and soundness of standardized approaches, such as the BSI Grundschutz or the NIST Cybersecurity Framework. Frequently, it also remains unclear which level of technical understanding is required from an employee to follow such guidelines at home successfully. From a company perspective, the main disadvantage of such guidelines is their incompatibility with certificates. Companies, that do not want to put their certified security strategies at risk, but send employees into home office, are forced to implement harsh measures that limit the usability of a home-office workplace.

One example for such a measure is to strictly disallow any company data on a private device, and to use screen forwarding from a remote machine at the company to the user's device via Virtual Private Networks (VPN). While this approach protects the integrity and confidentiality of the transmission and ensures the availability of the data at the company's side, it might be inadequate for many business tasks. One issue is that a malware at the user's device could interfere with the login process of the VPN or the remote machine. Another issue is that it is restricted to business processes that can be executed entirely on the remote machine. Furthermore, screen forwarding via VPN is too slow for many graphical tasks, including computer-aided design or multimedia content creation. A superior approach would be to extend the company's certified security concept to the user's home office.

In this paper, we analyze how the certifiable security level "Basic Protection" of the IT-Grundschutz Compendium can be executed in a home office. Furthermore, we find out whether the identified security requirements can be implemented by an employee without in-depth technical background knowledge, or need an expert from the employer. To this end, we restrict the focus of this paper on the technical parts of the IT-Grundschutz Compendium that are relevant for home offices, i.e., we only consider the module layers "Applications" (APP), "Concepts" (CON), "Detection and Reaction" (DER), "Operations" (OPS), "Networks" (NET) and "Systems" (SYS).

In particular, we make the following contributions:

- We model a minimal home-office scenario that contains customer data, together with respective roles for the employee in the home office and the company's IT-security expert.
- We execute a Basic Protection approach according to BSI Grundschutz on this scenario, and we say what must be modified if the scenario changes.
- For each security requirement identified, we examine whether it can be implemented by the employee.

We found out that, from a technical point of view, it is indeed possible to apply the Basic Protection of the BSI to a home office. This means that it is technically feasible to extend the scope of a certified security policy to workplaces at home. However, only 11 of the 103 security requirements needed to implement Basic Protection in our minimal scenario can be implemented by an employee without IT-security expertise that is beyond his or her working skills. All other requirements must be implemented by the employers IT-security experts, either by bringing-in the device, by call-center support or by a security expert visiting the workplace.

Section II describes the IT-Grundschutz basic protection and the basic terms of this work. We define a minimal home-office scenario and implement the basic protection in Section III. In Section IV, we check which of the identified basic requirements the user can implement independently. We discuss our findings in Section V. Section VI concludes.

## II. Related Work

In this section, we introduce the IT-Grundschutz Compendium, related standards and fundamental concepts.

### A. BSI IT-Grundschutz

Since 1991, the German Federal Office for Information Security (BSI) maintains a structured collection of guidelines to implement IT-security in large enterprises in a standardized way. The most recent collection is the IT-Grundschutz Compendium, version 2021 [1], together with supporting standards, such as BSI-Standard 200-2 "IT-Grundschutz Methodology" [10]. The BSI distinguishes security levels, such as "Basic", "Standard" and "Increased". The security levels can be audited and certified, and are compatible with the ISO 2700x series of standards [2] or the NIST cyber security framework [3]. In 2017, the BSI published the "Guide to Basic Protection based on IT-Grundschutz" [11]. It defines the steps shown in Figure 1 to secure a typical IT-infrastructure. We have aligned our research approach according to these steps. For this reason, we briefly describe them in the following.

### B. Basic Protection

The security level "Basic" requires to specify the scope of the protection, to map the information doman to BSI modules, and to implement adequate safeguards.

*a) Specification of the Scope:* The **information domain** is defined by means of a structural analysis. Either the entire IT-infrastructure of the company can be considered, or certain departments only. That essentially depends on the size of the individual departments or the company [10]. The information domain includes business processes (e.g., production), IT-systems (e.g., PC's, server), applications (e.g., Word, Dropbox), data (e.g., customer data), communication links (e.g., ethernet), rooms (e.g., offices), and organizational structures. The individual components of the information domain are described as a network plan.

After the information domain has been defined, it must be modeled by using the **IT-Grundschutz Compendium**. The IT-Grundschutz Compendium contains modules that map the elements of the information domain [1] to security requirements. The modules contain a clear introduction, a threat landscape and requirements on different protection levels. Furthermore the scope within each module is described. In the scope it is also pointed out in more detail which other modules should be considered when using this module.

The current version of the IT-Grundschutz Compendium [1] was released in 2021. However, this version is only available in German at the moment. We use the 2021 version as a basis for this paper, but we briefly describe the differences to the preceding version from 2019 [12], which is available in English: The module "APP.5.1 General Groupware" is no longer included in the 2021 version. The requirements contained in this module are now contained in other modules, such as "APP.5.3 General E-Mail Client and Server" The modules "SYS.4.5: Removable Media" and "APP.6 General Software" are not yet included in the 2019 version. We need to consider them in our work. The module "CON.2" only contains one basic requirement "Implementation of the Standard Data Protection Model". This requirement includes all basic requirements from the 2019 version. The Standard Data Protection Model complements the IT-Grundschutz Compendium regarding data protection and is also available in english [13]. In the 2021 version, some basic requirements have been omitted. That means, we do not have to consider them in our work. In the 2021 version the following basic requirements have been added: OPS.1.1.3.A15, OPS.1.1.3.A16, SYS.2.1.A42, SYS.3.1.A9 and APP.1.1.A17. We will consider them in our work.

*b) Selection and Prioritization (a.k.a. Modelling):* After the information domain has been defined, the **modelling** must be applied in the next step. For this purpose, all elements of the information domain are mapped to the respective modules in the IT-Grundschutz Compendium [1]. The modules contain definitions of possible risks that have to be considered when

Figure 1. "Basic Protection" according to BSI Standard 200-2

securing an element. Furthermore, requirements are described in each module that must be implemented to avert potential risks. For a more detailed description of the modules, we refer to one of our previous works [14]. This step is challenging, because elements can be linked with multiple modules, and modules frequently contain cross-references to other ones.

The result of the modelling is an IT-Grundschutz model of the information domain, which consists of various modules. The requirements for averting potential risks that are described in the modules represent a checklist that must be worked through. The IT-Grundschutz Check can now be started with this checklist.

*c) IT-Grundschutz-Check:* In the preceding step, relevant modules have been identified. Each of these modules contains basic requirements that must be implemented. However, some requirements might have been already implemented in the past, or the products used allow better options to fulfill a requirement than those named in a module. For this reason, the IT-Grundschutz Check provides as a **gap analysis**. For each basic requirement, it is checked whether and to what extent it has already been implemented. The following answers to the implementation status of the basic requirement are possible [11]:

- **Unnecessary:** The requirement can be omitted, because it is not relevant in the information system under consideration or has already been met due to alternative safeguards.
- **Yes:** Appropriate safeguards have been implemented completely for the requirement.
- **Partially:** The safeguards implemented so far do not entirely fulfill the requirement.
- **No:** The requirement has not been met yet, i.e., appropriate safeguards have not been implemented yet.

The result of the IT-Grundschutz Check is a list of requirements with implementation status "partially" or "no". The implementation of these requirements is the starting point for the next step in the Basic Protection. When implementing Basic Protection, the BSI stipulates that all requirements MUST be implemented. For this reason, we will not check which of the basic requirements can be waived, but consider all of them to be necessary.

*d) Implementation of the Safeguards:* Regarding the realisation of the requirements, it must be decided how and in what order the identified requirements have to be implemented. The BSI describes **implementation recommendations** for the requirements. These implementation recommendations are best practice approaches with many years of experience from experts in the field of information security.

## III. Basic Protection for Home Offices

In this section, we analyze to which extent an employee is able to implement the BSI protection level "Basic" to secure a typical home-office scenario. We start with our research method: First, we define the role "Home-Office User" as a person without in-depth background knowledge on IT-security. Second, We specify a home-office scenario, and we model its information domain according to BSI standard 200-2 [10]. Third, we apply the BSI protection level "Basic" on this scenario, i.e., we derive appropriate security requirements for this scenario from the BSI Grundschutz Compendium [1]. Fourth, we use our role definition from the first step as a reference to test if an employee can execute the respective IT-security requirements, or needs help from an expert from the employer. Finally, we discuss what changes if the minimal home-office scenario is extended due to further needs of the employee's business task.

### A. A Minimal Home-Office Scenario with Customer Data

With "home office", we refer to a situation where a home-office user fulfills (a subset of) his business tasks at home, in a domestic environment that is not strictly tailored for business, but also for daily (family) life, leisure, recreation, sports, etc. A room used for home office might also contain a TV or a smart speaker which could be banned on company premises. The room might be shared with other family members when it is not used for work. The PC used for work might be shared with others, with a different user account. We implement the BSI protection level "Basic" for the following scenario:

**Scenario:** *A health insurance company sends an employee from the customer service department into home office. Since the employee manages sensible data, the company requires that the room used for home office is locked when the employee is off. Furthermore, the company provides a work laptop with an operating system, applications for opening and editing documents, an e-mail client, a web browser and anti-virus software. Furthermore, the work laptop has an USB interface. The employee's private network has a router that acts as an Internet gateway and a personal firewall, and spans a WLAN network (WLAN0). To establish a network connection to the company, the employee connects his laptop via WLAN to the router, as shown in Figure 2.*

### B. The Role "Home-Office User"

In the context of this paper, we assume that an employee is an adequately-trained domain expert for the business task he executes, and we also assume that the employee has been trained to use computer equipment securely. However, we do

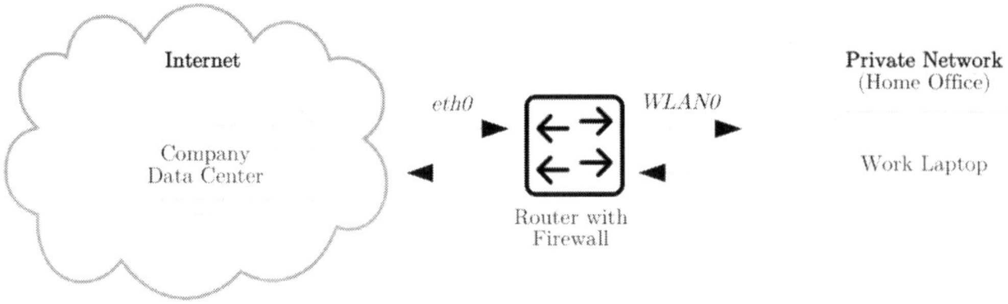


Figure 2. Network plan of a basic home-office scenario

not expect the employee to possess in-depth technical knowledge regarding IT-operations, IT-administration or IT-security. To approach a role specification for our home-office user that considers this, but is also in line with well-established best practices in industry and business, we adapt role definitions from the BSI. In standard 200-2 [10], the BSI describes a set of roles, such as "Information Security Officer", "Data User", "Data Owner" or "Data Creator". For our paper, we borrow the role "Home-Office User" from the BSI role "Data User".

While the BSI assumes that every employee can take the role "Data User" [10], our role "Home-Office User" is restricted to employees that are eligible for home office and have been trained for home office specific IT-components, e.g., how to establish a VPN connection to a company server, how to set up a video conference or how to lock the screen so that no family member gets insight into work data. Table I summarizes the properties and characteristics of this role definition. Note that the BSI defines the term "operations" according to ISO Standard 12207 [15]. This standard describes a software lifecycle that includes the primary processes of development, operation and maintenance. The ISO standard 15288 [16] describes the same for systems. In our work, we will also use this definition. Thus, our role definition is both compatible with BSI Grundschutz and the ISO standards.

TABLE I
ROLE "HOME-OFFICE USER"

| *Property* | *Role Characteristics* |
|---|---|
| **Tasks** | Execute business tasks on business data at home |
| **Operations** | Use work equipment and software applications at home |
| **Qualification** | Knowledge of the application domain and the IT systems used |
| **Eligibility** | Every employee whose function can be performed in home office |

With our minimal home-office scenario, the role home-office user is instantiated as follows:

**Scenario User:** *The employee works in customer service, has been qualified accordingly, and has years of working experience in that domain. His daily activities include answering customer requests, assessing and settling medical invoices or providing insurance contracts. For this purposes, he uses telephone and email. To do this, he uses the work laptop provided by the employer. Furthermore, the employee has been trained to use the laptop securely at home, i.e., he is able to change passwords, to allow automatic security updates for applications and operating system, and knows how to handle the anti-virus software.*

## C. The Information Domain

To implement the BSI Basic Protection on our scenario, we need its information domain. In the context of this paper, the scope of the information domain is limited to the technical home office setup of the employee, i.e., it ends with the router that provides Internet access.

In line with the BSI Grundschutz methodology, we model the the information domain for each of the levels "Data", "Communication", "Applications" and "IT-Systems" from the network plan (cf. Figure 2) and our scenario description (cf. Subsection III-A). The information domain for our scenario is shown in Table II. Observe that we do not make assumptions yet on the applications or operating systems installed.

TABLE II
INFORMATION DOMAIN OF THE PRIVATE NETWORK

| *ID* | *Object* | *Description* |
|---|---|---|
| **Data** | | |
| D1 | Customer Data | Personal data from customers |
| D2 | Content Data | Data of applications and services |
| D3 | Account Data | Login and authorization data of the user |
| **Communication** | | |
| N1 | Router/Firewall | Security gateway |
| **Applications** | | |
| A1 | System Software | Operating system, drivers and utilities |
| A2 | Applications | Applications to display and edit documents |
| A3 | E-Mail Client | Application for sending/receiving emails |
| A4 | Web Browser | Application to display web content |
| **IT-Systems** | | |
| S1 | Work Laptop | Laptop provided by the employer |

Data D1 to D3 represent different kinds of information from the daily work. For example, the work laptop is secured with a username and password (D3). The same applies to the login of the work e-mail account. Customer data, such as the names, addresses and customer IDs (D1), are processed together with other information (D2) on the work laptop (S1) due to the activity as a customer service employee. The employee's private Internet router (N1) serves also as a security gateway, because it contains a firewall. The applications A1 to A4 represent the various software needed for daily business.

### D. Implementing Basic Protection

To implement Basic Protection, we have to identify all modules from the IT-Grundschutz Compendium that address the elements of our information domain (Table II). Observe that the modules in the IT-Grundschutz Compendium are organized in a hierarchy. To secure the web browser, not only "APP.1.2 Web-Browser" needs to be considered, but also "APP.6 General Software". Furthermore, the scope definition of some modules contain cross references to others. For example, "SYS.3.1 Laptops" refers amongst others to "NET.2.2 WLAN usage" and "SYS.2.1 General Client". It is also possible that a requirement forces to implement another module. For example, basic requirement "NET.2.1.A8 Procedures in the Event of WLAN Security Incidents" makes it mandatory to consider "DER.2.1 Security Incident Handling". Finally, some requirements implicitly call for other modules. For example, Basic Requirement "SYS.2.1.A4 Regular Backups" is implicitly linked with "CON.3 Backup Concept". Table III shows all modules needed to model our scenario, and Table IV contains the list of all Basic requirements, we have identified. For a detailed description of the modules and its security requirements, see the IT-Grundschutz Compendium [1].

TABLE III
MODULES RELATED TO OUR INFORMATION DOMAIN

| *ID* | *Description* |
|---|---|
| APP.1.1 | Office Products |
| APP.1.2 | Web-Browser |
| APP.5.3 | General E-Mail Client and Server |
| APP.6 | General Software |
| CON.2 | Data Protection |
| CON.3 | Backup Concept |
| CON.6 | Deleting and Destroying Data and Devices |
| DER.2.1 | Security Incident Handling |
| DER.2.3 | Clean-Up of Extensive Security Incident |
| NET.1.1 | Network Architecture and Design |
| NET.1.2 | Network Management |
| NET.2.1 | WLAN Operation |
| NET.2.2 | WLAN Usage |
| NET.3.1 | Router and Switches |
| OPS.1.1.3 | Patch and Change Management |
| OPS.1.1.4 | Protection Against Malware |
| SYS.2.1 | General Client |
| SYS.3.1 | Laptops |
| SYS.4.5 | Removable Media |

Our starting point was a minimal home-office scenario with customer data. For this reason, this exhaustive list of Basic requirements must be fully implemented, in order to extend the certified security level "Basic Protection" from company premises to the workplace of a home-office user that handles any kind of customer data, personal data or other sensitive information.

Note that tasks like telemedicine or power plant control need a higher security level than "Basic Protection", because any security issue might endanger the life of a person or produce very high damages. In such scenarios, the list of requirements would be much larger. However, such scenarios are less suitable for home offices anyway.

## IV. Responsibilities for Requirements

To systematically approach at a distinction between requirements that can be implemented by the employee and requirements that need an expert from the employer, we define two prerequisites.

**Prerequisite 1:** The implementation of the requirement must be within the abilities defined in the role specification from Table I. In particular, for each requirement, we need the following questions answered with "yes":

- Has the requirement an impact on the user's professional tasks or business processes?
- Is the requirement within the user's typical activities with work equipment or software applications?
- Are the user's qualifications sufficient to appropriately meet the requirement?

**Prerequisite 2:** The requirement cannot be implemented at the employer's site.

If Prerequisites 1 and 2 are met, the user has the abilities and the responsibility to implement a requirement. If this is not the case, the requirement must be implemented by an expert.

Observe that some requirements for home-office users are among the typical tasks for an expert in the employer's IT department. It is the IT department which configures laptops, installs software or manages VPN tunnels. Thus, such tasks are addressed before the employee is sent into home office.

**Example:** *With our home-office scenario, an anti-virus application has been installed on the employee's laptop. This application is associated with Basic requirement SYS.3.1.A4 "Use of Anti-Virus Programs". Because the employee has been ordered to use it, it is part of his professional tasks. The employee needs to handle virus warnings or requests to accept fresh virus signatures, i.e., it is within his typical activities with the laptop. The employer has provided a training on how to use the anti-virus software. Finally, the daily use of the anti-virus application cannot take place at the employers site. Thus, Prerequisites 1 and 2 are met, and requirement SYS.3.1.A4 is within the responsibilities of the employee.*

Reconsider Table IV. All bold requirements fulfill both prerequisites and must be implemented by the home-office user in order to extend the company's security concept, level "Basic", to the user's home office.

To our surprise, this number of requirements is rather small. All other basic requirements must be implemented with the help of experts of the IT department, either via bringing-in the laptop, via hotline support, or by visiting the user.

TABLE IV
BASIC REQUIREMENTS FOR A MINIMAL HOME OFFICE

| *ID* | *Description* |
|---|---|
| **APP.1.1.A2** | **Limiting Active Content** |
| **APP.1.1.A3** | **Opening Documents from External Sources** |
| APP.1.1.A7 | Awareness of Specific Office Properties |
| APP.1.2.A1 | Using Sandboxing |
| APP.1.2.A2 | Encryption of Communications |
| APP.1.2.A3 | Using Certificates |
| **APP.1.2.A4** | **Version Checking and Updates for (...)** |
| APP.5.3.A1 | Secure configuration of e-mail clients |
| APP.5.3.A2 | Secure operation of e-mail servers |
| APP.5.3.A3 | Data backup and archiving of emails |
| APP.5.3.A4 | Spam and virus protection on e-mail servers |
| APP.6.A1 | Planning the software useage |
| APP.6.A2 | A requirements catalog for software |
| APP.6.A3 | Secure procurement of software |
| APP.6.A4 | Installation and configuration of software |
| APP.6.A5 | Secure installation of software |
| DER.2.1.A1 | Definition of a Security Incident |
| DER.2.1.A2 | Policy for Handling Security Incidents |
| DER.2.1.A3 | Responsibilities for Security Incidents |
| DER.2.1.A4 | Notification for Security Incidents |
| DER.2.1.A5 | Remedial Action for Security Incidents |
| DER.2.1.A6 | Recovering after Security Incidents |
| DER.2.3.A1 | Creation of a Management Committee |
| DER.2.3.A2 | Deciding on a Clean-Up Approach |
| DER.2.3.A3 | Isolation of Affected Network Segments |
| DER.2.3.A4 | Blocking and Changing Access Data (...) |
| DER.2.3.A5 | Closing the Initial Entry Route |
| DER.2.3.A6 | Returning to Production Operations |
| CON.2.A1 | Implementing the Standard Data Protection Model |
| CON.3.A1 | Determining the Factors for Backups |
| CON.3.A2 | Stipulating Backup Procedures |
| CON.3.A4 | Drawing Up a Minimum Backup Concept |
| CON.3.A5 | Regular Backups |
| CON.6.A1 | Regulations for Deleting/Destroying Information |
| CON.6.A2 | Disposal of Sensitive Resources and Information |
| CON.6.A11 | Deletion of Data by External Service Providers |
| CON.6.A12 | Minimum Requirements for Deletion |
| NET.1.1.A1 | Network Security Policy |
| NET.1.1.A2 | Documentation of the Network |
| NET.1.1.A3 | Specification of Network Requirements |
| NET.1.1.A4 | Network Separation in Security Zones |
| NET.1.1.A5 | Client-Server Segmentation |
| NET.1.1.A6 | End Device Segmentation for Networks |
| NET.1.1.A7 | Protection of Sensitive Information |
| NET.1.1.A8 | Basic Protection of Internet Access |
| NET.1.1.A9 | Communication with Untrusted Networks |
| NET.1.1.A10 | DMZ Segmentation for Internet Access |
| NET.1.1.A11 | Communication with the Internet |
| NET.1.1.A12 | Protection of Outgoing Communication |
| NET.1.1.A13 | Network Planning |
| NET.1.1.A14 | Implementation of Network Planning |
| NET.1.1.A15 | Regular Gap Analysis |

| *ID* | *Description* |
|---|---|
| NET.1.2.A1 | Network Management Planning |
| NET.1.2.A2 | Network Management Requirements |
| NET.1.2.A6 | Regular Backups |
| NET.1.2.A7 | Basic Logging of Events |
| NET.1.2.A8 | Time Synchronisation |
| NET.1.2.A9 | Network Management Communication |
| NET.1.2.A10 | Limitation of SNMP Communication |
| NET.2.1.A1 | Definition of a Strategy for WLAN Usage |
| NET.2.1.A2 | Selection of a Suitable WLAN Standard |
| NET.2.1.A3 | Selecting Crypto Methods for WLAN |
| NET.2.1.A4 | Suitable Location of Access Points |
| NET.2.1.A5 | Secure Basic Configuration of Access Points |
| NET.2.1.A6 | Secure Configuration of WLAN Clients |
| NET.2.1.A7 | Setting Up a Distribution System |
| NET.2.1.A8 | Procedures for WLAN Security Incidents |
| NET.2.2.A1 | Creating a User Policy for WLAN |
| NET.2.2.A2 | Awareness and Training of WLAN Users |
| NET.2.2.A3 | WLAN Usage in Insecure Environments |
| NET.3.1.A1 | Basic Configuration of a Router or Switch |
| **NET.3.1.A2** | **Installing Updates and Patches** |
| NET.3.1.A3 | Restrictive Granting of Access Rights |
| NET.3.1.A4 | Protection of Administration Interfaces |
| NET.3.1.A5 | Protection Against Fragmentation Attacks |
| NET.3.1.A6 | Emergency Access to Routers and Switches |
| NET.3.1.A7 | Logging on Routers and Switches |
| NET.3.1.A8 | Regular Backups |
| NET.3.1.A9 | Operational Documentation |
| OPS.1.1.3.A1 | Concept for Patch and Change Management |
| OPS.1.1.3.A2 | Specification of Responsibilities |
| OPS.1.1.3.A3 | Configuration of Auto-Update Mechanisms |
| OPS.1.1.3.A15 | Regular updating of IT systems and software |
| OPS.1.1.3.A16 | Searching for patches and vulnerabilities |
| OPS.1.1.4.A1 | A Concept for Protection Against Malware |
| OPS.1.1.4.A2 | System-Specific Protection Mechanisms |
| OPS.1.1.4.A3 | Virus Protection for End Devices |
| **OPS.1.1.4.A5** | **Operating Virus Protection Programs** |
| **OPS.1.1.4.A6** | **Updating Virus Protection and Signatures** |
| OPS.1.1.4.A7 | User Awareness and Obligations |
| **SYS.2.1.A1** | **User Authentication** |
| **SYS.2.1.A3** | **Activation of Automatic Update Mechanisms** |
| **SYS.2.1.A6** | **Use of Anti-Virus Programs** |
| SYS.2.1.A8 | Protection of the Boot Process |
| SYS.2.1.A42 | Use of cloud and online functions |
| SYS.3.1.A1 | Rules for Mobile Laptop Use |
| **SYS.3.1.A2** | **Laptop Access Protection** |
| **SYS.3.1.A3** | **Use of Personal Firewalls** |
| SYS.3.1.A9 | Secure remote access with laptops |
| SYS.4.5.A1 | Awareness for handling removable media |
| SYS.4.5.A2 | Loss or manipulation report |
| SYS.4.5.A10 | Volume encryption |
| SYS.4.5.A12 | Protection against malware |

## V. DISCUSSION

The focus of our work was to extend the company's security concept to the user's home office in a standardized way that is compatible with a certification from BSI. To approach at a minimal but comprehensive set of requirements, we have started with a minimal home office scenario that includes customer data. In consequence, the Basic requirements from Table IV must be fully implemented for any home-office scenario using customer data. We have found out that this includes much help from an security expert of the employer.

In some home-office scenarios, employers would equip their employees with additional devices, such as tablets or smartphones, or maybe with other categories of applications, such as database systems. The requirements for operating the company's own hardware and software in the home office can also vary greatly. In such cases, the list of requirements in Table IV must be extended. Recall that our minimal scenario did not make any assumptions on the operating systems and business applications used. Therefore, first candidates for further BSI modules are SYS.3.2.4 "Android", SYS.2.4 "macOS Clients" or SYS.2.2.3 "Windows 10 Clients".

The procedure to extend this list of requirements is identical to the research method we have used in this paper: It starts by widening the scope of the information domain. The next step is to research further BSI modules, followed by an assessment of the implementation status of the additional requirements with the IT-Grundschutz Check. The core protection of the BSI-standard 200-3 [17] uses the same approach. Core protection means to secure the most vulnerable subset of the information domain first, and to extend this protection at a later time.

Our approach is adaptable to other certifications, e.g., based on the NIST Cybersecurity Framework [3]. The IT-Grundschutz Compendium is organized in various process layers and system layers, while the Cybersecurity Framework is organized in the categories "Identify", "Protect", "Detect", "Respond" and "Recover". However, both approaches use a comparable methodology. The BSI role "Data User" [10]" corresponds to the NIST role "Information System User" [18]. Furthermore, the requirements in the modules of the IT-Grundschutz Compendium have their counterparts in the controls of the Cybersecurity Framework. For example, BSI module "CON.3 Backup Concept" names requirements that are a subset of the imperatives in the NIST control family "CP: Contingency Planning". Finally, both IT-Grundschutz Compendium and NIST Cybersecurity framework can be mapped to the ISO 2700x series of standards [2].

## VI. Conclusion

With the Basic Protection from the 200-2 standard, the BSI provides companies with a comprehensive guide to implement a defined level of IT-security in a company-wide IT-infrastructure. This security level can be audited and certified, which is mandatory in many sectors of industry and business. However, the BSI considers home-office users as a risk that is external to the company's infrastructure. In consequence, home-office users must have restricted access to company assets, which restricts the business tasks that can be carried out at home.

In this paper, we have investigated which requirements must be implemented in a minimal home-office scenario with customer data in order to obtain the BSI protection level "Basic". Furthermore, we have used a definition for a home-office user, to find out which of those requirements can be implemented by the user.

We have observed that the number of requirements that need a security expert from the company is manageable for a small home-office scenario, and we have discussed how to extend this scenario for more complex settings. Our findings are a first step towards creating an IT-Grundschutz profile for a home office, to simplify security management for employees in a home office, while ensuring a certified security policy at the same time.

## References


[1] Federal Office for Information Security, "BSI IT-Grundschutz Kompendium Edition 2021," https://www.bsi.bund.de/DE/Themen/Unternehmen-und-Organisationen/Standards-und-Zertifizierung/IT-Grundschutz/IT-Grundschutz-Kompendium/it-grundschutz-kompendium_node.html [accessed: July 2021], 2021.

[2] ISO/IEC/IEEE, "The ISO/IEC 27000 Family of Information Security Standards," https://www.itgovernance.co.uk/iso27000-family [accessed: July 2021], 2015.

[3] National Institute of Standards and Technology, "SP 800 series on Information Security and Cybersecurity Practice Guides," https://csrc.nist.gov/publications/sp800 [accessed: July 2021], 2020.

[4] FAZIT Communication GmbH in cooperation with the Federal Foreign Office Berlin, "The Federal Government informs about the Corona crisis," https://www.deutschland.de/en/news/german-federal-government-informs-about-the-corona-crisis [accessed: July 2021], 2021.

[5] M. Bispham, S. Creese, W. H. Dutton, P. Esteve-Gonzalez, and M. Goldsmith, "Cybersecurity in working from home: An exploratory study," Available at SSRN 3897380, 2021.

[6] S. Cooper, "How to secure your home wireless network," https://www.comparitech.com/blog/information-security/secure-home-wireless-network/ [accessed: July 2021], 2020.

[7] NortonLifeLock Inc., "Keep your home Wi-Fi safe in 7 simple steps," https://us.norton.com/internetsecurity-iot-keep-your-home-wifi-safe.html [accessed: July 2021], 2020.

[8] D. Nield, "How to Secure Your Wi-Fi Router and Protect Your Home Network," https://www.wired.com/story/secure-your-wi-fi-router/ [accessed: July 2021], 2020.

[9] Federal Office for Information Security, "IT-Sicherheit im Home Office," https://www.bsi.bund.de/SharedDocs/Downloads/DE/BSI/Cyber-Sicherheit/Themen/checkliste-home-office_mitarbeiter.html [accessed: July 2021], 2020.

[10] Federal Office for Information Security, "BSI-Standard 200-2: IT-Grundschutz-Methodology," https://www.bsi.bund.de/SharedDocs/Downloads/EN/BSI/Grundschutz/International/bsi-standard-2002_en_pdf.html [accessed: July 2021], 2017.

[11] Federal Office for Information Security, "Guide to Basic Protection based on IT-Grundschutz," https://www.bsi.bund.de/SharedDocs/Downloads/EN/BSI/Grundschutz/International/Basic_Security.html [accessed: July 2021], 2017.

[12] Federal Office for Information Security, "BSI IT-Grundschutz Compendium Edition 2019," https://www.bsi.bund.de/SharedDocs/Downloads/EN/BSI/Grundschutz/International/bsi-it-gs-comp-2019.html [accessed: July 2021], 2019.

[13] Conference of Independent German Federal and State Data Protection Supervisory Authorities, "The Standard Data Protection Model," https://www.datenschutzzentrum.de/uploads/sdm/SDM-Methodology_V2.0b.pdf [accessed: July 2021], 2020.

[14] C. Haar and E. Buchmann, "Securing Orchestrated Containers with BSI Module SYS.1.6," in Proceedings of the 7th International Conference on Information Systems Security and Privacy, 2021.

[15] ISO/IEC/IEEE, "ISO/IEC12207:2017 Systems and software engineering Software life cycle processes," https://www.iso.org/standard/63712.html [accessed: July 2021], 2008.

[16] ISO/IEC/IEEE, "ISO/IEC/IEEE 15288:2015 Systems and software engineering System life cycle processes," https://www.iso.org/standard/63711.html [accessed: July 2021], 2015.

[17] Federal Office for Information Security, "BSI-Standard 200-3: Risk Analysis based on IT-Grundschutz," https://www.bsi.bund.de/SharedDocs/Downloads/EN/BSI/Grundschutz/International/bsi-standard-2003_en_pdf.html [accessed: July 2021], 2017.

[18] National Institute of Standards and Technology, "NIST Special Publication 800-100: Information Security Handbook – A Guide for Managers," https://csrc.nist.gov/publications/detail/sp/800-100/final [accessed: August 2021], 2020.

# Identification of Automotive Digital Forensics Stakeholders

Kevin Gomez Buquerin
*C-ECOS*
*Technical University Ingolstadt*
Ingolstadt, Germany
e-mail: extern.kevinklaus.gomezbuquerin@thi.de

Hans-Joachim Hof
*C-ECOS*
*Technical University Ingolstadt*
Ingolstadt, Germany
e-mail: hof@thi.de

***Abstract*—New technologies and features emerging in modern vehicles are widening the attack surface for malicious tampering. As a result, security incidents including vehicles are on the rise. Automotive digital forensics investigations allow resolving such security incidents. This paper presents a stakeholder-based reference model for automotive digital forensics. It is essential to focus on stakeholders to provide the best possible automotive digital forensics investigation for them. We identified twelve distinct stakeholders relevant to automotive digital forensics and assigned them to the vehicle life-cycle's relevant phases. Furthermore, the stakeholders' questions for forensics investigations and their resources get analyzed. We created a Venn diagram to highlight differences and similarities between the stakeholders.**

***Keywords*—*automotive; digital forensics; forensic; cyber security; embedded; vehicle; car; automobile; stakeholder***

## I. Introduction

Features, such as car sharing or function-on-demand determine the design of modern vehicles. These use-cases are very attractive to customers. However, they allow cyber criminals to abuse novel use-cases for malicious purposes. Automotive Digital Forensics (ADF) must efficiently investigate and resolve resulting security incidents.

Vehicle manufacturer spend additional resources in security features and technologies. New security regulations such as the UNECE [12] or ISO-21434 [13] set new requirements for secure automotive systems and development of such. This change in the automotive domain, leads to additional stakeholders such as the UNECE approval authority. Also, the automotive industry sees a switch of focus from existing stakeholders in ADF. Addressing the needs and capabilities of stakeholders is important to ensure the best possible ADF investigation. This paper reports about our research on the questions: "*Which are ADF stakeholders?*" and " *What forensic questions are they interested in?*". The research on these questions contributes the following items:

- A list of twelve unique ADF stakeholders.
- Forensic questions asked by and relevant for ADF stakeholders.
- Forensic resources available to ADF stakeholders.
- Position of the ADF stakeholders in the vehicle life-cycle.
- A comparison between the ADF stakeholders based on defined close curves in a Venn diagram.

The paper is structured as follows: Section 2 presents related work on ADF and argues, why our work is unique. Section 3 provides a useful definition of ADF stakeholders. Section 4 summarizes methods to identify and describe ADF stakeholders. Section 5 presents the main contribution of our paper—the ADF stakeholders identified in our work. Section 6 elaborates differences in similarities of the identified stakeholders. Section 7 evaluates the quality of the identification of the stakeholders and shows, that indeed all relevant stakeholders were identified. Section 8 concludes the paper and gives an outlook on future work.

## II. Related Work

Several scientists from academy and industry already published research on ADF. Only a minority of papers focus on stakeholders or interest groups of the technologies and methods.

Armstrong [5] defines stakeholder groups in Digital Forensics (DF) programs and evaluated a bias for each towards their aim for prosecution. The author presents the victim group and associates, law enforcement, forensic scientists and experts, witnesses, perpetrator group and associates of the perpetrator, judiciary, technology providers, media, and the public as relevant stakeholders. Based on these groups, requirements for the program are defined. Furthermore, the author captures differences and similar interests between the groups. As a result, the DF programs are implemented based on the input collected from the primary users.

Al Fahdi et al. [6] interviewed different stakeholders to determine future challenges in DF. Based on those, the most relevant areas of research are defined. The paper identifies two distinct stakeholder groups, forensic researchers and practitioners. The authors list three top challenges for these stakeholders: cloud computing, anti-forensics, and encryption.

Mansor [4] presents automotive stakeholders in the area of security. The paper lists attack motivations, methods, and capabilities for each stakeholder. Based on this, a comprehensive understanding of each stakeholder is available. The authors define five stakeholder groups: Original Equipment Manufacturers (OEMs), users (e. g., car owner and drivers), service provides (e. g., dealers and workshops), insurance providers, and hackers (e. g., researchers, technical enthusiasts, thieves, and OEM competitors).

All available research focuses on general and offensive automotive security. To the best of our knowledge, we are the first to present stakeholders in the automotive domain for ADF and general defense techniques. However, a solid understanding of stakeholders in the automotive domain is of uttermost importance for the design and development of sufficient technologies and methods for ADF investigations.

## III. Definition of Automotive Digital Forensics Stakeholders

ADF utilizes DF techniques and methods within vehicular systems and the supporting infrastructure. It includes different data types and data sources. We define automotive systems as components installed in vehicles such as Electronic Control Units (ECUs) and modules connected to the vehicle such as manufacturer's backend, smartphones, or Vehicle to X (V2X) devices. X can be other vehicles, infrastructure components, smartphones, smart-home, backend-systems, and more. ADF includes many tasks, ranging from quickly collecting data from an in-vehicle black-box to in-depth analysis such as embedded forensics techniques. The general goal of ADF is answering questions asked by the entity that requests forensic investigation (vulgo stakeholder). The questions (6 WH's) include: *How*, *Why*, *Where*, *When*, *Who*, and *What*.

Freeman and Reed present two methods to define stakeholders. According to them, stakeholders are a "*group or [an] individual who can affect the achievement of an organization's objectives or who is affected by the achievement of an organization's objectives*" [1] or stakeholders are a "*group or [an] individual on which the organization is dependent for this continued survival*" [1]. Based on these definitions, the relevance for ADF stakeholders can be defined: "*ADF stakeholders are relevant if they have a significant negative or positive influence on digital forensics in the automotive sector. This includes in-vehicle systems and their supporting infrastructure.*".

## IV. Identification and Description of Automotive Digital Forensics Stakeholders

Bryson [2] presents multiple methods to identify and analyze stakeholders. He introduces two identification methods. The first method is a brainstorming technique, having multiple people determine relevant stakeholders. Bryson suggests to involve people which have "*information that cannot be gained otherwise*" [2], to ensure that the determined stakeholders are the most relevant for the specific domain. The second method is a snow-ball technique that is based on King et al. [10]. Each identified stakeholder gets contacted and asked to lists other potential stakeholders. This method utilizes the experience and knowledge of existing stakeholders and allows the initial determination of stakeholders to be general and incomplete.

Bryson presents multiple analysis methods. It contains power-versus-interests grids that show the level of interest on the X-axis and the level of power on the Y-axis. The method allows to determine crowds, subjects, context setters, and players in the different quadrants. In addition, Bryson constitutes stakeholder influence diagrams that expand on power-versus-interests grids. Here, lines are drawn between identified stakeholders and interest flows as well as directions of interests are identified. Influence diagrams allow to determine the most important stakeholders of a group.

We decided to use the brainstorming technique. The snowball method is neglected as it is not feasible for groups such as criminals and government organizations. In addition, no stakeholder analysis is performed. This research does not focus on public value or business interest for an ADF company. Instead, this work focuses on identifying stakeholders, including their interests in, resources for, and potential impact on ADF.

Three different groups of attendees for the brainstorming session were selected. First, from academia with a focus on automotive security, second vehicle manufacturer staff working in automotive security, and third a mixed session including automotive security researchers, vehicle manufacturer staff, car owners, supplier staff, and insurer staff. As a result, the different groups consist of car owners, a professor, PhD students, OEM employees, tier one supplier employees, and insurer employees.

There are multiple possibilities to describe ADF stakeholders. A bare listing of stakeholders is likely to be unclear and incomplete, and a reference to the automotive domain may not be evident. Hence, this work categorizes stakeholders based on the vehicle life-cycle that are *production*, *use*, and *end-of-life* [3]. The importance of ADF for a stakeholder is associated with the progression of the vehicle life-cycle. The advantage of such a categorization is the focus on ADF during specific steps of the manufacturing process. Our method is open to integration of additional stakeholders and to the adaption of existing collaborators in the future. To describe stakeholders, we use the following properties:

- The position in the vehicle life-cycle describes the stage in which the stakeholders has an impact on the vehicle or a focus on ADF.
- The stakeholders interests and exemplary forensic questions regarding the 6 WH's of DF.
- Resources available to the stakeholder. Capabilities of the stakeholder to perform or assist ADF investigations. Resources includes hardware, software, documentation, and experience.
- Examples for the stakeholder group.

We select a Venn diagram to visually present different stakeholders. Venn diagrams allow to easily recognize similarities as well as differences. Based on the brainstorming sessions, we identified different interests and focus areas of the stakeholder. Based on those, three closed curves are defined: *Trustworthiness, Functionality, and Law* as *A. Protection and Security* as *B. Misuse, Tampering, and Hacking* as $C$. Stakeholders in the closed curve $A$ focus on trustworthiness and functionality of the vehicle systems. Furthermore, their interest is in fulfillment of regulations. Protection of the intellectual property as well as ensuring security of the automotive systems do group stakeholders in $B$. Closed curve $C$ comprises stakeholders that try to misuse, tamper with, and hack automotive systems.

## V. Automotive Digital Forensics Stakeholder

Three brainstorming sessions were performed. All are based on Bryson's methodology presented in [2]. Within **session one**, one professor, four PhD students, and one master student were involved. The professor as well as all students are part of an automotive security research group at an university. Four PhD students with a focus on automotive security as well as two OEM employees and one tier one employee participated in the **second session**. **Session three** included one insurer employee, one tier one employee, two OEM employees, and two PhD students. All participants work in the area of automotive security and are car owners or business car users. We decided to have three brainstorming sessions in order to involve various relevant participants and stakeholders from different areas. All stated participants contribute to one session only. Further, PhD students as well as other contributors are not the same.

The following paragraphs present the identified stakeholders. Furthermore, forensic questions of the stakeholders, their position in the vehicle life-cycle and examples are presented. All results are from the brainstorming sessions.

*a) OEM:* OEMs are located in the *production* (vehicle development) as well as *use* (maintenance and sale of spare parts) phase of the vehicle life-cycle. OEMs are interested in identifying issues in their products. Forensic questions concern, among other things, the clarification of guilt questions such as *"Did a vehicle system cause the accident?"* or of legal questions such as *"Was there an inadequate handling of personal data in the vehicle?"*. Due to the development background and the system knowledge, there are effects on vehicle development. In addition, OEMs have access to internal information of the vehicles that is valuable in digital forensic investigations (e. g., manufacturer-specific Unified Diagnostic Services (UDS) identifiers). Examples are Audi, BMW, Daimler, Tesla, and Toyota.

*b) Business car owner:* Business car owners own a fleet of vehicles. The position in the vehicle life-cycle lies in the *use* phase. They are interested in protecting employee data and in low insurance costs. Forensic questions include *"Was the driver or the vehicle to blame in the accident?"* or *"Who extracted the personal data from the vehicle?"*. Business car owners have no system knowledge and sometimes use additional devices such as digital logbooks. Examples are companies such as Telekom or the police that own a vehicle fleet.

*c) Private car owner:* Private car owners have no additional resources to conduct ADF investigations. They *use* the car and are interested in the protection of personal data such as the travel route. Private car owners could also utilize ADF investigations to determine why their car is no longer reliable (e. g., a vulnerable device is installed and not properly patched). Examples are people who own a vehicle.

*d) Supplier:* Suppliers support the OEM in the development of vehicle components and functions during the *production* phase. This gives them partial system knowledge. However, this knowledge is very deep because a supplier implements certain subsystems. ADF supports suppliers in troubleshooting and resolving issues during investigations. In addition, suppliers have manufacturer-specific information (e. g., manufacturer-specific UDS identifiers). Examples are Continental, Bosch, and Faurecia.

*e) Mobility provider:* Mobility providers are in the *use* phase of the vehicle life-cycle. They protect their intellectual property and the personal data of their customers. Forensic questions are similar to those of the business car owner, such as *"Was the accident caused by the customer or the vehicle?"* or *"Who extracted the personal data from the vehicle?"*. Due to additional components such as tracking devices or tachographs, mobility providers sometimes have system knowledge. Examples are SIXT, Hertz, and DriveNow.

*f) Legal institution:* Legal institutions own official testers, maintenance equipment, and contracts with the manufacturer to carry out tests on vehicles. They use these resources to determine whether laws and regulations are being followed, which can lead to ADF investigations. They also offer services such as the extraction of Diagnostic Trouble Codes (DTCs). Legal institutions are located in the *production* and *end of life* phase of the vehicle life-cycle. Examples are the German TÜV, independent workshops, and the Federal Motor Transport Authority.

*g) Government organization:* Government organizations have an influence on ADF in the *use* and *end of life* phase. They protect vehicles with a sovereign role (e. g., the government fleet). ADF questions include *"Has the vehicle been compromised?"* and *"What data was collected by vehicle systems?"*. System knowledge is available by requesting necessary information from the manufacturer. In addition, there are special agreements on compliance with laws when the safety of vehicles with sovereign issues is affected. Examples are BND, NSA, CIA, MI5, and Mossad.

*h) Insurer:* Insurers affects ADF in the *use* phase of the vehicle life-cycle. They tend to determine whether the status of the vehicle permits registration and assess the insurance coverage. ADF questions are but are not limited to *"Has the vehicle accelerated by itself?"* and *"Has the vehicle been manipulated (tuned)?"*. System knowledge is partly given through the cooperation with manufacturers. Examples are DEKRA or Allianz.

*i) Criminal:* Criminals concentrate on ADF in the *production* and *use* phases of the vehicle life-cycle. They aim to activate chargeable services and products. In addition, criminals disable immobilizers and steal intellectual property or personal data. ADF questions include *"What personal information can be stolen"* and *"What intellectual property can be collected?"*. Their system knowledge varies between threat actors. Advanced attackers can be very skilled.

*j) Tuner:* Tuners are in the *use* phase of the vehicle life-cycle. Their goal is to achieve increases in performance and to carry out vehicle configurations. Therefore, ADF questions could be "*Where can you find specific information about a functionality in the vehicle?*" and "*Where is the configuration of the engine stored?*". Their system knowledge is high and there is networking as well as cooperation between the tuners. Hardware for communication with the vehicle is also available. Examples are Brabus, MTM, and MHD.

*k) Researcher:* Researchers are in the *use* phase of the vehicle life-cycle. Their aim is to carry out scientific research on vehicles and, for example, to identify problems within vehicle components. ADF questions include "*Which personal data are stored by modern vehicles*" and "*Which components contain forensically relevant data?*". System knowledge may be available. It is determined by open source resources and reverse engineering of components. The researchers are networked through conferences and publications. Examples are academic researchers, private researchers, and penetration testers.

*l) Approval authority:* Approval authorities position themselves in all three phases of the vehicle life-cycle. They determine the fulfillment of legal requirements. New regulations such as UNECE place demands on automotive security, security development, and forensics. An example for a model based security framework is presented by Volkersdorfer and Hof in [11]. Such research directly addresses challenges in security development and testing for modern automotive systems. ADF questions include "*Is personal data stored and protected in the vehicle?*" and "*What information is stored in vehicle systems?*". Approval authorities have no system knowledge. However, there is close cooperation with the manufacturers and they can collect documentation for components. One example is the approval authority for the UNECE standard.

## VI. Comparison of the Automotive Digital Forensics Stakeholder

To visualize all presented ADF stakeholders, a Venn diagram is created and presented in Figure 1. This research focuses on the main interests and areas of focus in ADF of the shown stakeholders. The results come from the brainstorming sessions. The authors are aware that multiple stakeholders do have interest in all areas. However, we categorized stakeholders based on *strong* interest in one of the closed curves: *Trustworthiness, Functionality, and Law* as *A*. *Protection and Security* as *B*. *Misuse, Tampering, and Hacking* as *C*. Various key interests were identified during the brainstorming sessions. The closed curves result from these.

Table I presents the results of the comparison. Set $A$ holds the insurer and approval authority. The business car owner is included in $B$, while the criminal is in Set $C$. Set $A \cap B$ contains the OEM, legal institution, researcher, and supplier. The tuner is located in Set $A \cap C$. Government organizations in Set $B \cap C$. Finally, Set $A \cap B \cap C$ contains the private car owner and mobility provider.

The Venn diagram visualizes similarities and differences. Similarities are shared between stakeholders in the same or adjoining sets. Differences are represented by closed curves in which there is a symmetrical difference. The symmetric difference is compared for all pairs of close curves, that is $A \triangle B$, $A \triangle C$, and $B \triangle C$.

TABLE I
COMPARISON OF AUTOMOTIVE DIGITAL FORENSICS STAKEHOLDER BASED ON A VENN DIAGRAM

| Set | Stakeholder |
|---|---|
| $A$ | Insurer, approval authority |
| $B$ | Business car owner |
| $C$ | Criminal |
| $A \cap B$ | OEM, legal institution, researchers, supplier |
| $A \cap C$ | Tuner |
| $B \cap C$ | Government organization |
| $A \cap B \cap C$ | Private car owner, mobility provider |

One example for the symmetric difference $A \triangle C$ is the insurer and the criminal. The insurer tends to not change automotive components and ensure their safety, while the criminal tampers with devices while not properly testing the safety of performance increases. Another example of the symmetrical difference $A \triangle B$ is the licensing authority and the government organization. Differences are represented by closed curves in which there is a symmetrical difference.

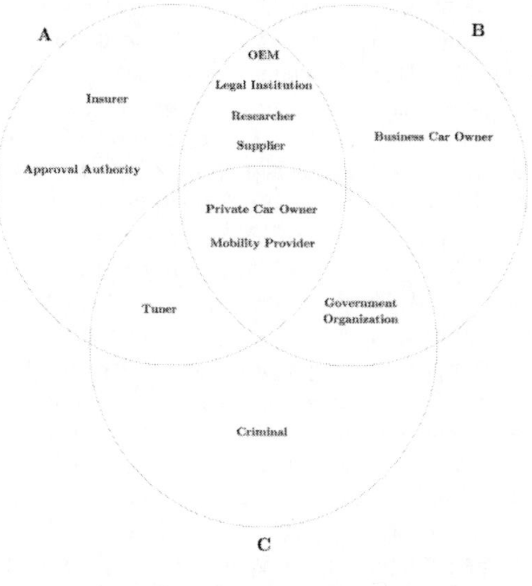


Figure 1. Automotive Digital Forensics Stakeholders in a Venn Diagram

## VII. Evaluation

The next step is to evaluated the shown results. It includes a validation for the methodology and the presented stakeholder table.

### *A. Completeness of the Automotive Digital Forensics Stakeholder Table*

To evaluate completeness of the stakeholder tables, we assessed them using the following list. The list is created based on prior research in stakeholder identification and analysis work:

- *A*: Used identification techniques are in the context of identification and analysis [7].
- *B*: Involved phases are included in the stakeholder identification process [7].
- *C*: Accessible resources are utilized [7].
- *D*: A suitable identification method is used [2] [10].
- *E*: Suitable factors to identify stakeholders are used [8].
- *F*: Legitimacy, urgency, and proximity of stakeholders are considered [9].

*a) A, B, C:* In [7], Luyet et al. stated that stakeholder identification techniques depend on the context of the identification and analysis, the phase involved, and the accessible resources. In case of this research, context and phase is "stakeholder identification". Accessible resources depend on the identification technique. As a result, evaluation is performed on techniques that focus on identification and not on stakeholder analysis. Furthermore, required resources are included in the evaluation criteria that comprises access to stakeholder groups (OEM employees, supplier employees, PhD students, master students, professors, insurer employees, and car owners), number of interviews (3), and interview type (physical and online).

*b) D:* In [2], Bryson presented 15 stakeholder identification and analysis techniques. To evaluate completeness of the automotive stakeholder tables we determine which identification method is used in all 15 techniques. In 12 of 15 techniques, brainstorming is mentioned for stakeholder identification. 3 of 15 techniques do not mention a stakeholder identification technique. Prior the stakeholder analysis, the method assumes that stakeholders have been identified. Furthermore, snow-ball technique by King et al. [10] is not feasible for ADF stakeholders, because no interviews are viable with government institutions or criminals.

*c) E:* Creighton implemented different factors to identify stakeholders [8]. Those include proximity, economy, and social values. Those characteristics are relevant for stakeholder identification in specific geographical areas. It is not feasible for ADF stakeholders because this topic of DF is not dependent on geographical areas. Hence, we did not include factors presented by the author.

*d) F:* In [9], Mitchell et al. identified stakeholders based on legitimacy, urgency, and proximity. These characteristics are covered by their position in the vehicle life-cycle. Legitimacy is covered because each stakeholder is part of the life-cycle—otherwise there would not be any impact from the stakeholder. Due to the different life-cycle phases, urgency and proximity is given for each stakeholder.

### B. Validation of Stakeholder List

We performed multiple interviews with identified stakeholders to validate the stakeholder list. To achieve sufficient coverage we aimed to interview at least one representative for each identified stakeholder group. During each interview, we described the aim of this research. Each representative was able to comment on the table and the shown results. Furthermore, they were instructed to specifically look into interests and resources for their associated stakeholder group. We were not able to contact a representative for government organizations, criminals, approval authority, or tuners. The following results were collected:

- 2 *OEM* representatives: Missed offensive stakeholders. The aim of this thesis is to identify automotive forensics stakeholders and not offensive security stakeholders.
- 2 *business car owner* representatives: No comments.
- 6 *private car owner* representatives: Missed *reliability of the car* as one of their interests. Added this interest to the table.
- 1 *supplier* representative: No comments.
- 1 *mobility provider* representative: No comments
- 1 *legal institution* representative: Missed *fulfillment of safety requirements* as one of their interests. We include those into *laws* since fulfillment of safety requirements is mandatory for a vehicle registration.
- 1 *insurer* representative: Missed *fulfillment of safety requirements* as one of their interests. We include those into *laws* since fulfillment of safety requirements is mandatory for a vehicle registration.
- 2 *researcher* representative: No comments
- 0 *government organization* representative: No interview performed.
- 0 *criminal* representative: No interview performed.
- 0 *tuner* representative: No interview performed.
- 0 *approval authority* representative: No interview performed.

We showed validity for 8 out of 12 presented stakeholders based on the stated interviews. Furthermore, we added missing interests mentioned by the stakeholders. However, additional interviews and surveys with stakeholder group would be beneficial.

### C. Limitations of the Presented List of Automotive Digital Forensics Stakeholder

The presented list of ADF stakeholders is a snapshot. The automotive industry is changing frequently. As a result, the list of stakeholders can change in the course of time. However, our method of adding new stakeholders or adapting interests and resources of existing stakeholders is independent of changes in the industry. New technologies and opportunities lead to adjustments of the stakeholders interests and resources. New regulations can add additional stakeholders—similar to the introduction of UNECE and the approval authority as a new stakeholder in automotive security.

We further emphasize that this research and the resulting stakeholder list is focusing on ADF only. We are aware that stakeholders as well as their interests and resources are similar to general and offensive automotive stakeholders. However, differences between the areas of research are present.

As mentioned in Section VII-B, we were not able to interview representatives for the stakeholder groups government organizations, criminals, approval authority, or tuners. Hence, results for these stakeholders are not sufficiently validated. In addition, more brainstorming sessions including relevant participates could result in more detailed results.

## VIII. Conclusion and Future Work

One challenge in automotive digital forensics is the amount of research questions and forensic problems. Knowing stakeholders relevant in this domain allows researchers to identify problems and ask valuable research questions. Furthermore, vehicles and their components are expensive. Extensive research with multiple evidence items is difficult to achieve. Hence, researchers must fall back to experience and questions asked by practitioners (i. e. stakeholders).

In this work, we determined twelve unique stakeholders relevant in the area of ADF. We were able to identity those, by adapting three brainstorming sessions with relevant participants from academia, the automotive industry, and insurance domain. To present the relevance and impact on each stakeholder, we determined their position on the vehicle life-cycle, their main interest in ADF, as well as their resources and capabilities in performing and assisting ADF investigations. To identify differences and similarities between all stakeholders, we created a Venn diagram with three closed curves.

Future work will focus on interviews of different stakeholders. Based on those, requirements for forensics investigations and DF questions can be determined. This opens new research areas in the field of ADF. Furthermore, constant refinement of the list of relevant stakeholders is required to work on a roster that is up to date. We will identify relevant research questions for the shown stakeholders. These research questions will allow us to create a more fundamental understanding of ADF.

## References


[1] R. Freeman and D. L. Reed, "Stockholders and Stakeholders: A New Perspective on Corporate Governance", California Management Review, vol. 25, pp. 88-106, April 1983.

[2] J. M. Bryson, "What to do when Stakeholders matter", Public Management Review, num. 1, vol. 6, pp. 21-53, March 2004.

[3] T. R. Hawkins, B. Singh, G. Majeau-Bettez, and A. Hammer Strømman, "Comparative Environmental Life Cycle Assessment of Conventional and Electric Vehicles", Journal of Industrial Ecology, num. 1, vol. 17, pp. 53-64, October 2012.

[4] H. Mansor, "Security and Privacy Aspects of Automotive Systems", Royal Holloway, University of London, July 2017.

[5] C. Armstrong, "Including Stakeholder Perspectives in Digital Forensic Programs", 45th Hawaii International Conference on System Sciences, January 2012.

[6] M. Al Fahdi, N. L. Clarke, and S.M. Furnell, "Challenges to digital forensics: A survey of researchers, practitioners attitudes and opinions", Information Security for South Africa, IEEE, August 2013.

[7] V. Luyet, R. Schlaepfer, M. B. Parlange, A. and Buttler, "A framework to implement Stakeholder participation in environmental projects", Journal of Environmental Management, Elsevier BV, pp. 213-219, November 2012.

[8] J. L. Creighton, "Managing Conflict in Public Involvement Settings: Training Manual for Bonneville Power Administration", Creighton and Creighton, 1986.

[9] R. K. Mitchell, B. R. Agle, and D. J. Wood, "Toward a theory of stakeholder identification and salience: the principle of who and what really count" Academy of Management Review 22, 1997.

[10] C. S. King, K. M. Feltey, and B. O. Sused, "The question of participation: toward authentic public participation in public administration" Public Administration Review 58 (4), 1998.

[11] T. Volkersdorfer and H. J. Hof, "A Concept of an Attack Model for a Model-Based Security Testing Framework", SECURWARE 2020, The Fourteenth International Conference on Emerging Security Information, Systems and Technologies, 2020.

[12] Economic and Social Council, "Proposal for a new UN Regulation on uniform provisions concerning the approval of vehicles with regards to cyber security and cyber security management system", UNECE WP.29 Standard, June 2020.

[13] ISO/SAE, "ISO/SAE 21434:2021: Road vehicles — Cybersecurity engineering", edition: 1, August 2021.

# Trust Management in Space Information Networks

Anders Fongen
Norwegian Defence University College, Cyber Defence Academy (FHS/CISK)
Lillehammer, Norway
Email: anders@fongen.no

***Abstract*—The concept of a Space Information Network (SIN) is evolving from a satellite transport infrastructure towards a provider of a range of services, including even Application-as-a-Service (AaaS). Client endpoints connected to a SIN will invoke services in other connected endpoints, as well as services inside the SIN itself. Interactions taking place between clients and SIN components will create trust relations that must be protected from the usual threats. Traditional cryptographic protocols can offer adequate protection from some threats, but the particular conditions of a satellite network requires modifications of the methods used for authorization control and key management. The amount of connectivity and transport capacity required by a traditional Public Key Infrastructure (PKI) configuration causes excessive use of SIN resources, and a modified approach to key deployment, credential validation and authorization control should be investigated.**

***Keywords*—*LEO satellites; trust management; space information networks; AaaS in space***

## I. INTRODUCTION

The term *satellite networks* indicates the evolution of satellites from being radio mirrors to form complex infrastructures where the spacecrafts cooperate for the provisioning of communication services. Satellite networks for communication services have been in operation for three decades and have proven the feasibility of their operation, capacity and utility. We foresee the further evolution of satellite networks into the *Application-as-a-Service* (AaaS) domain, where the network not only provides communication services, but also different kinds of discovery services, collaborative services and even platforms for general AaaS. The descriptive term for this evolving concept is *Space Information Networks* (SIN). Not only will a SIN provide global coverage, but also a very low Round Trip Time (RTT). A satellite at 300 km altitude can offer an RTT as low as 2 ms, much less than any terrestrial network path.

The evolution presented in the above paragraph creates service endpoints inside the network elements of the SIN, representing high value for both providers and customers, so trust management must be in place not only between client endpoints, but also inside the SIN infrastructure, as services in satellites are invoked from other satellites and client endpoints. Existing technology for authentication and authorization control may not be well suited for the particular properties of a SIN infrastructure, which this paper aims to address.

The illustration in Figure 1 shows the endpoints involved in transactions in or trough a SIN: The *Client Endpoints* (CE) are computers connected to the SIN (blue lines). A CE can both have client and server roles, but they are still clients to the SIN services. The service endpoints in satellites are called *Satellite Endpoints* (SE) and may be invoked from CEs as well as other SEs. There are a number of terrestrial endpoints called *Ground Stations* (GS), used by the satellites for communication with the Internet. Services offered by GS are never invoked from CE, only from SE. Red lines in the figure indicate intra-SIN communication endpoints not addressable for CE use.

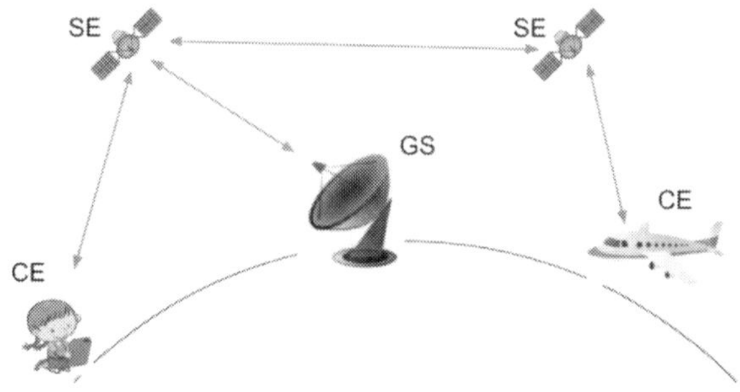


Figure 1. Service endpoint and links which forms the structure of a SIN

The general architecture principle of an AaaS oriented SIN has been published in a previous article [1], where a number of future research problems were presented. In the present paper, a model for SIN trust management will be described in some detail. The general principles of the proposed trust management architecture have originally been developed with tactical military networks in mind [2], and have been modified to match the properties of a satellite network.

A key property of Low Earth Orbit (LEO) satellites is the long idle periods as they fly over inhabited areas, and the predictability of the bursts of requests they receive as they fly over densely populated areas. Non-interactive tasks can thus be scheduled to idle periods, where data stores can be replicated, software updated, etc. Intelligent replication of frequently used resources can contribute to reduced latency and efficient use of infrastructure capacity. [1].

The contribution of this paper is a model for key management, authentication and authorization control using protocols well suited for the particular properties of a SIN. The identification of *Delay Tolerant* operations in credential management that can be scheduled to idle periods is essential in this respect.

The remainder of the paper is organized as follows: In Section II, a short survey of relevant research is presented. Section III identifies the shortcomings of the PKI design.

Section IV presents the author's alternative to X.509, the *Identity Statement*, and how its properties better serve the purpose of trust management and protected service invocation in a SIN. Section V summarizes the arguments of this paper and identifies future research activities.

## II. Related Research

The term *Space Information Network* (SIN) has been used to describe networks of satellites and high altitude aircrafts (drones, balloons) with different service levels. Existing satellite networks like Iridium and the upcoming Starlink [3] offer only communication services, the latter on a very large scale and with high bandwidth. A number of authors have proposed "Cloud Computing in Space" through the addition of larger satellites with sufficient energy and computing resources for taking on these tasks [4] [5].

In order to improve the communication capacity of SIN units, lots of research has gone into the development of antennas for spatial multiplexing (Space-Division Multiple Access, SDMA), beamforming, non-orthogonal multiple access, optical communication links, etc. [6] [7]

The proposals made in this position paper will not deal with technical details in the communication technology, but rather view the SIN as a distributed system which borrows its analysis and solutions from the field of distributed computing. The author is not aware of other efforts to investigate trust management and protection mechanisms specifically for a SIN. Efforts on trust management are made in related areas, as in Mobile and Distributed Systems [2], and in the area of Internet of Things (IoT). IoT systems seem to show little interest for traditional PKI, but rather look to the use of Blockchains. In [8], Blockchains are proposed as the distribution method for tamper-proof trust variables, which are formed through consensus processes and transitive trust. Given that Blockchains have scalability problems, [9] proposes a variant called Holochain, with better scalability properties since the distribution patterns are limited.

Proposals based on Blockchain/Holochain for trust management seem to overlook the importance of the trust chain which binds the technological domain to the managerial domain through cryptographic protocols, and the complexity of the resulting *key management*. Which is why these efforts are not used as a basis for this paper.

## III. Public Key Crypto and Infrastructure

The reader is assumed to be familiar with the fundamental principles of public key crypto, digital signatures, cryptographic hash functions and Public Key Infrastructure (PKI).

The PKI services can be divided in two categories:

1) Creation and deployment of key pairs and certificates
2) Assistance in the certificate validation process.

Operation (1) takes place for each End Entity (EE) after the existing certificate expires, while operation (2) takes place at short intervals or even every time a certificate is validated. It is the task of certificate validation which demands the highest connectivity and network capacity, which is why it is of interest for operation in a SIN.

### A. Certificate revocation

The decision that a certificate should no longer be validated is called *revocation*, and is made by the Certificate Authority (CA) and announced to the community in a variety of ways. A common method is to offer an interactive service through which EE can check the revocation status of a certificate by using the *Online Certificate Status Protocol* (OCSP) protocol. Another method is to disseminate a *revocation list* of certificates that are revoked but not yet expired. Experience indicates that approx. 10% of the certificate population is revoked and represented on a revocation list [10] through entries of (typical number) 37 bytes each.

The use of revocation lists has never been a good idea, and although attempts have been made to distribute delta lists and fragmented lists, the required network capacity for their dissemination is massive [11]. Besides, revocation lists raise lots of dilemmas in situations where the dissemination fails, which is considered to be out of scope for this paper [12].

### B. Authorization control through certificates

Certificates facilitate the authentication phase through binding a transaction or an object to an identifier. It does not indicate the *authorization* of the corresponding entity. Authorization control involves a new set of data sources and protocols for their distribution. Although standards have been published for its interoperability, e.g., XACML [13], they are not widely used. Most vendors offer their own proprietary solution.

In order to avoid the extra cost associated with separate authorization control, many systems choose to confuse authorization with authentication, and assume any valid certificate to be a token for authorization. This is a mistake, which greatly increases the need for revocation, since any changes in the authorizations of an entity requires a certificate to be revoked and a new certificate issued.

In a *constrained network*[14], both authentication and authorization control should be done using one set of data objects and protocols. The most popular standard format for certificates, the X.509, does not lend itself well to this combination, for which reason a different data structure is proposed: The *Identity Statement* (IdS).

## IV. The Identity Statement

For the purpose of authentication and authorization control in a constrained network, the protocols in use should have as few round-trips as possible with the smallest messages possible. For this purpose, the object class *Identity Statement* (IdS) has been constructed. It has many similarities with an X.509 certificate, but is simpler, and a block of named variables (name-value pairs) has been added to support Attribute Based Authorization Control (ABAC) operations. Its elements are:

- Identifier of subject, RFC-822 format address
- Public key

- Validity period
- Authorization attributes
- Issuer's Distinguished Name (X.500 form)
- Issuer's signature
- Room for cross-CoI extensions (described later)

The public key in the IdS can be used both for signature verification (during authentication) and encryption, but not for issuing new Identity Statements. There is no *keyUsage*-element, which means that keys can serve any purpose. As in a PKI, the trust chain depends on a small number of Trust Anchors, called *Identity Providers* (IdP). Their X.500 DN and digital signature are stored in each IdS and used for IdS validation. The group of clients which have the same IdP as their trust anchor is called a *Community of Interest* (CoI).

There is no revocation operation in this architecture. The IdS is irrevocably valid until it expires, before which it is re-issued unless it is invalidated in the mean time. The validity time may be set so short that it matches the *revocation latency* associated with revocation list (typically a small number of hours). The dissemination of re-issued IdS takes opp much less capacity than a similar arrangement based on revocation lists.

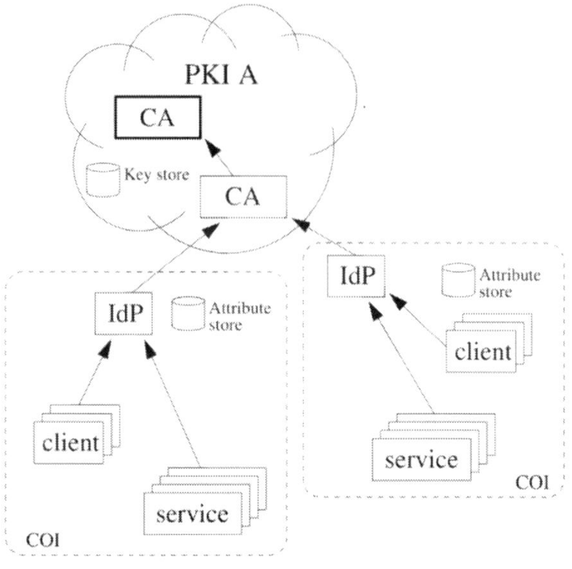


Figure 2. The functional components of trust management. The IdP serves one single CoI. Keys are issued by a PKI, attributes by the IdP.

### A. Issuing Identity Statements

The authority which issues Identity Statements is the Identity Provider (IdP). The structure of the issuing service is shown in Figure 2. The IdP keeps all EE information in a database (possibly gets it from a traditional PKI) and provides signed IdS at anyone' request through a simple HTTP interface. The IdS is a public object so no caller privileges is needed. The public key of the IdP must be installed and trusted by every EE in order for them to validate an IdS.

If the IdP receives an IdS issued by a different IdP, the IdP will issue a *Guest Identity Statement* with the same content and a selection of its authorization attributes, based on a *trust relation* between the two IdPs. This is a way for guest clients from a different CoI to invoke services in this domain. This approach to cross-CoI validation is vastly more efficient and secure than the cross-certificate approach proposed by the traditional PKI.

### B. Dissemination of re-issued Identity Statements

An endpoint (CE or SE) must possess a valid IdS of the corresponding party in order to validate an authentication request, cf. Section IV-C. Normally, it would be the responsibility of the requesting part to enclose a valid IdS with the request message, but several other communication patterns are possible. The validating party may store the IdS from earlier transactions, or may request it directly from the IdP service point.

Please keep in mind that all authentication operations should be *mutual*, i.e., both parties authenticate to the other, and both must have a valid IdS representing the other party at the time of authentication.

Since IdS are never revoked, sound practice for the IdP is to give them a short expiration time and renew them on demand. Anyone possessing an IdS will know the time for its expiration and can plan a suitable moment for its renewal. For this reason, the dissemination may be regarded as a *delay tolerant operation*, which takes place in a relaxed manner when the satellites are in a favorable position for the operation. The satellite can receive the IdS when it is directly communicating with a Ground Station (GS), and pass it on to the CE later when it is within range. In this way, the delay tolerant properties of the operation may allow for the satellite to be used as a *courier* rather than consuming infrastructure capacity.

For an IdS which represents the service endpoint in a satellite, the problem is simple. As the expiration time for the existing IdS is due, the satellite requests a new from the next GS in range.

For CEs, the courier approach raises interesting questions: (1) which satellite(s) should be chosen for the courier task, and (2) when is the CE in operation and ready to receive the IdS? The following observations apply for the analysis of possible solutions:

1) The CE has only one connection point, which is a satellite. The IdS may as well be stored in the satellite as in the terrestrial endpoint. Besides, the satellite has a shorter path to the IdP and higher communication capacity. The IdS will be a part of the client state during handover to trailing satellites before being discarded. A complicating factor for this arrangement to work is that the SE need to engage in the authentication protocol and inject the IdS into the message stream when needed.
2) If the CE is authenticating with an Internet endpoint, the other endpoint has the most network capacity to its disposal. It may as well acquire the IdS for the CE by itself, and cache it for subsequent invocations.

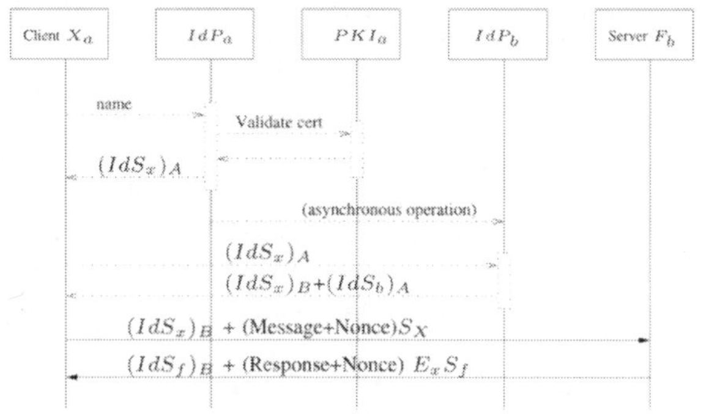


Figure 3. Trust management protocols for IdS issue and service invocation in a cross-CoI environment.

3) The IdS could be replicated on a subset of satellites, so that the CE may connect to one of them within a given time period (e.g., 60 minutes) to find a renewed IdS. With a handover frequency of 10 minutes (typical number) at least every 6th satellite passing over the CE should be able to offer the IdS. This fraction can be lower if the location of the CE is known or guessed, and the validity period of the IdS is less than a full orbital period. One can also take advantage of the fact that a southbound satellite pass will be northbound 12 hours later. There is a trade-off between the number of satellites involved and the operating demands on the CE, e.g., if the CE always has to be connected to the SIN.

As a fallback option, the endpoint may invoke the communication service to obtain an IdS from the IdP service point. Under the proposed scheme for IdS dissemination, this service is likely to be the choice when the CE computer is started and used immediately, if it cannot wait for the next pass of a courier satellite.

### C. *Invoking services with IdS*

The protocol for invoking a service should provide mutual trust establishment through a minimum number of messages. In the simplest scenario, the requester/client will send its IdS together with the request message and a nonce, signed by its private key. The responder/server will validate the IdS, verify the signature and execute the service. The response message will include the server's IdS and the service response and the nonce, encrypted with the client's public key and signed with server's private key.

Figure 3 illustrates a *cross-CoI* service invocation, which involves IdS issued by two IdPs, a guest IdS for client X issued by $IdP_b$, a cross-CoI $(IdS_b)_a$ for $IdP_b$ issued by $IdP_a$ for validation of the server's IdS by the client. Apart from these extra data elements, the cross-CoI invocation remains essentially similar to the base case, and there is no need for revocation status from foreign CoIs, which would otherwise complicate the validation of the guest IdS. The initial invocation of the IdP services and the enclosure of IdS in the service invocation messages are not strictly necessary since they may be cached in the parties from preceding operations.

## V. CONCLUSION

This paper describes the trust management components of an ongoing effort to outline the design of a Space Information Network with application service capabilities (AaaS). Its main focus is to preserve low latency through prudent protocols and data structures, as well as room for any number of credential-issuing authorities (called *Identity Providers*, IdP).

Why is the proposed trust management essential for the SIN operation? Because it allows cross-CoI service invocations to take place in a minimum of round trips and with minimal message size, allowing the SIN to offer services with unprecedented low latency, which is the most important motivating property for its design.

Other revocation free schemes could possibly work, like replacing the short-lived IdS with a combination of X.509 certificates and an OCSP response message which attests the validity of the certificate for a short period of time. This approach does not, however, lend itself well to the inclusion of authorization information in the trust protocols. Besides, the validation of an X.509 certificate involves a large number of poorly understood variables, which is often seen to create errors, ambiguities and interoperability problems.

Issuing and dissemination of IdS remains an unsolved problem though, which should take place in a *delay tolerant* manner to exploit the frequent idle period of satellites as they fly over inhabited areas. A simulation model is under construction for the study of possible solutions.

## REFERENCES

[1] A. Fongen, "Application services in space information networks," in *CYBER 2021*. Barcelona, Spain: IARIA, Oct 2021, pp. 113–117.

[2] ——, "Federated identity management in a tactical multi-domain network," *Int. Journal on Advances in Systems and Measurements*, vol. Vol.4, no 3&4, pp. 157–167, 2011.

[3] "Starlink web site," https://www.starlink.com/, [Online; accessed 19-Oct-2021].

[4] S. Briatore, N. Garzaniti, and A. Golkar, "Towards the internet for space: Bringing cloud computing to space systems," in *36th International Communications Satellite Systems Conference (ICSSC 2018)*, 2018, pp. 1–5.

[5] S. Cao *et al.*, "Space-based cloud-fog computing architecture and its applications," in *2019 IEEE World Congress on Services (SERVICES)*, vol. 2642-939X, 2019, pp. 166–171.

[6] X. Zhang, L. Zhu, T. Li, Y. Xia, and W. Zhuang, "Multiple-user transmission in space information networks: Architecture and key techniques," *IEEE Wireless Communications*, vol. 26, no. 2, pp. 17–23, 2019.

[7] Y. Su *et al.*, "Broadband leo satellite communications: Architectures and key technologies," *IEEE Wireless Communications*, vol. 26, no. 2, pp. 55–61, 2019.

[8] A. Lahbib, K. Toumi, A. Laouiti, A. Laube, and S. Martin, "Blockchain based trust management mechanism for iot," in *2019 IEEE Wireless Communications and Networking Conference (WCNC)*, 2019, pp. 1–8.

[9] R. T. Frahat, M. M. Monowar, and S. M. Buhari, "Secure and scalable trust management model for iot p2p network," in *2019 2nd International Conference on Computer Applications Information Security (ICCAIS)*, 2019, pp. 1–6.

[10] S. Berkovits, S. Chokhani, J. Furlong, J. Geiter, and J. Guild, "Public key infrastructure study: Final report," *Produced by MITRE Corporation for NIST*, April 1995.

[11] A. Fongen, "Optimization of a public key infrastructure," in *IEEE MILCOM*, Baltimore, MD, USA, Nov 2011, pp. 1440–1447.

[12] R. L. Rivest, "Can we eliminate certificate revocation lists?" in *Financial Cryptography*, R. Hirchfeld, Ed. Berlin, Heidelberg: Springer Berlin Heidelberg, 1998, pp. 178–183.
[13] "OASIS eXtensible Access Control Markup Language," https://www.oasis-open.org/committees/tc_home.php?wg_abbrev=xacml, [Online; accessed 19-Oct-2021].
[14] C. Bormann, M. Ersue, and A. Keränen, "Terminology for Constrained-Node Networks," RFC 7228, May 2014. [Online]. Available: https://rfc-editor.org/rfc/rfc7228.txt

# Board Games as Security Awareness Improvement Tools

Eszter Diána Oroszi
National University of Public Service
Budapest, Hungary
e-mail: oroszi.eszter@silentsignal.hu

*Abstract*—**Improving security awareness level of users is getting more important in all organizations. Experience shows that traditional training methods and campaign elements are not enough these days. This paper will show new gamified possibilities, and within that, it will introduce a security awareness board game, future works and partial results of a related research performed by author.**

***Keywords-security awareness; improvement; gamfication; board game; serious game.***

## I. INTRODUCTION

Information security is becoming more important in all organizations, and we can say that human factor is one of the most vulnerable elements at the workplace, the so-called weakest link in the chain of security [1]. Employees of companies could be targets of human-based attack types called Social Engineering, which means that attackers try to manipulate, and/or deceive users for example to compromise confidential data, and cause harm or loss to the organization. To reduce this risk, it is very important to improve the security awareness level of users.

Security awareness improvement actions could be trainings (for example, classroom or online presentations, workshops, e-Learning materials, etc.), or campaign elements (for example, posters, puzzles, quizzes, etc.). According to NIST 800-50 [2], the purpose of these actions is to inform and educate employees about the security policies and rules of the organization and the necessity of security aware behavior, improve skills and competences of users to work securely, and increase security awareness level [2]. Besides occasional or periodical trainings and educational events, it is important to maintain users' attention, and constantly remind employees of information security rules and best practices. To do this, organizing a security awareness campaign, or whole year improvement program could be a possible method, which can help employees remember the most important security rules and habits during their daily work, and which can show information security news, share actual knowledge elements for the audience. These events could be even a so-called awareness week, or cybersecurity month, like Cyber October, when the employees take part in trainings, presentations, answer questionnaires, participate in games; or it can be a general annual program with posters in the office, screensavers highlighting threats targeting the human factor, regular newsletters, and games improving security awareness.

According to the author's experiences, traditional security awareness training and campaign elements are quickly forgettable, and usually most of users think that these well-known messages are boring and contain unnecessary information. Finally, a significant problem regarding these is that they do not answer the most important questions: Why do we need information security? What could happen, if a user does not follow the rules? Which are our roles and responsibilities in security?

A useful and effective awareness program should answer the questions mentioned above and present the importance of security-aware behavior of employees. According to Rocha Flores and Ekstedt [3], using personalization in security related trainings and specialized content of educational material can make the security awareness improvement program more relevant and understandable for the participants, and combining the traditional methods with practical exercises will more likely lead to improved security behavior. The author's experience also supports the above-described statements: security awareness trainings are more effective, when the presentation is illustrated with real examples, and contain photos about results of Social Engineering audits. Another effective method is using gamified elements during the training [4]. Based on these, we must improve security awareness programs, and try to use unique and personalized campaign elements that involve employees into the information security. These kinds of actions could be active programs using gamification, games for formal prizes like "The most security aware employee of the month", or a photo competition about information security. The next parts of the paper will show how can we use gamification for security awareness improvement actions.

In Section II, the author presents gamified security awareness campaign elements, and in Section III, the focus is on board games as educational materials. Section IV contains the concept of a security awareness board game designed by the author. Section V shows the conclusions and the future work of the author.

## II. GAMIFIED ELEMENTS IN SECURITY AWARENESS

Gamification is getting more popular of a method in companies to motivate employees, improve performance, enhance experiences of trainings. A possible definition of this concept is the following: "Gamification is the use of game elements and game thinking in non-game environments to increase target behavior and engagement" [5].

According to Burke [6], the most important purpose of gamification is to increase motivation and improve engagement. Besides that, a key element of these methods is that "we most often want everyone to win", but it could have a collaborative-competitive approach, too – in this case, participants competing as teams, rather than individuals.

Typical gamified improvement elements could be badges, leaderboards, points or scores, levels, and challenges [7]. Applying these methods, participants could easily identify their progress and results and could motivate each other, too. Results could be recorded on Intranet sites of the organization, in the e-Learning solution, security awareness mobile application, or other training systems/framework. The essence of them is that users get points for participating in workshops, trainings, solving quizzes and tests, identifying, and participating in other campaign elements, games.

All previous mentioned elements have positive feedback, and it is an important aspect, when using gamification. Besides that, gamified methods provide the users with a sense of autonomy about the training, it is perceived as a fun experience, not as a mandatory task [8]. According to the author's experience, users really prefer positive feedback and "stories" in information security, for example, they are excitedly waiting for the results of phishing tests, and they would like to get better and better results, or they are proud, if someone recognizes a real or test-attack, or solves a security awareness game.

The first gamified method of the author was a security awareness escape room, which was designed in 2014, based on her experience of Social Engineering audits and security awareness trainings, but feedbacks of campaigns were also built into this special exit game. Besides the type of exercise, the most significant difference between a traditional exit room and an information security-based one is the scenario, or story of the game. In a traditional escape game, players are usually locked into the room of a non-realistic character (pirate, scientist, killer, etc.), but in case of the security awareness one, the escape room is mostly the office of a fictional assistant, boss, project manager, system administrator or other employee, who could be the target of any attacker [9]. A normal exit game, usually with two to six players can be solved in 60 minutes, in a security awareness escape room the time could be limited to 15 or 30 minutes, so shorter timeslots do not set back daily work, and managers can support the participation of their subordinates better. In this game the players are not locked in the room like in general cases, and the goal is not finding the key or code to unlock the door. To "escape" the room, and complete the mission, participants need to log into the computer of the targeted person and open a chosen file – if they can open it and read its content, they won, and the game ends. Feedbacks of security awareness escape rooms are very positive; participants really like these programs, and consider them not only exciting, but also useful. Based on these positive experiences, another game-based learning opportunity could be an applicable idea: board games.

## III. Board Games in Information Security

Board games as training materials are also new, gamified methods in several areas of education. The baseline of popularity is the same, as in case of escape rooms: tabletop games, puzzles, or card games are also well-liked nowadays, strategical-cooperative ones (for example, Pandemic, King of Tokio, Catan, Activity, etc.) have a serious target audience. Based on that, these games could be used for educational purposes, even in security awareness improvement.

Adam Shostack collected, and shortly introduced a few information security related board games on his website [10]. Some of them are more for fun, and include a little bit of security awareness topics and knowledge, but there are serious games, which are designed for use in corporate environment with less aim for enjoyment. These games show perfectly, what could be the purpose and role of the human factor in information security. To win the game, the players need to prevent attacks and defend against hackers, improve security countermeasures, design and develop securely, or they can even see the impact of a security incident on their assets. Increasing motivation, engagement and providing freedom are advantages that are particularly highlighted by these types of gamification elements. These serious games are not first and foremost designed for children, students or even individuals, rather for employees of organizations, average users, specialists, professionals and managers. For example, Cook et al. [11] introduced a board game called Simulated Critical Infrastructure Protection Scenarios (SCIPS), which is designed for decision makers of critical infrastructure, for showing consequences of cyber-attacks, and highlighting the importance of information security investments and controls.

Another security awareness board game is Riskio, which is a tabletop game for 3-5 players, even without technical knowledge. This game itself is not sold commercially, rather it could be played with the directions of an instructor, who is an information security expert [12]. In contrast, Control-Alt-Hack is a commercially available tabletop card game about white hat hacking, for 3-6 participants. According to the storyline of the game, players are ethical hackers performing audits and working for a security consulting company. Like classical board games, this one also has characters, different decks, and it is played in rounds, which are divided into 7 phases. To win the game, player must become the CEO of his own company [13]. Open source, free downloadable games could also be found on the Internet. For example, [d0x3d!] is a customizable, cooperative board game, focusing mainly on network security, so it is a special kind of security awareness games [14], or OWASP Cornucopia is a unique kind of security awareness card games, because it is designed only for a special user group, development teams, and the topic is secure development [15].

Although the main purpose of most games is to learn by playing, the above-mentioned games (according to the author's opinion, especially Riskio and OWASP

Cornucopia) could be useful in a corporate environment, too. Using these gamified methods, participation in security awareness trainings could be raised, and user satisfaction with information security could become better. Potential limitations of these games include being commercially available only on a limited basis, hard to find, according to the author's opinion, the main focus is not "to be a playful board game", and reaching target audience could be difficult. The author's assumption is that a well-advertised, commercially available security awareness related board game could be popular, and could help to improve security awareness level of both individuals and employees in an effective way. Availability as a classic board game could be more attractive than educational materials, and the audience could buy their own game, or they can try and use them as shared resource at the workplace, educational events (for example, family day, festival), board game cafes, etc.

## IV. Concept of a Security Awareness Board Game Designed by the Author

Based on Social Engineering audit and security awareness training experiences, the author of this paper also designed a board game with the purpose of improving security awareness. The board game is designed for an office environment, but development of a home edition, including for children is also in progress. The game focuses on general information security recommendations and awareness knowledge; thus, it is not limited to organizational rules and policies – special organizational editions could be implemented, but the main purpose of the basic game is to improve general security awareness knowledge of users, both at the workplace, and at home. Updates (for example, new threats, attack types, countermeasures) could be released as accessories, packages of additional cards, decks, characters, places, etc.

During the development of this board game, the author's goals were the following:

- Applying strategic-cooperative approach.
- Enables cooperative and competitive playing modes.
- Fit for organizational environment and private life.
- The game should highlight exploitable human traits (Solution: Character cards).
- The game should introduce assets to be protected (Solution: Asset tokens).
- The game should teach security awareness and useful countermeasures (Solution: Security awareness knowledge cards).
- The game should show threats and attacks affected by human factor (Solution: Action cards).
- Could be played with instructor at the workplace.
- Could be played alone at home (without instructor).
- Supports demo mode (applying time limit).
- Be realistic, but still a game (players sometimes need luck).
- Be commercially available, like traditional board games.
- The game should be expandable with accessories.

The game is designed for 6 players and have both cooperative and competitive modes: using the "security awareness meters", players can see the summarized results of the whole team, but in case of a competition, they can measure their own progress in the character cards. The parts of the game are introduced below and could be seen in Figure 1.

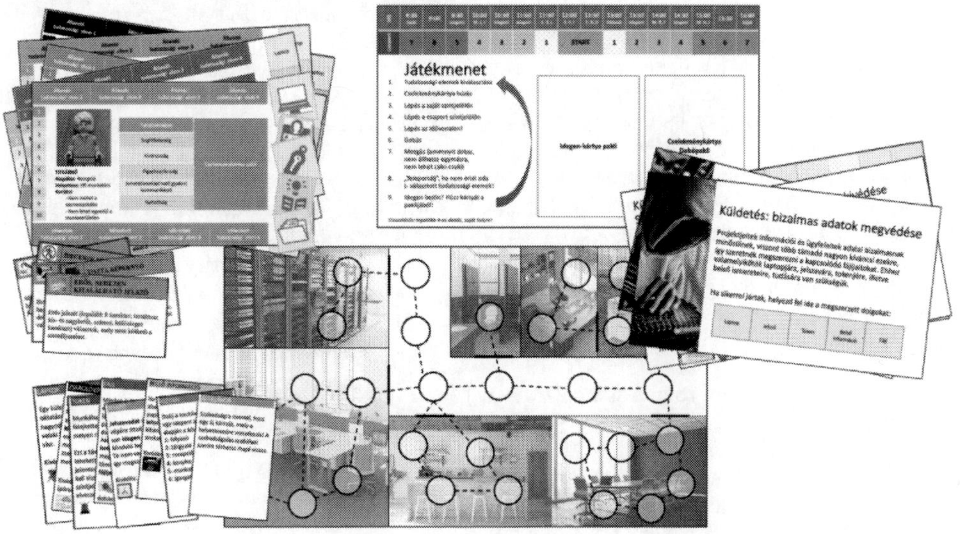


Figure 1. Elements of board game designed by the author

### *A. Game board*

The game board illustrates an office with lobby, open space workplaces, server room, director's office, meeting room, kitchen, corridors, and toilet. Characters can step on fields located within these areas.

### *B. Character cards*

The players can choose from 6 characters (director, secretary, lawyer, HR specialist, developer, and system administrator). Each character has different human traits and habits as vulnerabilities, which will become important when attacked, and they all have assets (notebook, token, password, knowledge, documents, files), which must be protected during the game. These elements are shown, or should be placed on the character cards.

### *C. Security awareness knowledge cards*

Each character has a deck of security awareness knowledge cards. Players can pick three fixed, and three variable options to protect their assets, and the variable cards can be exchanged after every round of the game, based on predicted actions, or according to the places, where the character is.

### *D. Mission cards*

In the current version, there are four missions in the game, which contain different goals and attack types (for example, defending passwords, securing top secret document, etc.), and have different difficulty, too. Players have to focus on the affected assets and protect them from the attacks. After a successful attack, the affected asset must be moved from the Character card to the Mission card. If all the targeted assets are on the Mission card, the players lose the game.

### *E. Action cards*

Attacks, or even positive (for example, security awareness training for bonus points) or general (like movement to another location) events happen by drawing Action cards. The action card deck is distributed among the players. These cards must be drawn by everyone in every round, and it will show, what happens. Attacks can be prevented by one of the relevant Security awareness knowledge cards shown in the Action card, which can be found on the Character card of the player (both fixed and variable cards could be used).

### *F. Timeline*

The timeline is showing the current round, symbolizing a workday divided into half hour slots. Fields of the timeline show subgoals, for example, some characters have to move to the meeting room, or there are timeslots, when unknown visitors arrive at the office, who could also become potential attackers, activated by Action cards. If players reach the last time slot (16:00), the game ends, and they win the game. (Timelines of demo games are shorter and divided into 8 hours.)

### *G. Security awareness meter*

Security awareness meter can be found both for the team, and on the character cards. If a player prevents the attack, he or she, and the team can both step forward on Security awareness meter(s), in case of successful attack, they have to step one field back. At the end of the game, players can see their results, how security-aware they are.

During the game, players have to move their characters every round, and to do this, they have to roll the dice. Direction of movement can be arbitrary, but certain points of the timeline show that certain characters have to be at a place at that time (for example, the developer has to be in the kitchen at 12:00).

The players win, if they are at the end of the timeline and completed the mission (have the needed assets), and the game is ended without success, if the characters fail the mission during the workday (if they cannot protect the assets according to mission).

This game is currently in end-user testing phase, and part of a security awareness research ending in 2022, but some partial results are shared in the next section.

## V. CONCLUSION AND FUTURE WORK

Gamification is nowadays a popular weapon to increase user motivation and engagement, and it is also a possible new method in improving security awareness level of employees. Besides traditional gamified actions (for example, gathering points, scores, leaderboards, achievements, levels, badges, etc.), games could be used also as educational materials. The paper introduced results of some conference papers and other related works, which are confirming the effectiveness and usefulness of gamified methods. Based on these statements, it is recommended to use gamified elements in security awareness improvement actions, like information security escape rooms or board games, which were presented in this paper.

Besides the popularity of these new methods, measuring their effectiveness is also important. As future work, the author has ongoing research, which is going to assess the effectiveness of different methods for improving security awareness. The author will compare six possible program elements, which are the following:

- In-person security awareness training,
- online security awareness training,
- using e-Learning materials,
- security awareness escape room,
- security awareness board game,
- security awareness campaign elements (posters, gifts, messages, etc.).

Each program element has the same timeframe (30 minutes) and content (ten chosen areas of knowledge), which makes them comparable with each other. To measure effectiveness, before and immediately after the participation in the improvement action, participants have to fill out an information security awareness survey, and one month later a post course questionnaire (containing same questions) will be performed. All of these surveys ask users to describe important security awareness rules, recommendations. As a result of the research, the author can identify, which are the most important new security awareness knowledge elements coming from the improvement action, which are the deepest knowledge elements (one month later), and how effective the investigated methods work. Participants of the research are 10 organizations, each of them with 30 employees, who are divided into six groups according to the tested methods. (Each user may participate in only one program element.)

The author's hypothesis in this research is that gamified elements will be more effective than traditional ones. Although the research is still in progress, partial results show that 75 percent of participants prefer gamified elements instead of traditional methods and in-person events are more effective than online based solutions. Based on the experiences to date, the highest amount of new knowledge elements was written after the security awareness board game – presumably, the reason could be that both Security awareness knowledge cards and Action cards contain useful information. According to the partial results of a questionnaire about the board game, 93.3 percent of the testers declared that they would like to play the game with their colleagues, 80 percent of the responders would like to use it also at home. 66.7 percent of players stated that they would like to use the game without the help of an instructor. These results suggest that there is a demand for such gamified security awareness improvement tools, like board games. Effectiveness of the gamified methods could be evaluated after performing the last surveys at the end of the research, probably finalizing in Q1, 2022.

## ACKNOWLEDGMENT

The author would like to thank Silent Signal LLC. that contributed to the development of the presented board game and supports ongoing research about evaluating effectiveness of security awareness improvement methods. Special thanks for friends and colleagues, who participated in testing the author's security awareness board game and contributed to the development with useful feedbacks and suggestions.

## REFERENCES

[1] K. D. Mitnick, and W. L. Simon, The Art of Deception: Contolling the Human Element of Security. Wiley, 2003, ISBN: 978-0764542800

[2] M. Wilson, and J. Hash, NIST 800-50 Building an Information Technology Security Awareness and Training Program, 2003

[3] W. Rocha Flores, and M. Ekstedt, Shaping intention to resist social engineering through transformational leadership, information security culture and awareness. Computers and Security, 59, pp. 26-44, 2016

[4] E. D. Oroszi, Security awareness escape room - a possible new method in improving security awareness of users. [Conference paper]. Cyber Science Cyber Situational Awareness for Predictive Insight and Deep Learning, C-MRiC.ORG., Oxford, pp. 170-173, 2019

[5] P. Van den Boer, Introduction to Gamification. Whitepaper. 2019. Available from: https://cdu.edu.au/olt/ltresources/downloads/whitepaper-introductiontogamification-130726103056-phpapp02.pdf [retrieved: January, 2019]

[6] B. Burke, Gamify: How Gamification Motivates People to Do Extraordinary Things. Gartner, 2014, ISBN: 978-1937134853

[7] Anadea, How Gamification in the Workplace Impacts Employee Productivity, 2018. Available from: https://medium.com/swlh/how-gamification-in-the-workplace-impacts-employee-productivity-a4e8add048e6 [retrieved: October, 2021]

[8] E. G. B. Gjertsen, E. A. Gjære, M. Bartnes, and W. Rocha Flores, Gamification of Information Security Awareness and Training. [Conference paper] 3rd International Conference on Information Systems Security and Privacy, pp. 59-70, 2017

[9] E. D. Oroszi, Security awareness escape room - a possible new method in improving security awareness of users. [Conference paper]. Cyber Science Cyber Situational Awareness for Predictive Insight and Deep Learning, C-MRiC.ORG., pp. 170-173, Oxford, 2019

[10] Online source, available from https://adam.shostack.org/games.html, 2021.08.08

[11] A. Cook, R. Smith, L. Maglaras H. Janicke, Using Gamification to Raise Awareness of Cyber Threats to Critical National Infrastructure [Conference paper]. 4th International Symposium for ICS & SCADA Cyber Security Research (ICS-CSR 2016), Belfast, pp. 84-94, 2016

[12] Online source, available from: https://www.riskio.co.uk, [retrieved: October, 2021]

[13] Online source, available from: https://boardgamegeek.com/boardgame/128408/control-alt-hack, [retrieved: October, 2021]

[14] Online source, available from: https://d0x3d.com/d0x3d/welcome.html, [retrieved: October, 2021]

[15] Online source, available from: https://owasp.org/www-project-cornucopia/, [retrieved: October, 2021]

# Differential Privacy Approaches in a Clinical Trial

Martin Leuckert
Faculty of Computer Science,
Otto-von-Guericke University
Magdeburg, Germany
e-mail: martin@leuckert.de

Antao Ming
Clinic of Nephrology, Hypertension, Diabetes and Endocrinology, Otto-von-Guericke University Magdeburg
Magdeburg, Germany
e-mail: antao.ming@med.ovgu.de

*Abstract*— **Clinical trials are essential for advancements in the medical field. The study subjects of clinical trials agree that the data may be used within the scope of the clinical trial and they trust the study center to not misuse the data. Limiting access and anonymizing the data is usually the only way of offering privacy to the subjects. Currently, the collected data may only be used within the scope of the respective study, and in the case of external entities evaluating the data, potential privacy risks occur. To improve the situation, we investigated the applicability of Differential Privacy approaches for clinical trials by looking into differentially private queries as well as differentially private Machine-Learning approaches. Different configurations have been tested for two Differential Privacy mechanisms. The Laplacian Mechanism is much more influenced by the chosen epsilon compared to the Functional Mechanism implemented in this study. However, both mechanisms trade accuracy for privacy. In summary, both queries and Machine Learning can be made secure by applying differential privacy approaches, but the implementation and configuration overhead is still likely to exceed the capacity of clinical trials, especially the smaller ones.**

***Keywords-Differential Privacy; Clinical Trial; Sensor Data; Machine Learning; Privacy Preservation; Data Security.***

## I. INTRODUCTION

There is an increasing number of companies collecting massive amounts of data about virtually every aspect of our lives. The availability of big data can be useful for many reasons, for instance, to gain statistical insights or to build Machine-Learning (ML) models. When it comes to confidential data, we expect entities that we trust our data with to release information only as long as privacy is maintained. Participants in medical trials expect their data to be handled with confidentiality, but, on the other hand, having as much available data collected as possible can be key to new scientific insights in medical trials.

In many cases, often including medical trials, the assumption is that anonymizing data suits this need. Often, it is considered safe to use pseudonyms and not release other identifying data, such as phone numbers and addresses. However, the Netflix prize dataset linkage attack performed by Narayanan and Shmatikov [1] in 2007 using the Internet Movie Database (IMDb) to successfully identify users is a good example of why pseudonymization and anonymization as the only means of privacy-preservation are insufficient.

The advances in privacy-preserving approaches are released proportionally to the increasing importance and awareness of privacy. The clinical implementation of privacy-preserving mechanisms, on the other hand, is often lagging many years behind because of the previously described misconception; and the data protection laws either do not require the implementation of advanced security functions or have, according to Koch et al. [3], insufficient requirements. On the basis of a real clinical study, we discuss an approach to improve the situation. This work focuses on the applicability of Differential Privacy (DP) in a specific medical trial scenario rather than surveying or evaluating different DP mechanisms to find the most suitable mechanism. However, the outcome of relevant surveys of DP ML in practice, such as Jayaraman and Evans [14], has been considered.

### A. *Problem Definition*

Initially, we explain the setup of a real-world scientific study to illustrate the privacy problem and how specific privacy-preserving mechanisms can be used to solve them. The research was carried out in the context of a clinical trial that studied ulcer prevention using a smart insole. The study, which is based on the findings in Armstrong et al. [2], found that the temperature at the affected foot regions increases weeks before the inflammation. The study, conducted in [6], aimed at providing 300 diabetics who suffer from comorbidities like nerve damage and are at risk of developing ulcers with a smart insole in order to intervene in time. The insole has multiple temperature sensors and transfers the measurement data to a smartphone app which then forwards the data to an electronic trials system located at the research facility.

Researchers then analyze the data to learn about potential diseases like ulcers, gout, or peripheral arterial occlusive disease that can be detected by continuously measuring the foot temperature. Further research intends to find automated alarm signals by using ML algorithms to identify arising ulcers early. In order to benefit the most from the data, it makes sense to involve third-party scientists specialized in data mining and ML.

First, the data subject must give explicit consent to all of the primary (article 6 (1)(a) of General Data Protection Regulation (GDPR)) and secondary research activities (article 6 (1)(b) of GDPR) involving their personal data:

"Personal data shall be collected for specified, explicit and legitimate purposes and not further processed in a manner that is incompatible with those purposes; further processing for archiving purposes in the public interest, scientific or historical research purposes or statistical purposes shall, per Article 89(1), not be considered to be incompatible with the initial purposes ('purpose limitation');"

This clinical trial setup relies on third parties to analyze the acquired data. Under the assumption that all requirements of the GDPR, including the explicit consent, are met, the privacy of the participants is at risk: Both the data queries and the ML models reveal data about the study participants. According to Jagannathan et al. [15]: "The difficulty of individual privacy is compounded by the availability of auxiliary information, which renders straightforward approaches based on anonymization or data masking unsuitable."

Significant progress was made when Cynthia Dwork [4] defined DP as retrieving useful information while maintaining privacy. Pre-eminently, DP uses randomized noise to protect individuals in a data set. The required range of noise that needs to be added to a query depends on the sensitivity of the respective function. The sensitivity describes the maximum difference between two queries on an underlying data set and is therefore proportional to the magnitude of the required noise to maintain privacy. Depending on the underlying data set, the amount of required noise can be very high if the global sensitivity is high. There are investigations to still achieve DP in these cases; Lundmark and Dahlman [5], for instance, address the issue of applying noise based on global sensitivity to reduce the required noise.

### B. Goals

First, this work will demonstrate why the security regulations required by European law and their national implementations are insufficient in the context of preserving the participant's privacy. This includes the General Data Protection regulation (art.70.1.b of the GDPR) and the Clinical Trials Regulation (CTR).

Second, we will demonstrate that it is possible to implement DP in the context of the clinical trial described in the problem definition to improve privacy without significantly affecting the usefulness of the results (utility). This is possible for both queries and ML operations. We will conclude this paper with a subjective assessment of the results.

### C. Setup

Implementing privacy-preserving mechanisms extending further than pseudonymization or anonymization might be hard to sell to physicians. They potentially fear for the usability of their data if encryption or noise of some sort is implemented. In the same vein, looking into the field of homomorphic encryption reveals many cases of rejection due to performance concerns [25]. Among other reasons, this is why most clinical trials implement legally required privacy measures without questioning them.

The open-label, prospective, and single-blinded study recruited participants with diabetes mellitus type I or II who are randomly assigned to the control (n=150) or the intervention group (n=150). All study participants are diagnosed with severe peripheral neuropathy (e.g., vibration perception $\leqslant 4/8$).

The study participant provides data by regularly measuring their foot temperature using smart insoles and a mobile application. The application uploads the raw data. Data analysts perform queries on the data with the goal of finding patterns that could help in developing and improving automatic ulcer detection algorithms. The analysts apply both Data Mining as well as ML approaches to make sense of the collected data and to predict future behavior (see examples described in Section IV).

Section II addresses related work that is the foundation of this study. Next, Section III describes possible attack scenarios. Section IV and section V describe DP queries and DP ML. The article closes with section VI summarizing the results and providing an outlook.

## II. Related Work

ML models are commonly used in the health care field. For instance, Orfanoudaki et al. [17] identify a non-linear Framingham stroke risk score using Optimal Classification Trees. With regard to the subject matter at hand, Tabaei et al. [18] use a logistic regression model to predict the likelihood of study subjects suffering from diabetes. Maniruzzaman et al. [19] expand on the aforementioned studies by addressing the impact of missing values and outliers and verified their results in different scenarios by testing six feature selection techniques and ten different qualifiers with Random Forest-based models showing the best performance. The given example and many more studies aim to create or improve their models and databases. Moreover, other studies focus on identifying various approaches to making ML algorithms privacy-preserving. This may partly be the case because the nature of the underlying ML algorithms is substantially different, but it is also driven by the system design and data flow. There are, among others, supervised, unsupervised, and reinforced ML algorithms that require different types of data and produce different types of results. Furthermore, the system can follow a local or a global privacy approach. Local privacy can be achieved by perturbating the individual input. Global privacy can be achieved by cost function or output perturbation, which will be explained in detail in Section IV and V. Privacy Preservation can be further expanded to other fields, like, for instance, Deep Learning. Phan et al. [9] proposed an adaptive Laplacian mechanism that can be used in a Deep Learning setting.

In [16], Bos et al. provide a good introduction to the topic of publicly available databases as well as privately compiled databases containing medical records. The authors expand on the point made in [15] that masked data records state privacy concerns when publicly available. Respectively, according to Bos et al. [16], publicly available databases provide the most benefit while also "creating the steepest privacy challenge". They first compared "conventional encryption" to homomorphic encryption, concluding that both encryption approaches can be used to assure privacy, but homomorphic encryption provides more operations on the encrypted data without the need for a decryption key. Second, they describe possible scenarios to conduct predictive analysis privately. In their outlook section, Bos et al. describe the need for performance improvements, which remains an issue with homomorphic encryption.

DP mechanisms use different ways of data perturbation to protect the privacy of individuals in a data set. Local DP approaches perturb the data on input time while global DP approaches do so when the data is queried by an adversary. The DP mechanisms range from applying random noise (e.g., coin toss) to more advanced systems using Laplacian noise [8]. Fundamental work and surveys by Dwork et al. can be found in [4], [8], [20], [21]. DP can be applied both to queries and ML approaches. For instance, Cheu et al. [22] introduce a system that works with sensitive data in a distributed setting and applies DP via shuffling.

Other contributions discuss the application fields of DP and that it has been successfully applied. Nguyen et al. [26] stated in 2013 that DP "[..] has become the de facto principle for privacy-preserving data analysis tasks". The application of DP on medical data is actively researched: Lee and Chung [24], for instance, propose "Informative attribute preserving anonymization" (IPA), which is further discussed in Section IV.

## III. ATTACKS ON DATA RECORDS AND MODELS

This section goes into detail about why and how the previously described medical trial raises privacy concerns for participants even though it acts within the legal requirements. The study participants agreed that their data may be shared with data analysts. Data analysts can access the masked data via a query interface using a secure channel, which allows for a similar linkage attack as described in Section I. Data analysts can query personal information like a subject's birthday, sex, diabetes type, and other known information regarding medication or medical anamnesis. The combination of the information becomes a quasi-identifier, rendering the pseudonymization meaningless.

### A. *Membership inference*

In medical trials, the ML models are trained on highly sensitive data of real persons and could potentially leak information about them. Membership inference attacks aim to prove the existence of a data record in a data set. According to [13], this is done by training an attack model which intends to distinguish the behavior based on input that was part of the training and input that was not. Publicly available ML models are usually block-boxes with unknown structures and parameters. Shokri et al. [13] propose multiple generic techniques to tackle this problem. For instance, they introduced "shadow training". Shadow training creates multiple models that imitate the original ML model's behavior with known training data.

### B. *Attribute Inference*

Attribute inference attacks are based on publicly available information about a person that is either provided directly by the user or gathered indirectly via their connections ("friends") on their social media accounts. The combined knowledge can then be used to infer or validate further information about an individual. Jayaraman and Evans [14] describe attacks on social network profiles of users and infer data about individuals by creating "social-behavior-attribute networks" and run different mechanisms like, e.g., "friends-based attack" on them.

The work of Shokri et al. [13] and Jayaraman and Evans [14] are examples of privacy breaches while potentially fulfilling the requirements of GDPR and CTR (see first goal in Section I), but both attacks can be mitigated by DP because there is plausible deniability or reasonable doubt about the presence or authenticity of data.

## IV. DIFFERENTIAL PRIVATE QUERIES

There are two stakeholders performing queries on the data set: the trial staff located at the study center observing the study data to intervene if necessary and the data analysts. Data analysts can be understood as adversaries in this setup and should be prohibited from finding sensitive information about individuals.

The original data may not be changed, which is why a preceding data perturbation is not a suitable solution but can be done on intermediate data sets. Purely syntactic approaches are also not suitable because the use case can be understood as a data mining problem rather than a data publication problem. Other means of anonymization and DP are mandatory to protect the privacy of individuals. This section describes different approaches to create differentially private versions of the queries. Transforming the queries into differentially private queries has an impact on the usefulness of the result due to reduced accuracy. We decided to go with the rather straightforward and well-known approaches to show their applicability in a real-world telemedical use case and do not focus on maximizing privacy or improving existing DP approaches.

### A. *Basic DP query mechanisms*

To evaluate a selection of differentially private analyses, the following example query will be used:

"Did study participant x have a foot ulcer in the past?"

This is revealing information and, therefore, worthy of being protected. Across all study participants, the percentage to answer the query with "yes" lies at $p=0.3$.

Each query on the medical database, including DP queries, reveals information about a patient and causes a certain amount of privacy loss. The privacy loss is defined by the parameter $\varepsilon$. The closer $\varepsilon$ gets to 0, the smaller the privacy loss will be for each query. However, smaller $\varepsilon$ also decreases the accuracy of the result due to the increased noise level. Fig. 1 illustrates how the usability increases when a larger n is available.

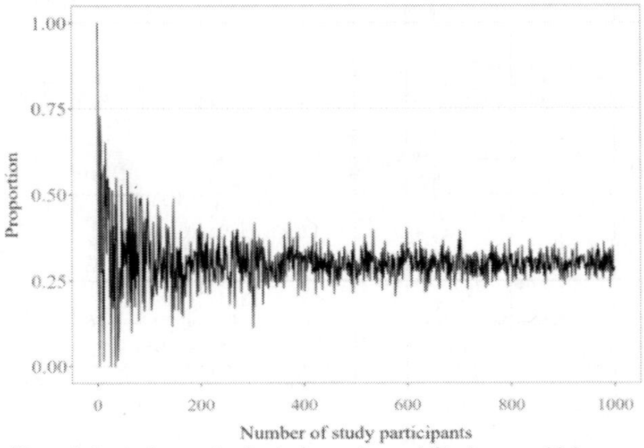

Figure 1: Laplacian mechanism's decreasing usability impact with larger n

The first global DP method is an ε-DP mechanism called the Laplacian method which is popular for numeric functions. Dwork [4] and Dwork and Roth [8] introduced solutions to (ε, $\delta$)-DP by applying Gaussian noise to query results. In [4] the summand

$$\sqrt{2\ln\frac{2}{\delta}} \times \frac{\Delta f}{\varepsilon}, \tag{1}$$

which was changed in [8] to

$$\sqrt{2\ln\frac{1.25}{\delta}} \times \frac{\Delta f}{\varepsilon}, \tag{2}$$

is added independently to each query answer for a query with L2 sensitivity $\Delta f$. The Gaussian mechanism does not satisfy ε-DP but achieves (ε, $\delta$)-DP for some $\delta \in [0, 1]$ while Laplacian achieves ε-DP.

Consequently, the Laplacian mechanism works best with low sensitivity and smaller amounts of queries. Vice versa, large amounts of queries require a larger ε, which produces less accurate results. The relaxed (ε, $\delta$)-DP definition and the smaller accuracy of the Gaussian mechanism turn out useful for vector-valued functions. The Laplacian mechanism requires the use of L1 sensitivity, while the Gaussian mechanism supports both L1 and L2 sensitivity. There are extensions and improvements to Gaussian and Laplacian mechanisms available with higher privacy results described, among others, in [7].

The Gaussian and Laplacian mechanisms are both focused on numerical queries. However, McSherry and Talwar [23] proposed a mechanism that is able to solve different types of problems that require retrieving a certain element of an existing set R that fits a query. A simple example could be: "What is the most common comorbidity of diabetic foot neuropathy?" from a set that could be

R = {"Ulcer", "Gait", "Macroangiopathy", "Fasciitis", "Angiopathy", "Arthrosis"}.

### B. *Medical DP queries*

Naturally, there are more complex queries than the query used for 5.1. Likewise, the requirements for DP queries exceed the possibilities of the basic mechanisms. It becomes both interesting and complex when different approaches are combined, may they be sequential or parallel compositions of DP functions.

The following somewhat simplified query is a realistic example that was run on the data in a similar fashion:

```
SELECT AgeGroup, Disease, COUNT(*)
FROM (
    SELECT FLOOR (Age/5) * 5 as AgeGroup, *
    FROM Patients
    WHERE Sex = 'male' AND DiabetesType = 1
) GroupedResults
GROUP BY AgeGroup, Disease
```

The query goes through the study subjects and divides them into age groups and diseases. A possible way of applying compositions of DP functions is the IPA approach proposed in Lee and Chung [24]. The IPA approach goes through a processing pipeline as illustrated in a simplified version in Fig. 2. The authors of [24] classify the data perturbation into different methods: generalization, suppression, and insertion. Each method achieves a different goal, such as reducing the number of counterfeit records or reducing information loss.

## V. Differentially Private Machine Learning

In the previous sections, we have introduced basic DP mechanisms. Now, we go a step further by implementing privacy-preserving ML using the same clinical trial as our use case. In contrast to the more theoretical Section IV, this section is more detailed and looks into the trade-off between the privacy parameter ε and the prediction quality of the ML model.

ML allows more stages to perturb data to make ML DP. We will consider output and cost function perturbation.

| Age | Sex | Weight | Diabetes | Disease |
|---|---|---|---|---|
| 66 | M | 86 | I | Ulcer |
| 79 | F | 74 | I | Angiopathy |
| 78 | M | 97 | II | Ulcer |
| ... | ... | ... | ... | ... |

Generalization, Insertion, Suppression

| Age | Sex | Weight | Diabetes | Disease |
|---|---|---|---|---|
| 65-69 | M | 86 | I | Ulcer |
| 75-79 | F | 74 | I | Angiopathy |
| * | * | * | * | Gait |
| ... | ... | ... | ... | ... |

Scoring & Selection

| Candidate | Score |
|---|---|
| v | 0.28 |

Figure 2: Simplified IPA model by Lee et al. [24]

This section will describe how output and objective perturbation have been applied to linear regression in a real-world application.

### A. *Differentially Private Linear Regression*

In our use case, we gather significant amounts of data from many different patients. One of our goals is to build a predictive model to identify inflammations or other diseases at an early stage and maybe even predict them before they occur. Using ML on the data sets has the potential to improve the accuracy of our prediction. However, this first example takes a step back and provides a forecast of the temperature development.

Let

$$y = f\left(\vec{x}, \vec{w}\right) = w_0 + w_1 x_1 + \ldots + w_D x_D, \tag{3}$$

where $\vec{x} = \left(x_1, \ldots, x_D\right)^T$ and $w_i$ are weights. With N data records, $X$ has dimension $\left(N \times D\right)$, which will become $\left(N+1 \times D\right)$-dimensional matrix $\bar{X}$ when accounting for $w_0$. Then $\vec{y} = \bar{X}\vec{w}$. When training a model from a data set, $\vec{y}$ can then be used to evaluate the chosen $\vec{w}$. A popular cost function can be the Mean Squared Error (MSE)

$$MSE = \frac{1}{N}\sum_{i=1}^{N}\left(y_i - y_i^*\right)^2. \tag{4}$$

To make the linear regression DP, we can add noise at several stages in the process including the dataset, the cost function, and the prediction output as shown in Fig. 3. As mentioned before, we will not alter the original datasets because the trial staff must have access to an immaculate dataset. Instead, we could create a secondary synthetic data set from the original data set that can be used to achieve a DP Linear Regression [10]. However, creating a synthetic data set was not part of this work. The linear regression is executed on a dataset of feet temperature measurements as described in Section I.

Several features are collected during the clinical trial as described in Ming et al. [6] and Section I. For simplicity reasons, no thought-out feature selection has been performed, but the features have been reduced to the available temperature data. The trained model has an MSE of 1.27.

The first example will add Laplacian noise to the prediction output of the linear regression. In order to do that, we need to calculate the sensitivity $l_1$. According to [8] the sensitivity $l_1$ is determined by finding $\Delta f$ of a function $f : N^{|x|} \rightarrow R^k$ over all pairs of neighboring databases. However, the pairs can only be found by making many

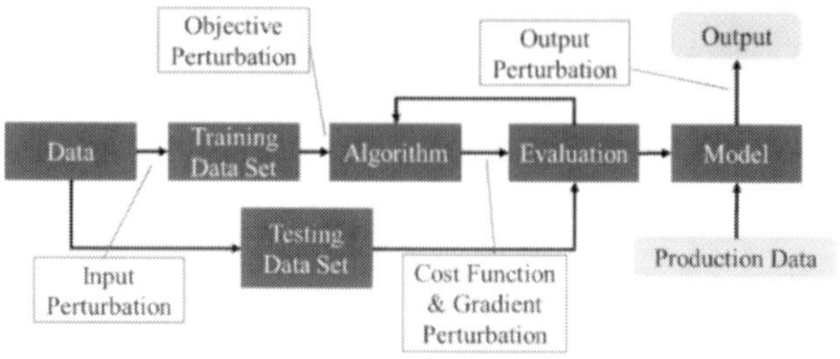


Figure 3: Perturbation approaches

assumptions about, for instance, the highest and lowest possible temperatures. Alternatively, we follow the approach proposed in Ji et al. [11] to find neighboring databases by deleting an element rather than changing it. Finding the element with the biggest impact on the model is still a challenging task; particularly if large amounts of data are gathered. Our use case allows applying a brute force approach because we have a maximum of 1,424 data records per study participant. We were able to identify a neighboring database with the highest difference in the MSE by deleting the element with the largest impact at index 64. Now that we have our original database and the one with the most differing outputs, the difference between their MSE can be used to find an approximated sensitivity of 0.62.

With the sensitivity value, we can now apply the following Lap(0, 0.62/ε) with ε being the selected security parameter. If ε is very small, e.g., 0.01, the noise addition will be very high, and the usability of the data gets very low due to a high mean error rate. With a higher value for ε, the error rate decreases but so does the privacy gained by the noise addition. Dwork [4] and Dwork and Roth [8] proposed a range between 0.01 and log3. Finding the "best value" for ε is not a trivial task and always needs to be a compromise between usability and privacy, depending on the requirements. If we use log2, for instance, and repeat the test using 10-fold cross-validation, we get an MSE of 5.74. The average processing time increased from approximately 7ms to 44ms on a machine with Intel Core i7-8665U with 48GB RAM.

To perturb the cost function of linear regression, we have to preprocess our data because it needs to be in the range [-1, 1]. This was achieved by scaling it using a min-max normalization

$$x' = \frac{x - x_{\min}}{x_{\max} - x_{\min}}. \tag{5}$$

Following the approach described by Zhang et al. in [12], we are not only able to perturb the cost function but also the function itself. This can be done by adding noise directly to the cost functions. Here, again, we used the noise from the Laplacian distribution. Following the definitions from [12], we define our problem to have a set of features $x_1$ to $x_n$ resulting from the temperature measurements and a Boolean $y$ indicating whether the participant has developed a disease.

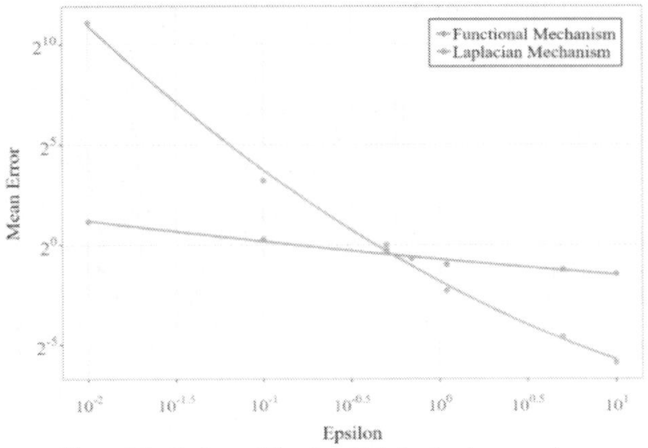


Figure 4: Laplacian and Functional Mechanism in comparison

This leaves us with a prediction function to predict $y = 1$ with probability:

$$p(x_i) = \frac{\exp(x_i^T \omega^*)}{(1 + \exp(x_i^T \omega^*))}, \quad (6)$$

Zhang et al. [7] describe $\omega^*$ as a vector of d real numbers that minimize a cost function:

$$\omega^* = \arg\min \sum_{i=1}^{n} \left( \log(1 + \exp(x_i^T \omega)) - y_i x_i^T \omega \right). \quad (7)$$

Using this function, a logistic regression on our dataset will be able to return a probability of a participant having an inflammation. To achieve DP by perturbing this function, we use the functional mechanism and the polynomial extension to this mechanism from [12], which have been proven to achieve DP for logistic regressions. The functional mechanism averaged at approximately 15ms on the same machine.

In Fig. 4 it can be seen that for the smallest ε=0.01 the Laplacian approach reaches a mean error of around 211 where the functional approach only reached 2.2, making the latter significantly more suitable. However, with decreasing ε the mean error also drops exponentially, eventually falling below the mean error of the Functional Mechanism. This explanation lies in the nature of the Laplacian algorithm which adds noise based on the underlying distribution. If all samples are very close together, it is much simpler to hide the original values but with strong outliers, much more noise needs to be added. The Functional Mechanism is better suited for smaller ε because it provides more accurate results than the Laplacian Mechanism.

## VI. Conclusion

ML problems can have different data types which are more or less suitable for the previously described DP mechanisms. If the data is strongly correlated, it gets even worse. Eventually, the practicability of the DP mechanisms remains dependent on the application. Sections IV and V have shown that it is a possible but not a trivial task to select the correct DP mechanism, since it requires a deep understanding of the (ML) task as well as DP. The exemplary privacy breaches from Section III can be prevented by choosing the right trade-off between usability and privacy.

The authors of this work are not aware of any openly available DP libraries which can be used for ML tasks, but existing open-source libraries can be integrated into, e.g., Microsoft's "ML.net" framework, which was one of the chosen approaches for this paper. Hence, each clinical study faces the problem of finding the correct DP approach to their individual ML tasks. Because of the unavailability of out-of-the-box solutions, smaller scale studies like our use case from Section I using DP correctly likely exceeds their possibilities and could be solved differently. However, when creating large databases like a diabetes register of a state with thousands of entries that could be used by multiple studies at once, DP becomes a more realistic approach.

Assuming the masked dataset is publicly available, it would allow for creating a huge learning data set. On the other hand, the public availability would pose a great privacy challenge. The privacy challenge can be addressed by applying differential privacy-preserving techniques, which enables users to query for approximate answers based on trained models. The suitability of DP techniques that build on ML training models requires further investigation [16]. Furthermore, the question remains whether this can be applied efficiently in the encrypted domain. Syntactic approaches were also not considered in this work and may be a valid solution for certain problems.

Privately compiled databases are a more typical scenario to handle patient data because companies and hospitals usually do not disclose their data freely. Regulations and applicable laws bind stakeholders to not only handle data confidentially but to use them for predetermined purposes. Nevertheless, both clinics and companies wish to learn as much as possible from their data and, consequently, to improve their work. Another approach to overcome this dilemma could be using a homomorphic encryption function. It may be possible to outsource the homomorphically encrypted storage and prediction model building and still maintain confidentiality.

The previously described use case is not as time-sensitive as, for example, an ECG evaluation. Nevertheless, a fast and efficient implementation is always desirable with respect to cost-efficiency. On the other hand, this approach may be adapted in a different medical use case that works with continuous data flows.

## References

[1] A. Narayanan, V. Shmatikov, "How To Break Anonymity of the Netflix Prize Dataset," Arxiv, 2006.

[2] D. G. Armstrong, A. J.M. Boulton, and S. A. Bus, "Diabetic Foot Ulcers and Their Recurrence," N Engl J Med., 376(24) pp. 2367-2375, 2017.

[3] H. Koch, B. Schütze, G. Spyra, and M. Wefer, "Datenschutzrechtliche Anforderungen an die medizinische Forschung unter Berücksichtigung der EU Datenschutz-Grundverordnung (DS-GVO)," GMDS e.V., Köln, 2017.

[4] C. Dwork, "Differential Privacy," International Colloquium on Automata, Languages and Programming, part II (ICALP 2006), vol. 4052, pp. 1-12, 2006.

[5] M. Lundmark, C. Dahlman "Differential privacy and machine learning: Calculating sensitivity with generated data sets," KTH, Stockholm, 2017.

[6] A. Ming, I Walter, A. Alhajjar, M. Leuckert, and P. R. Mertens, "Study protocol for a randomized controlled trial to test for preventive effects of diabetic foot ulceration by telemedicine that includes sensor-equipped insoles combined with photo documentation," Trials, vol. 20, 521, 2019.

[7] J. Zhao," Reviewing and Improving the Gaussian Mechanism for Differential Privacy," arXiv:1911.12060, 2019.

[8] C. Dwork and A. Roth, "The Algorithmic Foundations of Differential Privacy," Foundations and Trends in Theoretical Computer Science (FnT-TCS). vol. 9, no. 3-4, pp. 211-407, 2014.

[9] N. Phan, X. Wu, H. Hu, and D. Dou "Adaptive Laplace Mechanism: Differential PrivacyPreservation in Deep Learning," arXiv:1709.05750, 2017.

[10] J. Lei, "Differentially Private M-Estimators," Advances in Neural Information Processing Systems. pp. 361-369, 2011.

[11] Z. Ji, Z. C. Lipton, and C. Elkan, "Differentially Privacy and Machine Learning: A Survey and Review," arXiv:1412.7584. 2014.

[12] J. Zhang, Z. Zhang, X. Xiao, Y. Yang, and M. Winslett, "Functional Mechanism: Regression Analysis under Differential Privacy," arXiv:1208.0219, 2012.

[13] R. Shokri, M. Stronati, C. Song, and V. Shmatikov, "Membership Inference Attacks Against Machine Learning Models," 2017 IEEE Symposium on Security and Privacy (SP), San Jose, CA, pp. 3-18, doi: 10.1109/SP.2017.41, 2017.

[14] B. Jayaraman and D. Evans, "Evaluating Differentially Private Machine Learning in Practice," 28th USENIX Security Symposium, pp. 1895–1912, 2019.

[15] G. Jagannathan, K. Pillaipakkamnatt, and R. N. Wright, "A Practical Differentially Private RandomDecision Tree Classifier," Transactions on Data Privacy, vol. 5, pp. 273-295, 2012.

[16] J. W. Bos, K. Lauter, and M. Naehrig, "Private Predictive analysis on encrypted medical data," Journal of Biomedical Informatics, vol. 50, pp. 234-243, 2014.

[17] A. Orfanoudaki et al., "Machine learning provides evidence that stroke risk is not linear: The non-linear Framingham stroke risk score," PLoS ONE, 15(5), pp. 1-20, 2020.

[18] B. P. Tabaei and W. H. Herman, "A multivariate logistic regression equation to screen for diabetes: development and validation," Diabetes Care, 25(11):1999-2003, 2002.

[19] Md. Maniruzzaman et al., "Accurate Diabetes Risk Stratification Using Machine Learning: Role of Missing Value and Outliers," J Med Syst 42, 92, 2018.

[20] C. Dwork, "Differential Privacy: A survey of results," TAMC: Theory and Applications of Models of Computation, 5th International Conference, pp. 1-19, 2008.

[21] C. Dwork, "Differential Privacy in new settings," SODA, pp. 174-183, 2010.

[22] A. Cheu, A. Smith, J. Ullman, D. Zeber, and M. Zhilyaev, "Distributed Differential Privacy via Shuffling," Advances in Cryptology – EUROCRYPT 2019, 2019.

[23] F. McSherry and K. Talwar, "Mechanism design via differential privacy," FOCS, volume 7, pp. 94-103, 2007.

[24] H. Lee and Y. D. Chung, "Differentially private release of medical microdata: an efficient and practical approach for preserving informative attribute values," BMC Medical Informatics and Decision Making 20, pp. 1-15, 2020.

[25] M. E, Y. Geng, "Homomorphic Encryption Technology for Cloud Computing", Procedia Computer Science, pp. 73-83, 2019.

[26] H. Nguyen, J. Kim, and Y. Kim, „Differential Privacy in Practice", J. of Computing Science and Engineering, pp. 177-186, 2013.

# Threat Level Assessment of Smart-Home Stakeholders Using EBIOS Risk Manager

N'guessan Yves-Roland Douha, Doudou Fall, Yuzo Taenaka, and Youki Kadobayashi
*Division of Information Science*
*Nara Institute of Science and Technology*
Ikoma, Japan
email:douha.nguessan_yves-roland.dn6@is.naist.jp, doudou-f@is.naist.jp, yuzo@is.naist.jp, youki-k@is.naist.jp

***Abstract*—The smart home is among the emerging technologies designed to improve in-house quality of life by supplying many services, such as home automation, healthcare, and energy management. Recent cyberattacks on smart homes affecting home dwellers' privacy, safety, and security could slow down smart homes' adoption. To identify smart-home attack surfaces, we propose to use a risk analysis method called Expression of Needs and Identification of Security Objectives - Expression des Besoins et Identification des Objectifs de Sécurité (EBIOS) Risk Manager to evaluate the threat level of smart-home stakeholders in the role of threat agents. The contributions of this paper are assessing smart-home stakeholders and identifying attack scenarios in which they could be involved to extend the reflection on smart home security. We are the first to estimate the threat level of fourteen smart-home stakeholders through assessing many metrics. We use a 5-point Likert scale to collect data from security professionals to conduct this assessment. We classify the smart-home stakeholders into various threat zones and find that smart-home inhabitants and home automation service providers have the highest threat agent levels. This investigation will contribute to designing security systems and policies for strengthening the smart-home ecosystem's security.**

***Keywords-EBIOS RM; Internet of Things; Smart Home; Stakeholder; Security.***

## I. Introduction

A smart home is an Internet of Things (IoT) application that promotes technology-based living places. It includes various technologies such as devices (e.g., sensors, actuators, multimedia), networking (e.g., wireless, wired), mobile and web applications, cloud computing, and artificial intelligence [1] [2]. Statista estimates that the worldwide revenue of smart homes, US$78.9 billion in 2020, will increase to US$182.3 billion by 2025 [3]. This technology-based home attracts considerably, not only normal users, but also attackers. Recent cyberattacks exploiting home devices have revealed security risk concerns in smart homes [4] [5]. Hence, carrying out a risk assessment becomes necessary to identify and address the security flaws in smart homes to withstand future cyberattacks.

Recent research have shown interests in the risk assessment of the smart home security. Jacobsson et al. [6] propose an empirical evaluation and scenario-based study. Wongvises et al. [7] propose a Fault Tree Analysis to quantify security risks. Most studies have only focused on assets such as devices and networks. However, Cherdantseva et al. [8] emphasize that a risk assessment needs to include stakeholders to provide a complete set of risks. As stated in International Organization for Standardization (ISO) 27005, a stakeholder is a "person or organization that can affect, be affected by, or perceive themselves to be affected by a decision or activity [9]." To the best of our knowledge, prior work have not focused on smart-home stakeholders-based threat analysis so far. As mentioned by Bregman [10], the smart home intelligence requires developers, suppliers, and users to cooperate, specifically to transfer information. If one or many of these stakeholders get compromised by attackers or fail to secure information transmission, the smart home security could be affected. Stakeholders play an essential role in the smart home operations and could, without realizing it, contribute to the fulfillment of attack scenarios. Securing a smart home could require a deep understanding of every stakeholder connected to the smart home. Therefore, an assessment of how easy it is for an attacker to exploit a stakeholder to conduct a cyberattack on a smart home may provide security perspectives to reduce the attack surfaces.

Our approach uses EBIOS Risk Manager, referred to as EBIOS RM. It is a method based on the risk analysis and management methodology called EBIOS, which has proven to be effective for risk management in critical information infrastructures [11]. Furthermore, it includes stakeholder analysis.

The main contributions of this research are as follow:

- We introduce stakeholder-based risk analysis for smart home security.
- We evaluate the threat level associated with smart-home stakeholders to identify strategic scenarios that attackers could exploit.
- We propose an approach of threat classification for risk managers and compare our results with two other classification methods, including the EBIOS RM's.
- We identify and describe potential high-level attack scenarios that could involve smart-home stakeholders.

We organize the rest of the paper as follows: Section II describes the related work. Section III introduces EBIOS RM. Section IV analyzes the threat level of smart-home stakeholders using EBIOS RM. Section V discusses our results. Section VI concludes the paper.

## II. Related Work

This section presents previous work on smart home and stakeholder security risks.

### A. Smart-Home Security Risk

Wongvises et al. [7] use Fault Tree Analysis (FTA) to quantify security risks in a smart home. They show that security risks in smart homes might be high through the assessment of lighting systems. Ali et al. [12] use Operationally Critical Threat, Asset, and Vulnerability Evaluation (OCTAVE) Allegro to analyze information security risks in smart homes. The authors identify ten critical information assets (e.g., user credentials, log information, mobile application data, and various smart home-related information) and evaluate the risk scores associated with these information assets. We note that the paper does not present the calculation of risk scores. Kavallieratos et al. [13] use the Spoofing, Tampering, Repudiation, Information disclosure, Denial of service, Elevation of privilege (STRIDE) model to identify threats to smart homes. They identify threats that relate to devices such as IP cameras, smartphones, and alarm systems. The paper does not evaluate the threat levels. Jacobsson et al. [6] evaluate the risk exposure of a smart home by applying the Information Security Risk Analysis (ISRA) approach described in [14]. They used a questionnaire to collect the opinions of nine participants, including security experts, domain experts, and system developers of smart homes. The authors recognize that third-party stakeholders can access the whole smart home and collect private data on inhabitants.

The previous work show that risk assessment is essential to address smart home security. Furthermore, we can notice a lack of study on stakeholders assessment whereas Bregman [10] shows that they play a critical role in a smart-home environment.

### B. Stakeholder Security Risk

Grimble et al. [15] describe stakeholder analysis as a powerful tool for policy analysis and formulation that help understanding a system, and changes in it, by identifying and assessing key actors or stakeholders. Stakeholder assessments have been explored in many areas, such as human resource development, business management, or natural resource management [16]. However, the related papers in the cybersecurity area are limited. Mollaeefar et al. [17] propose a multi-stakeholder cybersecurity risk assessment for data protection. They focus their research on the estimation of the relation between the impact levels and risk exposures. We note that they consider the likelihood as the same for every stakeholder. Even if this consideration could be effective in the proposed configuration, it cannot be realistic in many areas, such as a smart home where stakeholders have various interests, intentions, and behaviors.

The limitations mentioned above motivate us to leverage a risk analysis method that complies with international cybersecurity standards and includes identifying and evaluating security issues associated with stakeholders. To the best of our knowledge, the related work has not explored this perspective. In this research, we adopt the EBIOS RM method to identify and assess the threat level of threat agents (stakeholders).

## III. Research Method

This section presents the background of EBIOS RM, the method used in this research.

### A. Method

We often express information security risk as a combination of the consequences (impacts) of an information security event and the associated likelihood of occurrence [9]. This research focuses on the likelihood assessment, and we use EBIOS RM to evaluate the threat level of stakeholders in the role of threat agents. We choose EBIOS RM because it is a flexible method covering any system, regardless of its size and sector of activity and whether it is under development or already developed. Furthermore, unlike most qualitative risk analysis methods, EBIOS RM introduces a new calculation of the threat level and an approach to identify and evaluate threat agents and attack scenarios.

Note that EBIOS is a methodology that was created in 1995 for risk management of information system security. It is maintained by the National Cybersecurity Agency of France - Agence Nationale de la Sécurité des Systèmes d'Information (ANSSI) with the support of Club EBIOS [18]. This methodology is a comprehensive tool that complies with security management policies and international standards such as ISO 27001, 27005, and 31000. Furthermore, it was used to address risk management in critical information infrastructures [11] and we believe it could be effective for a critical environment such as a smart home where the absence of dedicated cybersecurity teams to support home users could facilitate attackers activities to access users' privacy.

### B. EBIOS Risk Manager

Available since 2018, the so-called EBIOS Risk Manager (EBIOS RM) is the latest version of the EBIOS methodology. This method is iterative and includes two approaches: An approach through "conformity" that identifies the security baseline and through "scenarios" that analyzes potential attack scenarios based on the point of view of attackers. EBIOS RM comprises five workshops described as follows.

1) Workshop 1 (scope and security baseline): This workshop aims to identify the scope of our study, its assets, and its primary missions. Then, it determines the severity of feared events associated with its assets.
2) Workshop 2 (risk origins): The second workshop aims to identify the RO/TO pairs. This pair comprises risk origins (RO) and their high-level targets, namely target objectives (TO).
3) Workshop 3 (strategic scenarios): This workshop includes the threat level assessment, establishes a mapping of threat agents, and provides high-level scenarios, called strategic scenarios. These scenarios describe the attack paths a risk origin could use to reach its target objective.
4) Workshop 4 (operational scenarios): The purpose is to define technical scenarios that include the methods of attack that risk origins can use to carry out the strategic scenarios. This workshop also assesses the risk of each operational scenario.
5) Workshop 5 (risk treatment): In this workshop, the goal is to summarize all the identified risks, then define a risk

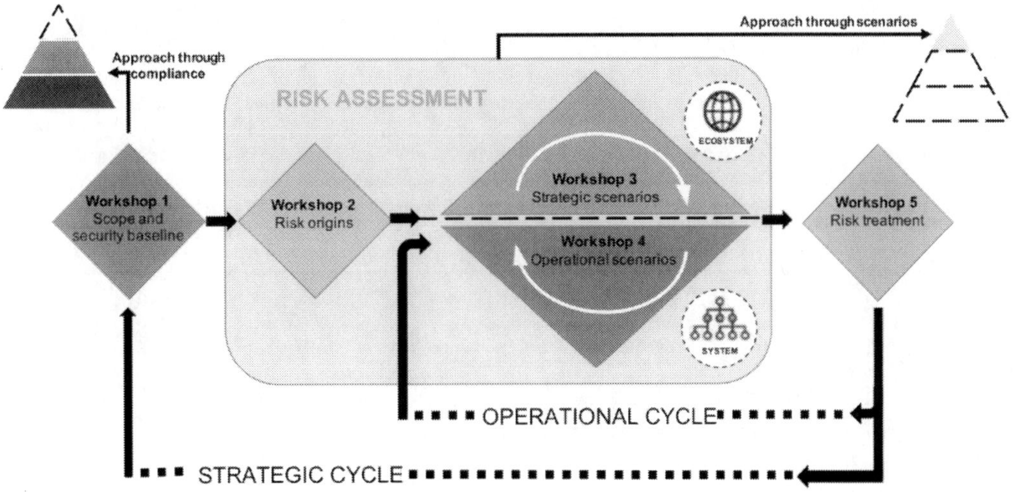


Fig. 1. A description of the general workflow of the EBIOS Risk Manager methodology [18].

treatment strategy. This workshop ends with a summary of the residual risks and the framework for monitoring risks.

Figure 1 shows the general flow of EBIOS RM. It presents two risk management cycles. The strategic cycle includes every workshop, and the operational relates only to Workshop 3, Workshop 4, and Workshop 5. We can see that Workshop 3 plays an indispensable role that consists of assessing threat agents and determining scenarios involving these agents. Furthermore, this workshop provides most of the information required to identify the operational scenarios (Workshop 4) and the appropriate risk treatment (Workshop 5).

We will focus exclusively on the first three workshops because our purpose is to evaluate the threat level of smart-home stakeholders.

## IV. Data Collection and Analysis

This section describes the participants of the study and presents data collection and analysis.

### A. Participants

In total, 17 participants (Academic Researcher (11.8%), Cybersecurity Specialist (29.4%), Chief Information Security Officer (5.9%), and IT Department/Information Management Team (52.9%)) responded to our survey questionnaire. Furthermore, 47.1%, 47.1%, and 5.8% of participants have respectively less than 5 years, between 5-10 years, and more than 10 years of experience in cybersecurity. 76.5% of participants are certified in one or many certifications: Cisco Certified Network Associate (CCNA), Certified Ethical Hacker (CEH), Certified Information Security Manager (CISM), Certified Information Systems Security Professional (CISSP), Control Objectives for Information and Related Technology (COBIT) 5 Foundation, ISO 27001, Information Technology Infrastructure Library (ITIL) V3, ITIL V4. These certifications are attributed to individuals who can distinguish IT services, analyze and mitigate risks, understand cyberattack methods, design security countermeasures, and prevent unauthorized intruders from accessing network systems.

We also interacted directly in private messages with six respondents who wanted to get more details in our research. Four of them were security professionals who wanted to confirm that our study is real and legitimate. The two others were IoT/smart home professionals who informed us that they do not have the required skills for risk analysis. In a nutshell, the participants are likely to be qualified and experienced enough to assess the security of complex IT systems. Therefore, we assume that they are all eligible to evaluate the threat level of smart-home stakeholders.

### B. Data Collection

We created an online Google Form and carried out the survey questionnaire over two weeks through two primary social networking services: LinkedIn for professionals and researchers and ResearchGate for academic researchers. We choose this short period of time to prevent eligible individuals to repeatedly take the only form and ineligible individuals to fill out the form. Our target was to reach cybersecurity professionals, top managers, and IoT/smart home specialists. To ensure the representativeness of the sample, we identified several private groups on LinkedIn related to IoT security/Cybersecurity, IoT/smart home professionals, risk managers, and Chief Information Security Officer (CISO).

The survey questionnaire provided six pages for a total of 13 questions, including five grid questions, which can be filled in 15-20 minutes. The questions we asked included:

### C. Data Analysis

First, we asked the participants' opinions regarding the stakeholders we selected. To the question *"Do you think that these stakeholders are part of the smart home ecosystem?"*, more than 70% of participants responded *"Yes, I*

TABLE I
DESCRIPTION OF SEVERITY LEVELS REGARDING THE POTENTIAL IMPACTS OF FEARED EVENTS.

| Severity level | Description |
|---|---|
| S4 (Critical) | Incapacity for the smart home to ensure all or a portion of its functioning. Severe impacts on the safety and security of dwellers, data, and assets. |
| S3 (Serious) | High degradation in the performance of the smart home. Significant impacts on the safety and security of dwellers, data, and assets. |
| S2 (Significant) | Degradation in the performance of the smart home. No direct impact on the safety and security of dwellers, data, and assets. |
| S1 (Minor) | Minor or no impact on operations or performances of the smart home. Minor or no impact on the safety and security of dwellers, data, and assets. |

*do*" to 10 out of 14 propositions: *Energy service provider* (76.5%), *Healthcare service providers* (76.5%), *Home automation service providers* (88.2%), *Courier service providers* (23.5%), *Network service providers* (88.2%), *IoT cloud service providers* (88.2%), *Sensor/IoT device manufacturers* (70.6%), *IoT application developers* (88.2%), *IoT/smart home regulators* (97.1%), *Real estate agents* (11.8%), *Dwellers friends* (17.7%), *Dwellers collaborators* (11.8%), *Smart home owners (dwellers)* (76.5%), and *Other smart home inhabitants (dwellers)* (70.6%). We can see that three stakeholders, i.e., *Courier service providers*, *Real estate agents*, *Dwellers' friends*, and *Dwellers' collaborators*, did not get many favorable votes.

Furthermore, we asked the participants: *"Please rate the Dependency, Penetration, Cyber Maturity, and Trust levels between each stakeholder and the smart home on a scale of 1 to 5."* to measure the metrics recommended by EBIOS RM and calculate the threat levels. We used a five-point Likert scale to measure the participants' responses. The choice of this measure is motivated by Boone et al. [19], who stated that if one designs a series of questions that, when combined, measure a particular trait, then one has created a Likert scale. In this case, the authors recommended the mean and standard deviation to describe the scale.

## V. THREAT LEVEL ASSESSMENT OF STAKEHOLDERS

This section describes the threat level assessment of smart-home stakeholders using EBIOS RM.

### A. Scope and Security Baseline

The scope of this investigation is about the smart-home services (functions) that relate to stakeholders. According to Mendes et al. [20], we can distinguish four functions (i.e., energy efficiency and management, healthcare, entertainment, and security) in a smart home. The analysis of smart home devices discussed in [21] guided us to consider five essential functions in a smart home: energy management, safety and security, healthcare, home automation, and entertainment. These functions could be associated with one or many feared events (FEs). For each essential function identified, we associate the feared events, their impacts, as well as their severity. Table I summarizes each instance of severity.

**Energy management**: This function helps to avoid wasting energy and to supply power when a power failure occurs.

- FEs: *Triggering power outage*, *tampering consumed energy amount*, and *alteration of heating, ventilation, and air conditioning*. These FEs could impact the quality of service (QoS), comfort, safety, security of dwellers, and financial losses (Severity: S3 or S4).

**Safety and security**: The goal of this function is to ensure data and information confidentiality, integrity, and availability.

- FEs: *Disabling of alarm system, smart door lock*, or *network security services*, and *detection of human activities by an attacker*. These FEs could impact the QoS, data security, privacy, safety, and security of dwellers (Severity: S2, S3, or S4).

**Healthcare**: This function remotely monitors and manages the health of dwellers in the smart home.

- FEs: *Leaking medical data records of dwellers* and *altering medical data records*. These FEs could impact the safety and privacy of dwellers and involve financial losses (Severity: S3 or S4).

**Home automation**: Smart homes automate the in-home daily tasks of dwellers. This function controls and manages the smart home appliances. Furthermore, it automatically monitors and manages dwellers' activities in the smart home.

- FEs: *Altering the automation configuration and remote control by an attacker*. These FEs could impact the comfort, privacy, safety, and security of dwellers (Severity: S1, S2, or S3).

**Entertainment**: This function provides amusement moments (e.g., music, movies, games) to dwellers.

- FEs: *Leaking personal data of dwellers*. These FEs could impact the safety and privacy of dwellers and involve financial losses (Severity: S3 or S4).

Our research does not include the security baseline because it is only necessary for risk treatment in Workshop 5, which is beyond this research scope. However, it is essential to note that the security baseline of smart homes may include ISO 27030 and ISO 24391, which are currently under development.

### B. Risk Origins

Bugeja et al. [22] classify the attacker profiles into six profiles: *"State-related", "terrorist", "competitor and organized crime", "hacktivist", "thief", and "hacker"*. In addition to this classification, we consider the *"amateur"* profile as script kiddies who use malicious codes and programs created

TABLE II
DESCRIPTION OF RO/TO PERTINENCE.

| Identification | | Scoring | | Assessment |
|---|---|---|---|---|
| Risk origins (RO) | Target objectives (TO) | Motivation | Resources | Pertinence |
| Amateur | Challenge | Low | Limited | Low |
| Avenger | Obstacle to functioning; Spying | Low | Limited | Low |
| Competitor and organized crime | Profit; Strategic pre-positioning; Terrorism | High | Significant | Fair |
| Hacker | Challenge; Profit; Spying; Strategic pre-positioning | High | Significant | Fair |
| Hacktivist | Terrorism | Fair | Significant | Fair |
| Inadvertent attacker | N/A–does not intend to attack | Very low | Limited | Low |
| Specialized outfits | Profit; Challenge; Spying; Strategic pre-positioning | High | Considerable | High |
| State-related | Terrorism; Spying | High | Unlimited | High |
| Terrorist | Terrorism; Spying | Highly motivated | Considerable | High |
| Thief | Spying; Obstacle to functioning; Profit | Fair | Significant | Fair |

by more experienced attackers, the "avenger" corresponding to profiles in bad relations with smart home inhabitants. An example of an avenger could be a disgruntled service provider. Furthermore, we consider the *"specialized outfits"* profile as cyber-mercenaries who are often at the origin of the design and creation of attack kits and tools. Lastly, we consider the *"inadvertent attacker"* profile as another risk origin because many recent attacks were due to human errors [23].

Note, the target objectives of attacker profiles are mostly well-known and could relate to *challenges* (e.g., fun, curiosity, or social recognition), *profit* (e.g., moneymaking by selling dwellers' private information), *spying* (e.g., access to dwellers' privacy), *obstacle to functioning* (e.g., making smart home services unavailable), *strategic pre-positioning* (e.g., using smart home devices to perform another attack–case of DDoS attacks), or *terrorism* (e.g., impacting smart home dweller security for political or economic purposes.).

Detecting risk origins (ROs) and target objectives (TOs) led us to determine the most critical attacker profiles to the smart home security. We assess the RO/TO pertinence as described in Table II by relying on the motivation level (i.e., very low, low, fair, or high) and potential financial, technical, human, and time resources (i.e., limited, significant, considerable, or unlimited) of attackers to compromise a smart home. Based on this assessment, the most relevant ROs are *terrorists*, *specialized outfits*, and *States-related*. Next, the least relevant but pertinent ROs are *thieves*, *hacktivists*, *hackers*, and *competitors and organized crimes*. Finally, the least pertinent ROs are *inadvertent attackers*, *avengers*, and *amateurs*. We will build the strategic scenarios on the most relevant ROs and the smart-home stakeholders.

### C. Strategic Scenarios

*1) Smart-Home Stakeholders:* EBIOS RM recommends distinguishing internal stakeholders to the system from the externals to identify the stakeholders to be taken into account. Regarding the internal stakeholders, we decided to choose dwellers, i.e., people living in smart homes. They comprise smart-home owners and other smart-home inhabitants such as children. About the external stakeholders, the information collected in various academic papers [20] [24]–[26], led us to consider service providers, manufacturers, IoT developers, IoT/smart home regulators, real estate agents, dwellers' friends, and dwellers' collaborators. Note that services providers enrich smart homes with many services. They are energy providers, home automation providers, healthcare service providers, courier service providers, network service providers, and IoT cloud service providers. Manufacturers provide smart homes with actuators, sensors, and IoT devices. Developers create web and mobile applications that control one or more aspects of the smart home. Then, IoT or smart home regulators contribute to ensuring the quality of services by accreditation. Real estate agents encourage people that seek new properties to buy smart homes. Home dwellers' friends or collaborators may have direct or indirect access, depending on their intimacy with smart homes' owners and other dwellers.

*2) Assessment of Stakeholders:* This assessment is based on a formula recommended by EBIOS RM. The formula comprises four metrics (i.e., *Dependency*, *Penetration*, *Cyber Maturity*, and *Trust*). *Dependency* and *Penetration* represent the level of exposure to the system. More specifically, *Dependency* evaluates the degree of relationship between the stakeholder and the smart home. *Penetration* assesses how far the stakeholder could access the smart home assets (including physical and remote access). Then, *Cyber Maturity* and *Trust* give information on cyber reliability. *Cyber Maturity* measures the ability of stakeholders to understand and implement cybersecurity best practices in their daily activities. *Trust* measures the level of confidence the system should have regarding the intention of stakeholders. Each metric is scored on a scale from 1 to 4. When the threat level score of threat agents (stakeholders) is close or equal to 4, it is highly feasible that an attacker exploits the related stakeholder to compromise a smart home.

$$Threat\ Level = \frac{Dependency \times Penetration}{CyberMaturity \times Trust} \quad (1)$$

[18]

*3) Measurement of Threat Levels:* The EBIOS RM method recommends an assessment on a scale of 1 to 4 for each metric: *Dependency*, *Penetration*, *Cyber Maturity*, and *Trust*. As we used a five-point Likert scale in our survey questionnaire, we consider the participants' evaluations in the range of 0 to 4

TABLE III
EVALUATION OF THE "DEPENDENCY" (D), "CYBER MATURITY" (M), "PENETRATION" (P), AND "TRUST" (T) METRICS WITH MEANS AND STANDARD DEVIATIONS FOR EACH SMART HOME STAKEHOLDER.

| | Number of n-points | | | | | Total points | Means | Standard Deviations |
|---|---|---|---|---|---|---|---|---|
| | 0-point | 1-point | 2-points | 3-points | 4-points | | | |
| | (D) (M) (P) (T) | (D) (M) (P) (T) | (D) (M) (P) (T) | (D) (M) (P) (T) | (D) (M) (P) (T) | (D) (M) (P) (T) | (D) (M) (P) (T) | (D) (M) (P) (T) |
| Energy service providers | (0) (0) (0) (0) | (1) (5) (2) (2) | (5) (8) (7) (11) | (6) (4) (7) (3) | (5) (0) (1) (1) | (49) (33) (41) (37) | (2.88) (1.94) (2.41) (2.18) | (0.90) (0.73) (0.77) (0.71) |
| Healthcare service providers | (0) (0) (0) (0) | (0) (7) (3) (1) | (8) (7) (9) (9) | (5) (3) (5) (6) | (4) (0) (0) (1) | (47) (30) (36) (41) | (2.76) (1.76) (2.12) (2.41) | (0.81) (0.73) (0.68) (0.69) |
| Home automation service providers | (0) (0) (0) (0) | (0) (2) (1) (3) | (1) (7) (6) (10) | (10) (7) (8) (4) | (6) (1) (2) (0) | (56) (41) (45) (35) | (3.29) (2.41) (2.65) (2.06) | (0.57) (0.77) (0.76) (0.64) |
| Courier service providers | (5) (5) (3) (1) | (6) (9) (4) (7) | (4) (2) (9) (8) | (2) (1) (1) (1) | (0) (0) (0) (0) | (20) (16) (25) (26) | (1.18) (0.94) (1.47) (1.53) | (0.98) (0.80) (0.85) (0.70) |
| Network service providers | (0) (0) (0) (0) | (0) (1) (1) (4) | (1) (0) (5) (9) | (6)( 12) (7) (3) | (10) (4) ( 4) (1) | (60) (53) (48) (35) | (3.53) (3.12) (2.82) (2.06) | (0.61) (0.68) (0.86) (0.80) |
| IoT cloud service providers | (0) (0) (0) (0) | (0) (0) (2) (3) | (2) (2) (4) (8) | (7) (11) (8) (5) | (8) (4) (3) (1) | (57) (53) (46) (38) | (3.35) (3.12) (2.71) (2.24) | (0.68) (0.58) (0.89) (0.81) |
| Sensor/IoT device manufacturers | (0) (0) (0) (0) | (1) (1) (3) (1) | (2) (7) (9) (12) | (7) (7) (2) (3) | (7) (2) (3) (1) | (54) (44) (39) (38) | (3.18) (2.59) (2.29) (2.24) | (0.86) (0.77) (0.96) (0.64) |
| IoT application developers | (0) (0) (0) (0) | (1) (1) (4) (4) | (5) (7) (6) (10) | (6) (8) (5) (3) | (5) (1) (2) (0) | (49) (43) (39) (33) | (2.88) (2.53) (2.29) (1.94) | (0.90) (0.70) (0.96) (0.64) |
| IoT/smart home regulators | (0) (0) (0) (0) | (1) (1) (4) (0) | (3) (8) (9) (8) | (9) (6) (3) (9) | (4) (2) (1) (0) | (50) (43) (35) (43) | (2.94) (2.53) (2.06) (2.53) | (0.80) (0.78) (0.80) (0.50) |
| Real estate agents | (3) (4) (3) (0) | (7) (10) (7) (8) | (5) (2) (7) (7) | (1) (0) (0) (2) | (1) (1) (0) (0) | (24) (18) (21) (28) | (1.41) (1.06) (1.24) (1.65) | (1.03) (0.94) (0.73) (0.68) |
| Dwellers friends | (4) (5) (2) (4) | (6) (8) (6) (6) | (5) (3) (6) (6) | (2) (0) (3) (1) | (0) (1) (0) (0) | (22) (18) (27) (21) | (1.29) (1.06) (1.59) (1.24) | (0.96) (1) (0.91) (0.88) |
| Dwellers collaborators | (4) (4) (4) (4) | (6) (8) (9) (6) | (6) (4) (4) (6) | (1) (1) (0) (1) | (0) (0) (0) (0) | (21) (19) (17) (21) | (1.24) (1.12) (1) (1.24) | (0.88) (0.83) (0.69) (0.88) |
| Smart home owners (dwellers) | (0) (3) (0) (0) | (1) (7) (2) (1) | (4) (5) (7) (9) | (4) (1) (8) (7) | (8) (1) (0) (0) | (53) (24) (55) (40) | (3.12) (1.41) (3.24) (2.35) | (0.96) (1.03) (0.68) (0.59) |
| Other smart home inhabitants (dwellers) | (1) (5) (0) (1) | (1) (6) (3) (2) | (5) (4) (1) (8) | (2) (1) (6) (6) | (8) (1) (7) (0) | ( 49) (21) (51) (36) | (2.88) (1.24) (3) (2.12) | (1.23) (1.11) (1.08) (0.83) |

rather than 1 to 5. Thus, metrics that obtained 1 point during the assessment will get 0 points.

*Mean* and *standard deviation* describe the scale of the dataset.

$$\bar{x} = \frac{\sum x}{N} \qquad (2)$$

The mean evaluates the average of points–where $x$ is the point value for each evaluation and $N$ represents the number of evaluations.

$$\sigma = \sqrt{\frac{\sum_{i=1}^{N}(x_i - \bar{x})^2}{N}} \qquad (3)$$

Standard deviation is a statistical measurement that evaluates dataset variability. It helps to understand the distribution of the dataset relative to the mean.

Table III presents the evaluation results of the *Dependency (D)*, *Penetration (P)*, *Cyber Maturity (M)*, and *Trust (T)* metrics. We calculate the means and standard deviations and evaluate the threat level of each stakeholder using the obtained means.

*4) Threat Classification:* It provides a clear insight into how critical the threats are and contribute to prioritizing the countermeasures. Table IV presents the results of threat level assessments.

Figure 2 maps the threat levels of smart-home stakeholders according to the classification provided by EBIOS RM, i.e., the danger (red) zone is determined by considering 10% of the stakeholders with the highest threat levels. The control (yellow) zone is determined by considering 40% of the following stakeholders. The watch (green) zone is determined by considering 40% of the next stakeholders. The remaining

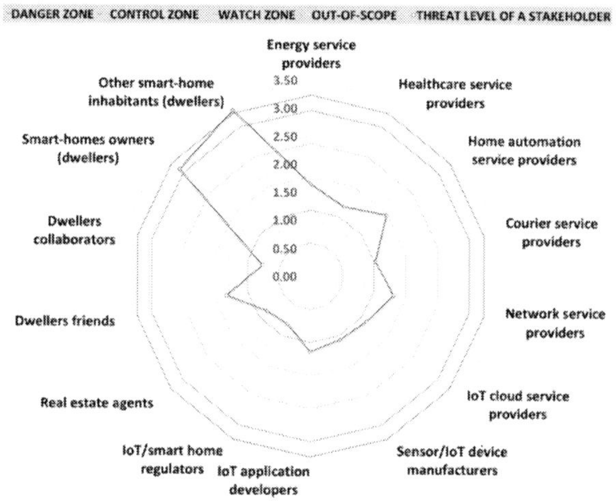


Fig. 2. A description of threat agents using EBIOS RM classification.

10% covers the out-of-scope. This classification indicates that the danger zone contains *Smart-homes owners (dwellers)* and *Other smart-home inhabitants (dwellers)*. The watch zone contains the other stakeholders.

Given that the EBIOS RM recommends a threat assessment in the range 1-4, a simplified classification could follow this pattern: Danger zone ($3 \leq$ Threat level $\leq 4$); Control zone ($2 \leq$ Threat level $< 3$); Watch zone ($1 \leq$ Threat level $< 2$); Out-of-scope ($0 \leq$ Threat level $< 1$). Figure 3 maps the threat levels. According to this classification, the danger zone contains *Smart-home owners (dwellers)* and *Other smart-home inhabitants (dwellers)*, the out-of-scope contains *Dwellers collaborators* and *IoT/smart home regulators*. The watch zone

TABLE IV
LIKELIHOOD ASSESSMENT OF SMART HOME STAKEHOLDERS.

| | Dependency | Cyber Maturity | Penetration | Trust | Threat Level |
|---|---|---|---|---|---|
| Energy service providers | 2.88 | 1.94 | 2.41 | 2.18 | 1.64 |
| Healthcare service providers | 2.76 | 1.76 | 2.12 | 2.41 | 1.38 |
| Home automation service providers | 3.29 | 2.41 | 2.65 | 2.06 | 1.76 |
| Courier service providers | 1.18 | 0.94 | 1.47 | 1.53 | 1.21 |
| Network service providers | 3.53 | 3.12 | 2.82 | 2.06 | 1.55 |
| IoT cloud service providers | 3.35 | 3.12 | 2.71 | 2.24 | 1.30 |
| Sensor/IoT devices manufacturers | 3.18 | 2.59 | 2.29 | 2.24 | 1.26 |
| IoT applications developers | 2.88 | 2.53 | 2.29 | 1.94 | 1.34 |
| IoT/smart home regulators | 2.94 | 2.53 | 2.06 | 2.53 | 0.95 |
| Real estate agents | 1.41 | 1.06 | 1.24 | 1.65 | 1.00 |
| Dwellers friends | 1.29 | 1.06 | 1.59 | 1.24 | 1.56 |
| Dwellers collaborators | 1.24 | 1.12 | 1 | 1.24 | 0.89 |
| Smart home owners (dwellers) | 3.12 | 1.41 | 3.24 | 2.35 | 3.05 |
| Other smart home inhabitants (dwellers) | 2.88 | 1.24 | 3 | 2.12 | 3.29 |

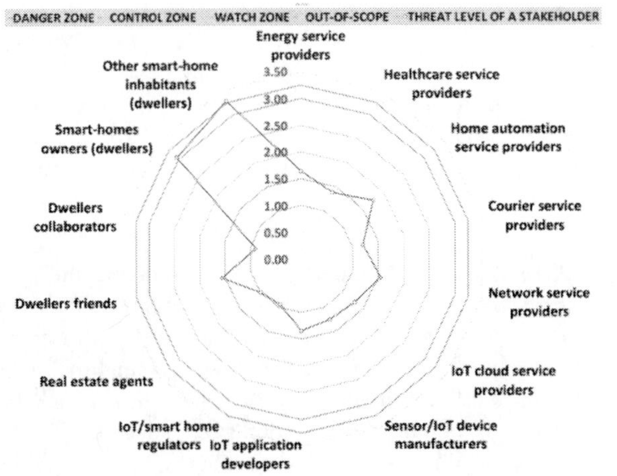


Fig. 3. A description of threat agents using a simplified classification.

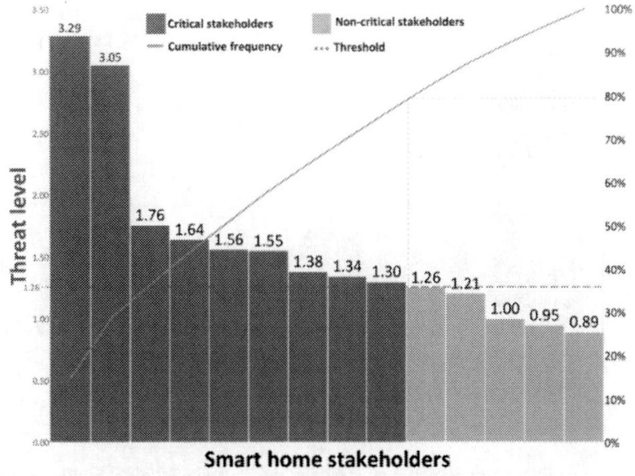


Fig. 4. A description of distinction between the critical and non-critical threats using a Pareto chart.

contains the other stakeholders.

We can notice that Figures 2 and 3 give different results. Furthermore, they do not distribute the threats onto each threat zone, which could be troublesome for decision-makers.

To cope with this limitation, we propose to use the Pareto principle [27] to determine the threat zones associated with each stakeholder. According to the Pareto principle or "80/20 rule", only a few vital inputs contribute to the greatest outputs. In our context, this principle contributes to identifying the most critical stakeholders who represent 80% of the total threats. Figure 4 presents a distinction between the critical and non-critical threats using a Pareto chart. Our proposed classification consists of iterating the Pareto Chart three times to determine respectively the stakeholders included in the following zones: *out-of-scope*, *watch*, *control*, and *danger*. We present the first iteration in Figure 4. The *non-critical stakeholder* obtained represents the *out-of-scope*. The second iteration uses the *critical stakeholders* obtained in the first iteration to identify the *non-critical stakeholders* included in the *watch zone*. Then, the third iteration uses the *critical stakeholders* obtained in the second iteration to identify the *non-critical stakeholders* included in the *control zone*. Finally, the remaining *critical stakeholders* of the third iteration is included in *danger zone*. Figure 5 presents the outcome when we classify the smart-home stakeholders per threat zone using a three-level Pareto chart. The danger zone contains *Smart-homes owners (dwellers)* and *Other smart-home inhabitants (dwellers)*, and *Home automation service providers*. The control zone contains *Energy service providers*, *Dwellers friends*, and *Network service providers*. The watch zone contains *Healthcare service providers*, *IoT application developers*, and *IoT cloud service providers*. The out-of-scope contains *Sensor/IoT device manufacturers* and *Courier service providers*, *Real estate agents*, *IoT/smart home regulators*, and *Dwellers collaborators*.

We summarize and compare the results of each classification method in Table V. The table illustrates that the Pareto-based classification can distribute the stakeholders' threats to every threat zone identified. Hence, a three-level Pareto chart can

TABLE V
COMPARISON OF THREE CLASSIFICATION APPROACHES OF THREAT AGENTS DISTRIBUTION PER ZONE.

| | Danger zone | | Control zone | | Watch zone | | Out-of-scope | |
|---|---|---|---|---|---|---|---|---|
| | Range of the likelihood (L) | Number of stakeholders | Range of the likelihood (L) | Number of stakeholders | Range of the likelihood (L) | Number of stakeholders | Range of the likelihood (L) | Number of stakeholders |
| EBIOS RM's classification | $4 \geq L \geq 2.96$ | 2 | $2.96 > L \geq 1.77$ | 0 | $1.77 > L \geq 0.59$ | 12 | $0.59 > L \geq 0$ | 0 |
| Simplified threat classification | $4 \geq L \geq 3$ | 2 | $3 > L \geq 2$ | 0 | $2 > L \geq 1$ | 10 | $1 > L \geq 0$ | 2 |
| Proposed Pareto's classification | $4 \geq L > 1.64$ | 3 | $1.64 \geq L > 1.38$ | 3 | $1.38 \geq L > 1.26$ | 3 | $1.26 \geq L \geq 0$ | 5 |

TABLE VI
DESCRIPTION OF THREE CRITICAL ATTACK PATHS.

| | Risk Origins (RO) | Target Objective (TO) | RO/TO Pertinence | Fear Events (FEs) | Severity | Threat Agents (Smart-Home Stakeholders) | Likelihood |
|---|---|---|---|---|---|---|---|
| Attack path 1 | Specialized outfits | Profit | High | Leaking personal data of dwellers; Leaking medical data records. | S4 | Smart-home dwellers; Smart-home dwellers' friends. | Danger zone; Control zone. |
| Attack path 2 | Terrorists | Terrorism | High | Triggering power outage; Disabling of network security services. | S4 | Energy service providers; Network service providers. | Control zone; Control zone. |
| Attack path 3 | State-related | Spying | High | Leaking personal data; Leaking medical data records; Altering medical data records. | S4 | Home automation service providers; Network service providers; Smart-home dwellers' friends. | Danger zone; Control zone; Control zone. |

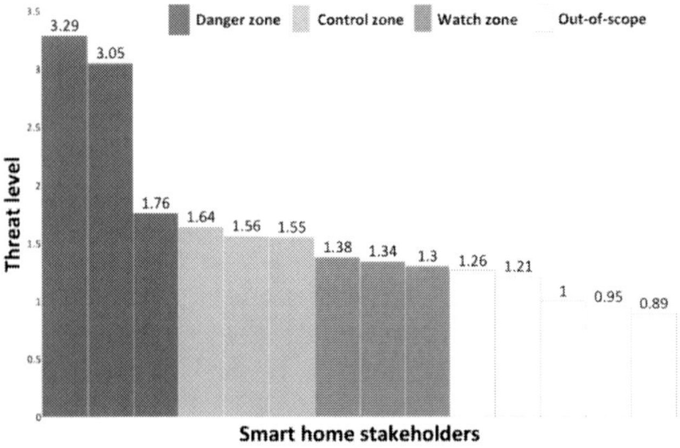


Fig. 5. A description of threat agents using a Pareto chart.

provide better results than the two other approaches.

*5) Identification of Strategic Attack Scenarios:* The attack scenarios present briefly which attacker's profile may want to exploit a particular vulnerability in smart homes, for what purpose, and how they can realize that. Table VI describes the needed information (e.g., RO/TO pertinence, feared events, and threat level) to identify three strategic attack scenarios.

**Strategic attack scenario 1**: *Experienced hackers with specialized outfits use social engineering techniques (e.g., phishing) to trick smart-home dwellers or their friends and get unauthorized access to a smart home. The attackers could sell their personal data or medical data records on the dark web to make profit (Severity: S4).*

**Strategic attack scenario 2**: *Terrorists put many smart homes out of service and spread fear among citizens by disabling access to Internet-based services after attacking network service providers or triggering power outages of many smart homes simultaneously after compromising the infrastructure of energy service providers (Severity: S4).*

**Strategic attack scenario 3**: *A government spies and gets confidential and sensitive information on opposition leaders or other state leaders to blackmail them for national security, political or economic purposes. The state-related profile performs the attack after taking advantage of the strategic positions of home automation service providers, network service providers, and dwellers' friends (Severity: S4).*

Figure 6 summarizes the three strategic attack scenarios.

## VI. DISCUSSION

There are no easy solutions when discussing the security issues of complex systems such as smart homes. We are aware of the importance of developing robust systems to empower the security of home networks, mobile apps, and IoT software and hardware. Furthermore, we believe that attackers are continuously looking for weak links to achieve their ends. As in the recent attacks on the European aerospace giant Airbus in which attack scenarios first targeted Airbus' suppliers (external stakeholders) [28], attackers could take advantage of one or many stakeholders to harm a smart home and its inhabitants. Hence, to prevent such attack scenarios, we used EBIOS RM to evaluate the threat levels to which an attacker could compromise a smart-home stakeholder.

**Threat level calculation**: In our work, we have used the threat level equation proposed by EBIOS RM to evaluate the likelihood of threat agents. However, in risk assessment, many authors estimate the likelihood without the use of an equation. For example, Nurse et al. [29] used a 3-point Likert scale to estimate the likelihood directly, without considering an estimation of relevant metrics. As these authors mentioned, it is difficult to estimate the likelihood of risks. We believe that an approach, such as that of EBIOS RM, that evaluates many metrics to calculate the likelihood may provide more reliable results than a direct assessment. We encourage future research to investigate and provide new metrics and equations to estimate the likelihood of threat agents and cyberattacks in qualitative risk assessment.

**Threat level of stakeholders**: Our results showed that the security education of smart-home dwellers is crucial to reduce attack scenarios targeting these internal stakeholders. Further-

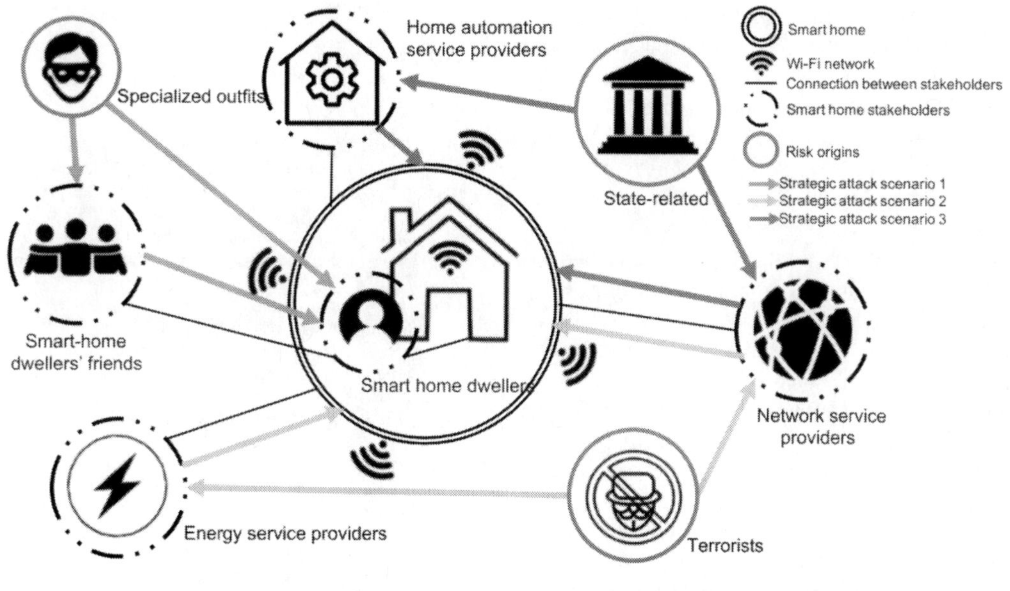


Fig. 6. A description of proposed attack scenarios on smart homes involving stakeholders.

more, there is an imperative necessity to set up a regulatory agency to check on home automation service providers and the other smart-home stakeholders to ensure they comply with the security standards of smart homes for the benefit of all. This cybersecurity compliance will increase the values of *Cyber Maturity* and *Trust*, and reduce the *Threat Level* given the calculation proposed by EBIOS RM.

**Classification of stakeholders**: Risk managers always have to make crucial decisions based on priorities to ensure the security of the assets they are in charge of. As presented in Table V, EBIOS RM could not distribute the stakeholders in every threat zone. To address this issue and provide a more effective classification to risk managers, we proposed a three-level Pareto chart. By extension, an $(n-1)$ level Pareto chart could distribute the threat agents on $(n)$ threat zones effectively.

**Attack scenarios**: We defined the strategic attack scenarios based on information (e.g., risk origins, target objectives, fear events, threat agents, and threat level) we collected through our investigation. These scenarios support our claim regarding the importance of assessing the stakeholders for smart home security. However, it could be challenging to discuss how realistic these scenarios are. To address these issues, note that EBIOS RM recommends an assessment of every strategic attack scenario in Workshop 4, which is out of the scope of this paper.

**Limitations**: Given the complexity of smart home ecosystems, one limitation of this paper could be the identification of key smart-home stakeholders. "The Principle of Who or What Really Counts" rests upon the assumptions and perception of risk managers [30]. That being said, a comprehensive survey study to identify the smart-home stakeholders in regards to critical attributes, such as *power*, *legitimacy*, and *urgency* proposed by [30], is necessary. Moreover, the results of our research, especially those described in Table III and Table IV, rely on the stakeholders we choose and participants' responses to our questionnaire. Since we used an online questionnaire, we could not guarantee the integrity of the collected data. Furthermore, the results could have changed with fewer or more stakeholders and participants. It is necessary to remark that risk assessment is evolutionary. Threats are constantly evolving, and ecosystems are changing. Therefore, our results are not timeless. We recommend a more global investigation with considerable financial and human resources to perform a benchmark for significant smart-home stakeholders in many countries and collect evaluations of thousands of participants to provide more robust and reliable results.

Our findings sound the alarm on the security of smart homes, but mostly its stakeholders. This research fills a gap in the literature since none of the previous works have considered this perspective.

## VII. Conclusion and Future Work

Cyberattacks regularly involve sophisticated means that could be challenging to detect, mainly when they target a dynamic and complex environment such as a smart home. This paper elaborates the security risk analysis of a smart home using EBIOS RM with a focus on the threat level assessment of smart-home stakeholders in the role of threat agents. The goal is to identify realistic attack scenarios to smart homes involving these stakeholders. We provide high-level attack scenarios involving smart-home stakeholders after a step-by-step process to identify risk origins, target objectives, fear events and their severity, threat agents and their threat level, as recommended by EBIOS RM. This perspective of the smart home security with a focus on stakeholders security issues have not been explored in the previous studies.

We develop a questionnaire based on a 5-point Likert scale to assess the threat level of threat agents. We propose a three-level Pareto chart to classify the smart-home stakeholders into different threat zones. This approach distributes the threat agents into every threat zone, unlike the proposed distribution suggested by EBIOS RM. Our results show that the threat levels of successful attack scenarios involving smart home inhabitants and smart home automation service providers are very high.

Forthcoming work will cover the identification and risk assessment of each operational scenario (Workshop 4) and the risk treatment (Workshop 5). More broadly, the present findings might contribute to extending the discussions on smart home security to the security of stakeholders who make smart home operations effective. Including stakeholders when rethinking the security design of smart homes becomes essential. Furthermore, multi-layered security cooperation for smart home security could be possible in the future. Future work will cover the designing of security systems and policies considering stakeholders for smart home security. We invite interested readers to engage in smart-home stakeholders analysis to provide other perspectives and results.

## ACKNOWLEDGMENT

Part of this study was funded by the ICS-CoE Core Human Resources Development Program.

## REFERENCES

[1] M. R. Alam, M. B. I. Reaz, and M. A. M. Ali, "A review of smart homes—Past, present, and future," *IEEE transactions on systems, man, and cybernetics, part C (applications and reviews)*, vol. 42, no. 6, pp. 1190–1203, 2012.

[2] P. P. Gaikwad, J. P. Gabhane, and S. S. Golait, "A survey based on Smart Homes system using Internet-of-Things," in *2015 International Conference on Computation of Power, Energy, Information and Communication (ICCPEIC)*. IEEE, 2015, pp. 0330–0335.

[3] Statista, "Smart Home Report 2021," 2021, retrieved: October, 2021. [Online]. Available: https://www.statista.com/study/42112/smart-home-report/

[4] Proofpoint, "More than 750,000 Phishing and SPAM emails Launched from "Thingbots" Including Televisions, Fridge," 2014, retrieved: October, 2021. [Online]. Available: https://www.proofpoint.com/us/proofpoint-uncovers-internet-things-iot-cyberattack

[5] E. Blumenthal and E. Weise, "Hacked home devices caused massive Internet outage," 2016, retrieved: October, 2021. [Online]. Available: https://www.usatoday.com/story/tech/2016/10/21/cyber-attack-takes-down-east-coast-netflix-spotify-twitter/92507806/

[6] A. Jacobsson, M. Boldt, and B. Carlsson, "A risk analysis of a smart home automation system," *Future Generation Computer Systems*, vol. 56, pp. 719–733, 2016.

[7] C. Wongvises, A. Khurat, D. Fall, and S. Kashihara, "Fault tree analysis-based risk quantification of smart homes," in *2017 2nd International Conference on Information Technology (INCIT)*. IEEE, 2017, pp. 1–6.

[8] Cherdantseva et al., "A review of cyber security risk assessment methods for scada systems," *Computers & security*, vol. 56, pp. 1–27, 2016.

[9] ISO, "ISO/IEC 27005:2011(en) Information technology — Security techniques — Information security risk management," 2011, retrieved: October, 2021. [Online]. Available: https://www.iso.org/obp/ui/#iso:std:iso-iec:27005:ed-2:v1:en

[10] D. Bregman, "Smart home intelligence–the ehome that learns," *International journal of smart home*, vol. 4, no. 4, pp. 35–46, 2010.

[11] W. Abbass, A. Baina, and M. Bellafkih, "Using EBIOS for risk management in critical information infrastructure," in *2015 5th World Congress on Information and Communication Technologies (WICT)*, 2015, pp. 107–112.

[12] B. Ali and A. I. Awad, "Cyber and physical security vulnerability assessment for IoT-based smart homes," *Sensors*, vol. 18, no. 3, p. 817, 2018.

[13] G. Kavallieratos, V. Gkioulos, and S. K. Katsikas, "Threat analysis in dynamic environments: The case of the smart home," in *2019 15th International Conference on Distributed Computing in Sensor Systems (DCOSS)*. IEEE, 2019, pp. 234–240.

[14] T. R. Peltier, *Information security risk analysis*. CRC press, 2005.

[15] R. Grimble and K. Wellard, "Stakeholder methodologies in natural resource management: a review of principles, contexts, experiences and opportunities," *Agricultural Systems*, vol. 55, no. 2, pp. 173–193, 1997, socio-economic Methods in Renewable Natural Resources Research. [Online]. Available: https://www.sciencedirect.com/science/article/pii/S0308521X97000061

[16] R. M. Yawson and B. Greiman, "Stakeholder analysis as a tool for systems approach research in hrd," in *Leading Human Resource Development through Research. Proceedings of the 21st Annual AHRD International Research Conference in the Americas. Houston, Texas, USA*, 2014.

[17] M. Mollaeefar., A. Siena., and S. Ranise., "Multi-stakeholder cybersecurity risk assessment for data protection," in *Proceedings of the 17th International Joint Conference on e-Business and Telecommunications - SECRYPT*, INSTICC. SciTePress, 2020, pp. 349–356.

[18] ANSSI, "EBIOS Risk Manager – The method," 2021, retrieved: October, 2021. [Online]. Available: https://www.ssi.gouv.fr/en/guide/ebios-risk-manager-the-method/

[19] H. N. Boone and D. A. Boone, "Analyzing likert data," *Journal of extension*, vol. 50, no. 2, pp. 1–5, 2012.

[20] T. D. Mendes, R. Godina, E. M. Rodrigues, J. C. Matias, and J. P. Catalão, "Smart home communication technologies and applications: Wireless protocol assessment for home area network resources," *Energies*, vol. 8, no. 7, pp. 7279–7311, 2015.

[21] V. Williams, S. Terence J., and J. Immaculate, "Survey on internet of things based smart home," in *2019 International Conference on Intelligent Sustainable Systems (ICISS)*, 2019, pp. 460–464.

[22] J. Bugeja, A. Jacobsson, and P. Davidsson, "An analysis of malicious threat agents for the smart connected home," in *2017 IEEE International Conference on Pervasive Computing and Communications Workshops (PerCom Workshops)*. IEEE, 2017, pp. 557–562.

[23] S. Harris, "China's cyber-militia," 2008, retrieved: October, 2021. [Online]. Available: https://www.nextgov.com/cio-briefing/2008/05/chinas-cyber-militia/42113/

[24] M. R. Alam, M. B. I. Reaz, and M. A. M. Ali, "A review of smart homes—past, present, and future," *IEEE Transactions on Systems, Man, and Cybernetics, Part C (Applications and Reviews)*, vol. 42, no. 6, pp. 1190–1203, 2012.

[25] R. H. Jensen, Y. Strengers, J. Kjeldskov, L. Nicholls, and M. B. Skov, *Designing the Desirable Smart Home: A Study of Household Experiences and Energy Consumption Impacts*. New York, NY, USA: Association for Computing Machinery, 2018, p. 1–14. [Online]. Available: https://doi.org/10.1145/3173574.3173578

[26] S. Ul Rehman and S. Manickam, "A study of smart home environment and its security threats," *International Journal of Reliability, Quality and Safety Engineering*, vol. 23, no. 03, p. 1640005, 2016. [Online]. Available: https://doi.org/10.1142/S0218539316400052

[27] V. Pareto, *Trattato di sociologia generale [The mind and society]*. G. Barbèra, 1916, vol. 2.

[28] AFP, "Airbus Hit by Series of Cyber Attacks on Suppliers: Security Sources," 2019, retrieved: October, 2021. [Online]. Available: https://www.securityweek.com/hackers-target-airbus-suppliers-quest-commercial-secrets

[29] J. R. C. Nurse, A. Atamli, and A. Martin, "Towards a usable framework for modelling security and privacy risks in the smart home," in *Human Aspects of Information Security, Privacy, and Trust*, T. Tryfonas, Ed. Cham: Springer International Publishing, 2016, pp. 255–267.

[30] R. K. Mitchell, B. R. Agle, and D. J. Wood, "Toward a theory of stakeholder identification and salience: Defining the principle of who and what really counts," *The Academy of Management Review*, vol. 22, no. 4, pp. 853–886, 1997. [Online]. Available: http://www.jstor.org/stable/259247

# Software Based Glitching Detection

Jakob Löw
*Technische Hochschule Ingolstadt*
Ingolstadt, Germany
jakob@löw.com

Dominik Bayerl
*Technische Hochschule Ingolstadt*
Ingolstadt, Germany
dominik.bayerl@carissma.eu

Prof. Dr. Hans-Joachim Hof
*Technische Hochschule Ingolstadt*
Ingolstadt, Germany
hof@thi.de

***Abstract*—Clock glitching is an attack surface of many microprocessors. While fault resistant processors exist, they usually come with a higher price tag resulting in their cheaper alternatives being used for small embedded devices. After describing the effects of fault attacks and their application to modern microprocessors, this paper presents a novel software based approach at protecting programs from fault attacks. Even though the protection mechanism is automatically added to a given program in a special compiler step, its use case is not to protect the full program. The approach comes with heavy performance implications, making it only useful for protecting important parts of programs, such as initialization, key exchanges or other cryptographic implementations.**

***Index Terms*—computer security, clocks, microcontrollers, program compilers, program control structures**

## I. Introduction

Hardening software against glitching attacks manually is a tedious task and requires a trained developer. Hardware based glitch detection on the other hand increases cost of production. Thus the most efficient approach in order to protect against glitch attacks is with generalized and automated software mechanisms. The goal of this paper is to introduce a novel software based approach protecting a program from clock glitching attacks.

In order to introduce this approach, first, the nature and effects of glitching attacks in general and clock glitching attacks in particular are described in Section II. Section III discusses state of the art software based protection mechanisms. Then a novel approach detecting glitch attacks is introduced in Section IV. Finally in Section IV-D the performance impact of the novel approach is rated given its impact on common compiler optimizations.

## II. Glitching Attack Models

In embedded IT Security, glitching attacks are a special kind of side channel attacks. Their target is to trigger misbehaviours of the target processor in order to alter execution or data flow. A typical goal of a glitch attack is changing the execution flow such that one instruction is skipped. For example, when glitching the conditional branch instruction of a signature check, the check is skipped and the program continues even if the signatures did not match. Triggering a glitch while the processor is loading a value from memory can cause the memory load to not finish correctly and often results in a zero value being loaded instead. Thus, glitching the data flow is often used to attack cryptographic algorithms by glitching the load of keys from memory or by glitching arithmetic operations [1].

The next Subsection will first describe clock glitching attacks, which this paper focuses on, in detail. Afterwards Section II-B will cover the exact effects of clock glitches targeting AVR Microprocessors.

### A. Clock Glitching

Clock glitching is a specific form of glitching attacks. A glitch in the target processor is triggered by altering the provided clock signal. Normally a clock signal is generated by an oscillator with a constant frequency; Rising that frequency is called overclocking. Each processor has a maximum operating frequency, if the clock frequency rises above this threshold the processor starts to behave abnormally.

In a classical clock glitching attack, only a single targeted glitch is inserted into the clock signal, i.e., a second high signal is inserted causing the current instruction to not complete before the next one starts its execution. The effects depend on various parameters as well as on the processors architecture and design.

Figure 1 shows the electrical potential of a clock line during a clock glitch attack. The first Section, labeled as cycle A, shows a regular clock cycle, while cycle B shows a clock cycle with a glitch inserted [4].

### B. Effects of Clock Glitches on AVR Microprocessors

The research by Balasch et. al [4] goes into detail about what exactly happens when a microprocessor is attacked by a glitching attack. They used a Field Programmable Gate Array (FPGA) to generate a clock signal for ATMega163 based smart cards. The FPGA allows clock signal modifications, such as inserting a glitch at a specific location. The ATMega runs a special firmware, which places all registers in a known state, executes the instruction targeted by the glitch and then examines the state of all registers of the microprocessors. From the transformations between the start state and the result state the executed instruction can be derived. This, however, is a non trivial task. For example when before the instruction the value `0x0f` was in register `r18` which changed to `0xf0` afterwards the executed instruction could either be a 4-bit left shift or an addition with `0x51`. Multiple runs with the same glitch period, the same instruction but different input states have to be performed in order to be able to identify the actual executed instruction.

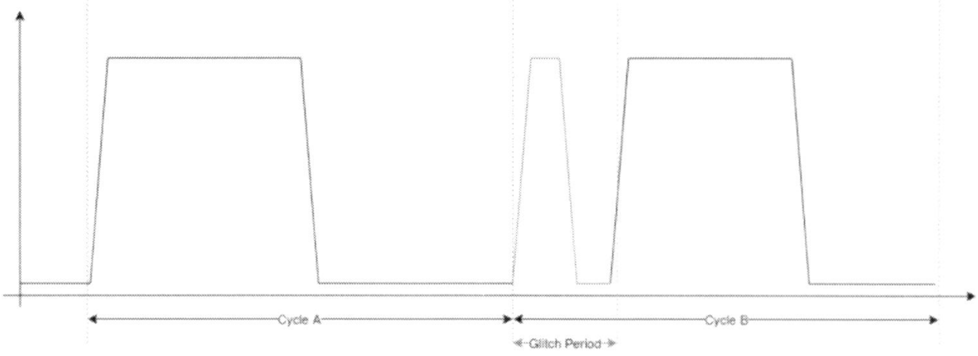


Fig. 1: Injection of a Clock Glitch

With these methods [4] shows the actual effect of clock glitches with different glitch periods on a target instruction. During instruction fetching the value of the instruction to execute next changes from the previous instruction to zero and then to the value of the following instruction. By injecting a glitch into this transition, depending on the length of the glitch period, either a decayed version of the previous instruction or a decayed, i.e. not yet fully loaded, version of the current instruction can be executed. Figure 2 shows this behaviour for a *Set all Bits in Register* (`SER`( instruction followed by a *Branch if Equal* (`BREQ`) instruction. In this specific case, for a glitch period up to 28 ns a decayed version of the `BREQ` instruction is executed. From 32ns and upwards an intermediate value of the transition from zero to `SER` is executed [4].

| Glitch period | Instruction | Opcode (base 2) |
|---|---|---|
| | TST R12 | 0010 0000 1100 1100 |
| - | BREQ PC+0x02 | 1111 0000 0000 1001 |
| | SER R26 | 1110 1111 1010 1111 |
| $\leq$ 57ns | LDI R26,0xEF | 1110 1110 1010 1111 |
| $\leq$ 56ns | LDI R26,0xCF | 1110 1100 1010 1111 |
| $\leq$ 52ns | LDI R26,0x0F | 1110 0000 1010 1111 |
| $\leq$ 45ns | LDI R16,0x09 | 1110 0000 0000 1001 |
| $\leq$ 32ns | LD R0,Y+0x01 | 1000 0000 0000 1001 |
| $\leq$ 28ns | LD R0,Y | 1000 0000 0000 1000 |
| $\leq$ 27ns | LDI R16,0x09 | 1110 0000 0000 1001 |
| $\leq$ 15ns | BREQ PC+0x02 | 1111 0000 0000 1001 |

Fig. 2: Instruction decay based on glitch period

## III. Existing Software based Glitch Detection Techniques

With one of the first papers covering fault based attacks on cryptographic implementations dating back to 1997 [1], there are already multiple papers covering protection mechanisms against fault attacks using software or hardware based countermeasures. The software based countermeasures are usually based on either duplicating instructions or validating computations. The following sections describe some of the common approaches at glitch detection by example, before a novel approach is discussed in Section IV.

### A. *Instruction duplication mechanisms*

A very common approach at protecting code from glitch attacks is instruction duplication or even triplication. It is usually implemented at a very late stage in the compilation process and works by simply duplicating memory load or even arithmetic instructions and checking their results for equality. A simple ARM64 assembly example is shown in Figure 3. Instead of only loading the value at `x0` once into register `w0` it is loaded a second time into `w1`. If a glitch occured in one of the two instructions, i.e. a wrong value was read from memory, the comparasion check fails and an error handler is called.

```
ldr     w1, [x0]
ldr     w0, [x0]
cmp     w1, w0
bne     glitch_error
```

Fig. 3: Validation using instruction duplication

While this approach is simple to implement it is flawed, especially when using modern microcontrollers with multi stage pipelines. As shown by Yuce et. al in [6] injecting a single glitch can affect multiple instructions. This is possible, because the two load instructions are not executed one after another, but rather go simultaneously through various stages in the processor pipeline.

In general placing the validation of an instruction too close to the instruction itself renders the validation vulnerable to single glitch attacks.

### B. *Loop count validation*

In [8], Proy et. al describe an automated compiler based glitch detection mechanism. Instead of validating arbitrary expressions as shown later in this paper, the approach from [8] focuses on validating loop exit conditions and iteration counts. The goal is to prevent attacks which weaken the

security of cryptographic algorithms by reducing the number of encryption rounds.
A special compilation pass is added to LLVM, a very common compiler infrastructure. When encountering a loop with a iteration variable this optimization pass add a a second iteration variable which gets incremented or decremented the same as the original variable and thus allows to validate the loop exit condition after the loop exited. For example, the loop shown in 4a is modified to include a second variable and a condition check turning it into code for the loop shown in 4b.

```
int i = 0;
while(i < 10) {
        // ...
        i++;
}
```

(a) Loop with iteration variable

```
int i = 0;
int j = 0;
while(i < 10) {
        // ...
        i++;
        j++;
}

assert(j >= 10);
```

(b) Loop from 4a with validation

Fig. 4: Basic loop validation example

This optimization works best for loops with simple iteration calculation, i.e. adding or subtracting a constant from the iteration variable each iteration. Loops which contain `break` statements or which use a complex iteration modification however increase complexity of correct validations. The code listings in Figure 5 demonstrate these special loop forms.
A glitch attack on the calculation of `x` in Figure 5b would affect not only the iteration variable, but also a possible validation variable. Thus for glitch robustness not only the iteration variable needs to be duplicated and recalculated, but also all variables used to modify it. In [8] this is achieved by tracing through the expressions used to modify the iteration variable and recalculating all these expressions.
The following section describes a similar, but broader approach, which not only validates loop conditions but rather all expressions calculated in a function.

```
int i = 0;
while(i < 10) {
        // ...
        int x = // ...
        if(x == 42)
                break;
        i++;
}
```

(a)

```
int i = 10;
while(i > 0) {
        // ...
        int x = // ...
        i -= x;
}
```

(b)

Fig. 5: Advanced loop validation examples

## IV. Detecting Glitches using Expression Validations

Traditionally, glitch detection techniques use instruction duplication or even triplication. While this works for some architectures, as described in Subsection III-A, a duplicate instruction is still vulnerable to a single fault on processors featuring a multi stage pipeline. Thus in order to increase the robustness of glitching detection mechanism the validation has to be placed as far away from the original computation as possible. In compiler engineering functions a divided into multiple blocks through which execution flows linearly. Moving validations out of the basic block of the original computation, means the number of instruction executed between computation and validation can vary between just a few computations to multiple calls to other functions. Placing validations farther away from their original computations makes it harder for an attacker to glitch both computation and validation.
The following sections describe how to find the optimal locations for validations and how to validate both computations and conditional branches.

### A. *Identifying Locations for Validations*

As described in Subsection III-A glitch detection mechanisms are still vulnerable to a single glitch fault when the duplicated instruction, in our case the second computation, is placed close to the original instruction. Placing the validation as far away from the original computation as possible ensures its robustness against single fault attacks.
The last possible location for a validation check is usually the end of the scope a value is defined in. For a value defined in a conditional or loop body this results in the check being placed at the end of the conditional or loop respectively. For a value defined in a function the last possible check is right before the function returns. Figure 6 shows an example with these two cases.

```
int main(int argc, char **argv)
{
        int x = argc * 10 - 2;
        if(argc > 1)
        {
                int y = x * 3;

                if(argc > 2)
                        puts(argv[1]);

                // <— validate 'y' here
        }

        // <— validate 'x' here
        return x;
}
```

Fig. 6: Example Code

While it is trivial to find the optimal location for immutable variables in program code, a mutable variable might be changed between its first initialization and the end of the scope. In order to correctly validate all values of a mutable variable the location has to be determined during a later stage in the compilation process. The Static Single Assignment (SSA) form is a very common form of representing a program in compilers. In SSA form each variable is immutable and only assigned once, variables which are originally mutable and set multiple times are split up into seperate variables for each assignment. Additionally a function in SSA form is usually represented as basic blocks rather than loops and branches. Figure 7 shows how *gcc* represents the code listed in Figure 6 internally after SSA creation.

The validation of x, labeled x_5 in Figure 7, can be placed in block 5 ($B_5$). But there does not exist a block for the optimal location to validate y_7. It cannot be placed in $B_5$, as that block is also reachable from $B_2$ where y_7 does not exist. Thus a new block has to be created, with $B_3$ and $B_4$ as predecessors and $B_5$ as successor. The edges $B_3 \rightarrow B_5$ and $B_4 \rightarrow B_5$ have to be removed. The validation of y_7 can then be placed inside the newly created block.

In general a variable $x$ created in block $B_x$ can only be validated in $B_x$ itself or in a block $B_i$ where all predecessors $prec(B_i)$ are direct or indirect successors of $B_x$. The optimal location for the validation is by definition the block that is the farthest away from $B_x$ while still meeting the required condition.

Figure 8 shows the SSA block graph of Figure 6 with validations. Block $B_5$ is the newly inserted block and $B_6$ the former block 5.

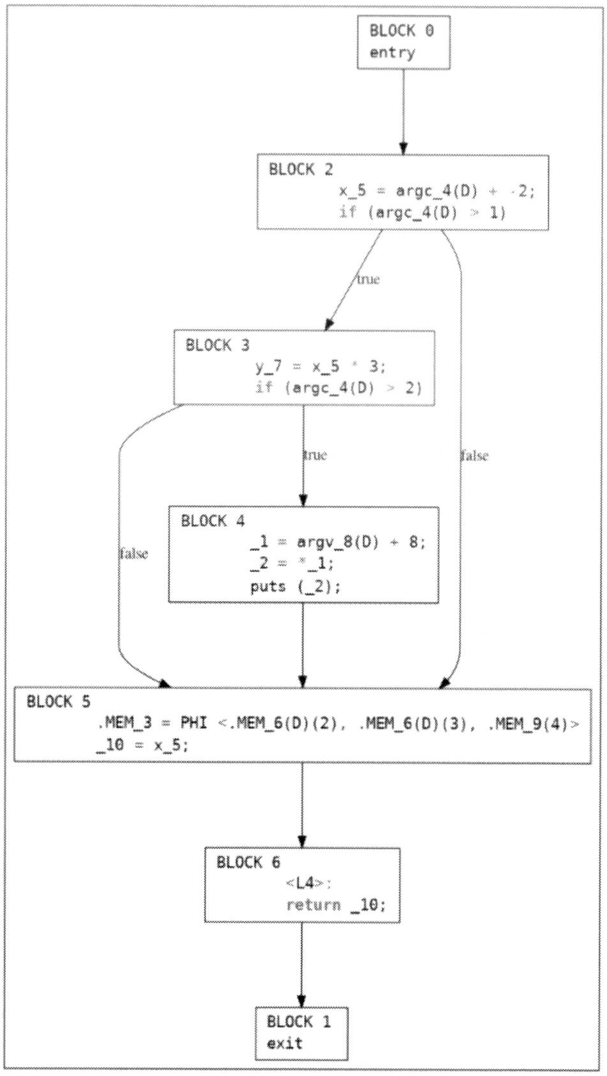


Fig. 7: Basic Block graph in SSA form of 6 without validations

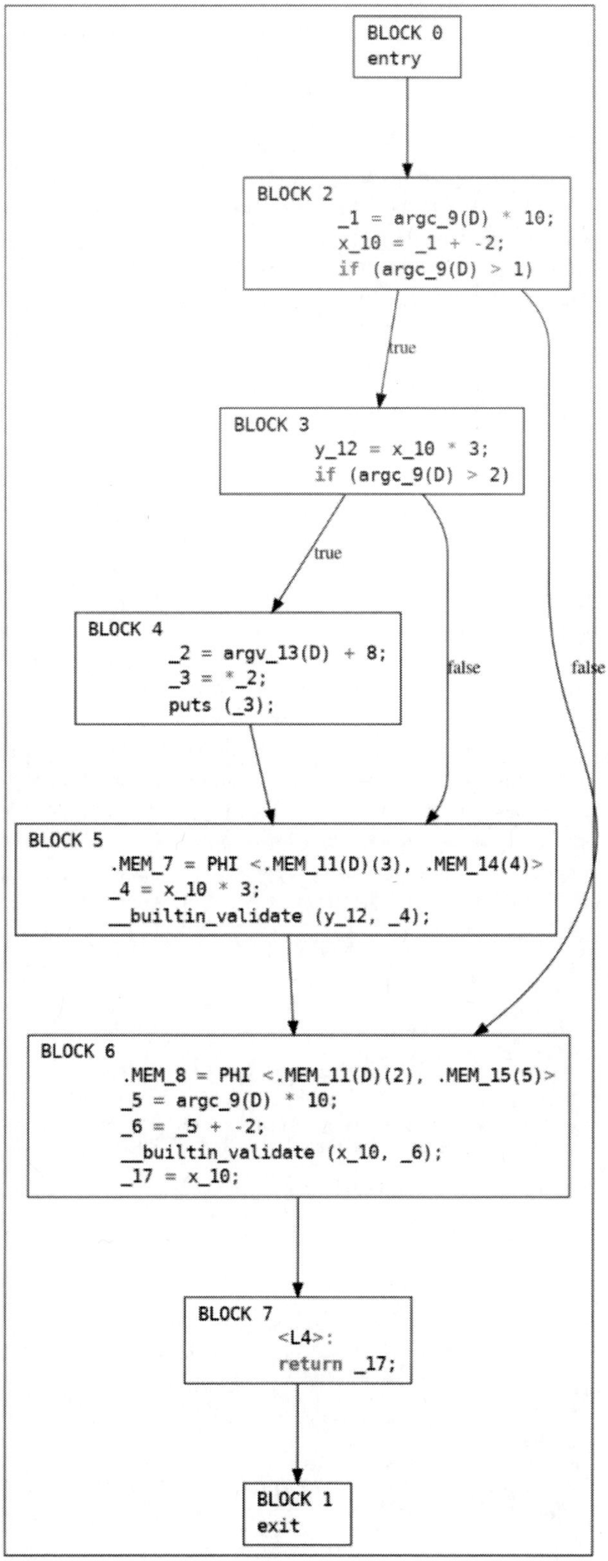


Fig. 8: Basic Block graph in SSA form of 6 with validations

### *B. Validating Calculations*

Without deeper knowledge of the implemented algorithm validating calculations often boils down to simply recomputing all values and thus duplicating the entire calculation.
For example, the statement `int x = argc * 10 - 2;` from Figure 6, results in the SSA shown in the following listing:

```
_1 = argc_9(D) * 10;
x_10 = _1 + -2;
```

For a full validation both the SSA values `_1` and `x_10` have to be recalculated and validated:

```
_5 = argc_9(D) * 10;
__builtin_validate (_1, _5);
_6 = _5 + -2;
__builtin_validate (x_10, _6);
```

A simpler approach is to only validate the outermost result of one or more chained calculations. For the above example this is achieved simply by removing the first instance of `__builtin_validate` resulting in the code shown in 8. For larger entangled calculations removing redunant validations allows to greatly reduce the amount of validations required. For instance all variables in the following C code can be validated using a single validation of `z` instead of having to validate all variables or even all intermediate SSA values one by one.

```
int x = a * 10 + 3;
int y = x / 7;
int z = x * y * 13;
```

The `__builtin_validate` function acts similar to an assert equals function, it continues with execution if the two values are identical and cancels execution otherwise. In a production environment the function can be inlined producing an inequality check and a conditional jump to an error function, resulting in code similar to what gcc produces for calls to `assert`. Figure 9 shows the validation of `x` from Figure 6.

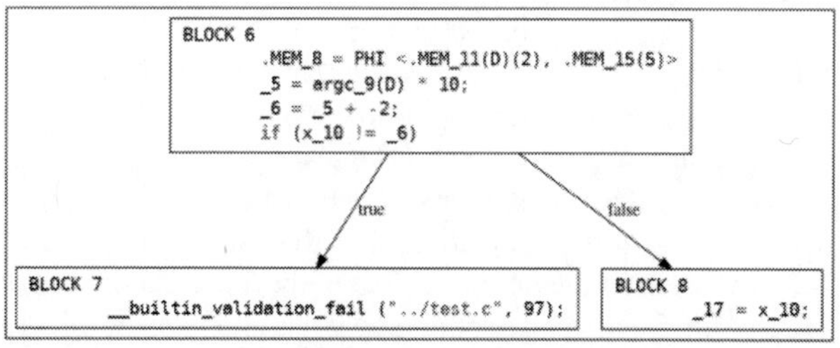


Fig. 9: Validation in production

### *C. Validating Comparasions and Conditional Jumps*

In *gcc* the condition of a branch can not only be a single SSA value, but also a comparasion operation. An example is the `if (argc_4(D) > 1)` statement at the end of block 2 in Figure 7. This is because in most processor architectures a comparasion of two values used for a conditional jump is done without storing the result in a common register, i.e. the comparasion result is only stored in a flags register which is then immediately used by the following conditional jump instruction.

As there exists no SSA name for the result of such comparasions in *gcc* it cannot be validated as described in Subsection IV-B. A block with a conditional branch at the end always has two successors, one for when the condition is true, one for when its false. Therefore in order to validate the condition, two validations, one for each successor have to be created. Each validation follows the same rules as described in Subsection IV-A with their initial blocks being the targets of the conditional edges.

In general, for a block $B_i$ with multiple successors, the branching condition can be validated using one validation placed as if a value $j$ has been created in $B_j$ for all edges $B_i \rightarrow B_j$.

If one of the successors $B_j$ is also a direct or indirect successor of any of the other successors of $B_i$ a new block between $B_i$ and $B_j$ has to be inserted. This is usually the case for loops and if statements without an else block. For example, in Figure 7 the validation for the condition of $B_2$ being false cannot be placed in $B_5$, as $B_5$ is also a successor of $B_3$.

### *D. Performance Considerations of Expression Validations*

Simple instruction duplication mechanisms as described in III-A duplicate the runtime of the protected instructions. This holds true for simple microprocessors where each instruction takes a fixed amount of clock cycles. For advanced processors which incorperate memory caching a second load of a specific address will result in a cache hit, which is usually faster than a load from memory.

The novel glitch detection approach described in Section IV also duplicates instructions and thus has similar effect during runtime. The bigger impact, howver, is its prevention of possible compiler optimizations resulting in the generation of less performant instructions. Normally a compiler analyzes the lifetime of variables and the collisions between those lifetimes. The lifetime of a variable starts when the variable is first set and ends with its last usage. Two lifetimes collide when they are both alive at any given point in the function. When two lifetimes do not collide they can be placed in the same processor register. With too many lifetime collisions the compiler might run out of registers to assign and has to place variables in memory instead [5]. By definition, the optimal location for validation, as given in Subsection IV-A, extends the lifetime of variables to the maximum possible. Thus, with the novel detection approach, the register allocator of the compiler will have to place variables in memory more often, resulting in more memory accesses and decreased performance.

For example the SSA variable `y_12` of Figure 8 would normally live only for a short time in $B_3$. Its validation in $B_5$ extends its lifetime, making it collide with the SSA variables `_2`, `_3` and `_4`.

In order to decrease the performance impact expression validation can only be enabled for security relevant functions such as cryptographic implementations or credential checks by disabling validations for all functions and adding a special compiler attribute to relevant ones.

## V. Conclusion

After giving an introduction to glitching attacks and clock glitches in particular, we discussed various software based approaches at hardening against glitching attacks. While the common protection mechanism discussed in Subsection III-A can easily be applied to a program via an additional compilation pass, it is also shown to be ineffective [6]. The protection mechanism discussed in Subsection III-B by Proy et. al [8] can easily be applied to existing codebases, but only validates loop conditions and loop iterators.

The novel approach described in Section IV tries to combine the best traits of the three described previous mechanisms. It is similar to the mechanism by Proy et. al [8] as it also comes in the form of a compiler pass and it also adds validations of existing computations to the program. However, it not only validates loop conditions, but rather generalizes validation of arbitrary computations and branch conditions. This allows it to also protect the program from glitch attacks targeting value computations or substitutions, instead of only protecting against attacks aimed at modifying loop execution counts.

As discussed in Subsection IV-D this novel approach comes with a big performance impact, doubling the execution time in the best case scenario, but usually having an even worse impact. Thus the approach is best applied only selectively to specific parts of a program, keeping performance impact low while still providing protection to curcial code parts.

## References


[1] Dan Boneh, Richard A. DeMillo, and Richard J. Lipton, "On the Importance of Checking Cryptographic Protocols for Faults", Advances in Cryptology — EUROCRYPT '97, pp. 37-51, 1997.

[2] D.I. Crecraft and S. Gergely "Analog Electronics - Circuits, Systems and Signal Processing" Elsevier Science, 2002.

[3] C. Aumüller, P. Bier, W. Fischer, P. Hofreiter, and J.-P. Seifert, "Fault Attacks on RSA with CRT: ConcreteResults and Practical Countermeasures", Cryptographic Hardware and Embedded Systems - CHES 2002 pp. 260-275, 2002.

[4] J. Balasch, B. Gierlichs, and I. Verbauwhede, "An In-depth and Black-box Characterizationof the Effects of Clock Glitches on 8-bit MCUs", 2011 Workshop on Fault Diagnosis and Tolerance in Cryptography, 2011, pp. 105-114, 2011.

[5] Keith D. Cooper and Linda Torczon, "Engineering a Compiler", 2nd edition, Elsevier Science, 2012.

[6] B. Yuce et. al, "Software Fault Resistance is Futile: Effective Single-Glitch Attacks", 2016 Workshop on Fault Diagnosis and Tolerance in Cryptography (FDTC), pp. 47-58, 2016.

[7] S. Patranabis, A. Chakraborty, and D. Mukhopadhyay, "Fault Tolerant Infective Countermeasure for AES", J Hardw Syst Secur 1, pp. 3-17, 2017.

[8] J. Proy, K. Heydemann, A. Berzati, and A. Cohen, "Compiler-Assisted Loop Hardening Against Fault Attacks", ACM Trans. Archit. Code Optim. 14, 4, pp. 1-25, 2017.

[9] B. Selmke, F. Hauschild, and J. Obermaier, "Fault Injection into PLL-Based Systems via Clock Manipulation", Proceedings of the 3rd ACM Workshop on Attacks and Solutions in Hardware Security Workshop, pp. 85-94, 2019.

# Quantifying Information Leakage of Probabilistic Programs Using the PRISM Model Checker

Khayyam Salehi
*Dept. of Computer Science*
*Shahrekord University*
Shahrekord, Iran
email: kh.salehi@sku.ac.ir

Ali A. Noroozi
*Dept. of Computer Science*
*University of Tabriz*
Tabriz, Iran
email: noroozi@tabrizu.ac.ir

Sepehr Amir-Mohammadian
*Dept. of Computer Science*
*University of the Pacific*
Stockton, CA, USA
email: samirmohammadian@pacific.edu

*Abstract*—**Information leakage is the flow of information from secret inputs of a program to its public outputs. One effective approach to identify information leakage and potentially preserve the confidentiality of a program is to quantify the flow of information that is associated with the execution of that program, and check whether this value meets predefined thresholds. For example, the program may be considered insecure, if this quantified value is higher than the threshold. In this paper, an automated method is proposed to compute the information leakage of probabilistic programs. We use Markov chains to model these programs, and reduce the problem of measuring the information leakage to the problem of computing the joint probabilities of secrets and public outputs. The proposed method traverses the Markov chain to find the secret inputs and the public outputs and subsequently, calculate the joint probabilities. The method has been implemented into a tool called PRISM-Leak, which uses the PRISM model checker to build the Markov chain of input programs. The applicability of the proposed method is highlighted by analyzing a probabilistic protocol and quantifying its leakage.**

***Index Terms*—*Information leakage; Quantitative information flow; Confidentiality; PRISM-Leak.***

## I. INTRODUCTION

Confidentiality is a major concern in cybersecurity that deals with protecting potentially sensitive data against illegitimate disclosure. Considering different application domains, secret data may range over different kinds of information, for instance, medical records in healthcare systems, financial records in banking systems, and passwords and other factors being used in authentication systems. Disclosure of sensitive data to low-confidentiality users has been identified as one of the common weaknesses in system deployment [1], and Open Web Application Security Project has identified it as one of the top ten privacy risks with "very high impact" [2].

Upon executing a program, a low-confidentiality user, henceforth called an attacker, may gain insight into the program secret data by observing its public outputs. This is known as *information leakage*. For example, assume that `h` is a 4-bit secret variable and `l` is a publicly available data container, i.e., it can be freely read by the attacker. Then, in the program `l := h | ` $(1100)_b$, the attacker can infer the two rightmost bits of `h` by observing `l`.

A widely-studied formalism to avoid these leakages is noninterference [3][4]. It enforces the policy that no output should be affected by secret inputs. Although this ensures the security of programs by capturing all explicit and implicit flows, it is too restrictive in at least two respects: (1) Noninterference is a hyperproperty [5], and thus only applicable in meta-level analysis of programs, i.e., it cannot be enforced at runtime. To overcome this in practice, flow analysis is restricted to explicit flows only, e.g., through taint trackers [6][7]; (2) Noninterference is too conservative in many application domains by labeling many intuitively secure programs as insecure. For example, the password-checking program `if user-input = password then success else failure fi` leaks information about what `password` is not when the user cannot login, and hence, it does not satisfy noninterference. This is while, for most applications an acceptable amount of leakage can be tolerated. This limitation can be addressed by quantifying the amount of leakage and considering the ones lower than a predefined threshold as secure, instead of enforcing a no-leakage policy. Quantifying information leakage has been widely used in different realms of cybersecurity, e.g., differential privacy [8][9], the analysis of OpenSSL Heartbleed vulnerability [10], and the evaluation of cryptographic algorithms [11].

This work aligns with the second aforementioned issue of noninterference and in particular, focuses on probabilistic programs, i.e., programs that exhibit probabilistic characteristics. These characteristics are required for modeling systems in different application domains, including randomized and distributed algorithms, unreliable and unpredictable system behaviors, and model-based performance evaluations [12].

Consider a basic scenario in which the program has a secret input `h` and a public output `l`. The attacker has an *initial uncertainty* about `h` and might infer some information after running the program and observing `l`. In this case, the attacker's *remaining uncertainty* is reduced and the difference between the initial uncertainty and the remaining uncertainty is equal to the amount of leaked information. Information theory suggests entropy, e.g., *Shannon entropy* [13], as a solution to quantify uncertainty [14].

Several methods have been proposed to quantify the information leakage of various programs. For example, Klebanov [15] uses symbolic execution besides self-composition to manually compute the leakage of deterministic programs. Biondi et al. [16] develop a tool, HyLeak, for estimating the leakage of simple imperative programs. The method proposed in our work is fully-automated and computes the exact value for the leakage. Noroozi et al. [17] use model checking to compute the leakage of multi-threaded programs. They consider two assumptions, which are required to measure the leakage of concurrent programs: the attacker can select a scheduler and observe intermediate values of the public variable. Since we focus on sequential programs, there is no scheduler and the attacker can only observe final values of the public variable. This is the case in many information flow methods that analyze sequential programs [15][18]–[21].

### A. Security and threat model

Any terminating sequential program exhibiting probabilistic characteristics is the subject of our study. These programs may include data associated with different levels of confidentiality, as well as zero or more neutral components. We assume the existence of at least two levels of confidentiality: secret and public. Neutral data specify temporary and/or auxiliary components of the runtime program configuration that are not assigned to a certain confidentiality level by nature, e.g., the stack pointer and loop indexes. The secret input is fixed and does not change during program execution. This is the case in any analysis in the context of confidentiality that assumes data integrity to be out of scope, e.g., [22][23]. Furthermore, the attacker is assumed to have access to the program source code, but she cannot modify it. The secret data are received by the program as input, and thus reading the source code does not directly reveal secret data. On the other hand, the attacker can execute the program arbitrary number of times and observe the public output after execution, i.e., the attacker does not have access to intermediary values, e.g., through debugging the code.

### B. An illustrative example

In what follows, we describe an illustrative simple example. We will come back to this example in later sections, to explain different aspects of our formal study. Consider the following program:

```
while l1 < h mod 2 do
    l1 := l1 + 1;
    l2 := random(2);
od                                          (P1)
```

Let us assume that h is a secret variable, $l_1$ and $l_2$ are public variables with initial values set to 0, and random(2) produces 0 or 1 randomly. After executing the program, the attacker can infer information about h by observing the final value of $l_1$. In this paper, we are attempting to propose a method that can measure the amount of leaked information from h to $l_1$. As mentioned earlier, the quantification of the leakage implies a more flexible and granular security policy enforcement.

### C. Contributions

The contributions of this work are as follows:

1) We propose a novel automated method for computing the information leakage of sequential programs with probabilistic characteristics. We model operational semantics of the programs by Markov chains, in the same style as [12][17]. The proposed method explores the Markov chain in a depth-first manner and finds all possible paths, from which it computes joint probabilities of the program's secrets and public outputs. It then calculates the exact value of information leakage using these joint probabilities.
2) The method has been implemented into a tool, called PRISM-Leak [24]. Input programs of PRISM-Leak are written in the PRISM language [25]. PRISM-Leak constructs the Markov chain of the input program using the PRISM model checker [25]. PRISM is a well-established tool for formal modeling and analysis of programs with probabilistic characteristics. It has been used to analyze a wide range of algorithms, protocols, and systems in various application domains such as cybersecurity, computer networking, biology, game theory, etc.
3) Finally, we demonstrate the applicability of our proposed method in a case study by analyzing the grades protocol [26]. This opens the path for evaluating confidentiality of real-world security protocols.

### D. Paper outline

The paper proceeds as follows. Section II provides preliminaries of the paper, including formal definition of Markov chain and how we use it to model operational semantics of probabilistic programs. In Section III, the proposed method for computing the information leakage is discussed. Implementation and the case study are discussed in Section IV. Section V reviews related work. Finally, Section VI concludes the paper and discusses future work.

## II. Basic Definitions

Let $\mathcal{X}$ be a random variable. A probability distribution $Pr$ of random variable $\mathcal{X}$ is a function $Pr : \mathcal{X} \mapsto [0,1]$, such that $\sum_{x\in\mathcal{X}} Pr(x) = 1$.

A well-established measure to compute uncertainty of a random variable is *Shannon entropy*, which is the average number of bits required to predict a value, considered in the distribution of the random variable.

*Definition 1 (Shannon entropy):* The *Shannon entropy* of a random variable $\mathcal{X}$ is defined as $\mathcal{H}(\mathcal{X}) = -\sum_{x\in\mathcal{X}} Pr(\mathcal{X} = x).\log_2 Pr(\mathcal{X} = x)$.

We use Markov chains to model operational semantics of probabilistic programs. In what follows, we define Markov chains abstractly. In Section III, we instantiate them for probabilistic programs.

*Definition 2 (Markov chain):* A (discrete-time) Markov chain (MC) is a tuple $\mathcal{M} = (S, \mathbf{P}, \zeta)$, where

- $S$ is a set of states,
- $\mathbf{P} : S \times S \mapsto [0,1]$ is a transition probability function such that for all $s \in S$, $\sum_{s'\in S} \mathbf{P}(s,s') = 1$, and
- $\zeta : S \mapsto [0,1]$ is the initial distribution of states, i.e., $\sum_{s\in S} \zeta(s) = 1$.

An MC is called finite if $S$ is finite. A state $s$ contains the values of variables (secret, public, and neutral) as well as the program counter in each execution of the program. Given states $s$ and $s'$, the function $\mathbf{P}$ defines the probability $\mathbf{P}(s, s')$ of moving from $s$ to $s'$ in one step. $\zeta$ specifies the likelihood of being an initial state of the program. The set of initial states of Markov chain $\mathcal{M}$ is indicated by $Init(\mathcal{M})$, i.e., $Init(\mathcal{M}) = \{s \in S : \zeta(s) > 0\}$. The set of posterior states of each state is defined as $Post(s) = \{s' \in S : \mathbf{P}(s, s') > 0\}$. A state $s$ is terminating if $Post(s) = \emptyset$. A path $\pi$ in $\mathcal{M}$ is defined as a sequence of states $s_0 s_1 \ldots s_n$, in which $s_0$ is an initial state, $s_n$ is a terminating state, and $s_{i+1} \in Post(s_i)$ for $i \in \{0, 1, \ldots, n-1\}$. The occurrence probability of $\pi$ is defined as

$$Pr(\pi = s_0 s_1 \ldots s_n) = \begin{cases} \zeta(s_0) & \text{if } n = 0, \\ \zeta(s_0). \prod\limits_{0 \le i < n} \mathbf{P}(s_i, s_{i+1}) & \text{otherwise.} \end{cases}$$

## III. Computing the Information Leakage

In this section, we show how to compute the final leakage of probabilistic programs. Let $P$ be a terminating probabilistic program, with a random secret variable $h$, a public variable $l$ and possibly some neutral variables. For the cases where there are more than one secret variable, we concatenate them to form a single secret tuple. The same is done for public and neutral variables. This way, we simplify the formal analysis and only track the flow of a single secret data structure to a single public output channel. This results in quantifying the aggregate amount of flow from secrets to public outputs. Indeed, quantification of individual flows in the presence of multiple secrets and public outputs is feasible in our framework by revising the confidentiality labels that are assigned to different variables. For instance, one may only tag single input $\mathtt{h}_i$ as secret and the remaining inputs as neutral to solely study the flow of $i$th input to the public domain.

We model program $P$ with a Markov chain $\mathcal{M} = (S, \mathbf{P}, \zeta)$. Each state $s \in S$ is a tuple $\langle \bar{l}, \bar{h}, \bar{n}, pc \rangle$, where $\bar{l}$, $\bar{h}$, and $\bar{n}$ are values of the public, secret, and neutral variables, respectively, and $pc$ is the program counter. The transition probability function $\mathbf{P}$ defines probabilities of transitions between states. $\zeta$ is determined by $\zeta(s_0) = Pr(h = \bar{h})$ for each initial state $s_0$ and $s_0 = \langle \cdot, \bar{h}, \cdot, 0 \rangle$. Therefore, the definition of $\zeta$ captures the attacker's knowledge about program secrets.

When constructing $\mathcal{M}$ for $P$, loops of $P$ are unfolded and considering that $P$ is terminating, $\mathcal{M}$ becomes a directed acyclic graph (DAG). Initial states are roots and terminating states are leaves of each DAG. In the following example, we review the MC of program `P1`.

***Example 1: MC of*** **`P1`*.*** The MC of `P1` is depicted in Figure 1, where `h` is a 2-bit value and thus either 0, 1, 2, or 3. For the sake of brevity, $pc$ is not shown in the graph. Moreover, there are not any neutral values in this simple example. In each state, `l` is defined as $\langle \mathtt{l}_1, \mathtt{l}_2 \rangle$. Note that branches are due to assigning a random value (0 or 1) to $\mathtt{l}_2$.

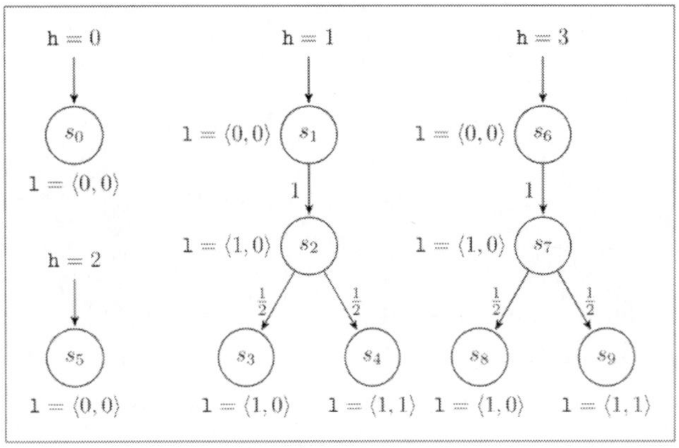


Figure 1. MC of the program `P1`.

The attacker runs the program and observes the public outputs. The public outputs are the values of `l` in terminating states and denoted by $o$. The prior distribution $Pr(h)$ specifies the initial uncertainty of the attacker and the posterior distribution $Pr(h \mid o)$ specifies the remaining uncertainty of the attacker, which is obtained after running the program and observing the output $o$. Therefore, the final leakage of $\mathcal{M}$ is computed as

$$\mathcal{L}(\mathcal{M}) = \mathcal{H}(h) - \mathcal{H}(h \mid o). \tag{1}$$

In (1), $\mathcal{H}(h)$ is the initial uncertainty and computed as

$$\mathcal{H}(h) = -\sum_{\bar{h} \in h} Pr(h = \bar{h}). \log_2 Pr(h = \bar{h}).$$

$\mathcal{H}(h \mid o)$ is the remaining uncertainty in (1) and calculated as

$$\mathcal{H}(h \mid o) = \sum_{\bar{o} \in o} Pr(o = \bar{o}).\mathcal{H}(h \mid o = \bar{o}). \tag{2}$$

In (2), $\mathcal{H}(h \mid o = \bar{o})$ is defined as

$$\mathcal{H}(h \mid o = \bar{o}) = \\ -\sum_{\bar{h} \in h} Pr(h = \bar{h} \mid o = \bar{o}). \log_2 Pr(h = \bar{h} \mid o = \bar{o}),$$

and $Pr(h = \bar{h} \mid o = \bar{o})$ is computed by

$$Pr(h = \bar{h} \mid o = \bar{o}) = \frac{Pr(h = \bar{h}, o = \bar{o})}{Pr(o = \bar{o})}.$$

$Pr(h = \bar{h}, o = \bar{o})$ is the joint probability of $h = \bar{h}$ and $o = \bar{o}$. $Pr(o = \bar{o})$ is the occurrence probability of the output $\bar{o}$ and is computed as

$$Pr(o = \bar{o}) = \sum_{\bar{h} \in h} Pr(h = \bar{h}, o = \bar{o}).$$

Thus, computing the remaining uncertainty is reduced to computing the joint probabilities $Pr(h, o)$. Assuming we have all paths of $\mathcal{M}$ and their probabilities, the joint probability $Pr(h = \bar{h}, o = \bar{o})$ can be calculated as the sum of the

$$Pr(h = 0, o = \langle 0, 0\rangle) = Pr(\pi = s_0) = 1/4$$
$$Pr(h = 1, o = \langle 1, 0\rangle) = Pr(\pi = s_1 s_2 s_3) = 1/8$$
$$Pr(h = 1, o = \langle 1, 1\rangle) = Pr(\pi = s_1 s_2 s_4) = 1/8$$
$$Pr(h = 2, o = \langle 0, 0\rangle) = Pr(\pi = s_5) = 1/4$$
$$Pr(h = 3, o = \langle 1, 0\rangle) = Pr(\pi = s_6 s_7 s_8) = 1/8$$
$$Pr(h = 3, o = \langle 1, 1\rangle) = Pr(\pi = s_6 s_7 s_9) = 1/8$$
$$Pr(o = \langle 0, 0\rangle) = Pr(h = 0, o = \langle 0, 0\rangle) + Pr(h = 2, o = \langle 0, 0\rangle) = 1/2$$
$$Pr(o = \langle 1, 0\rangle) = Pr(h = 1, o = \langle 1, 0\rangle) + Pr(h = 3, o = \langle 1, 0\rangle) = 1/4$$
$$Pr(o = \langle 1, 1\rangle) = Pr(h = 1, o = \langle 1, 1\rangle) + Pr(h = 3, o = \langle 1, 1\rangle) = 1/4$$
$$Pr(h = 0 \mid o = \langle 0, 0\rangle) = 1/2, \quad Pr(h = 1 \mid o = \langle 1, 0\rangle) = 1/2$$
$$Pr(h = 1 \mid o = \langle 1, 1\rangle) = 1/2, \quad Pr(h = 2 \mid o = \langle 0, 0\rangle) = 1/2$$
$$Pr(h = 3 \mid o = \langle 1, 0\rangle) = 1/2, \quad Pr(h = 3 \mid o = \langle 1, 1\rangle) = 1/2$$

Figure 2. 1) Joint probabilities, $Pr(h, o)$, 2) public output occurrence probabilities, $Pr(o)$, and 3) the posterior probabilities, $Pr(h \mid o)$, in `P1`.

occurrence probabilities of all paths that lead to a terminating state $s_n = \langle \overline{o}, \overline{h}, \cdot, \cdot \rangle$, i.e.,

$$Pr(h = \overline{h}, o = \overline{o}) = \sum_{s_0 \in Init(\mathcal{M}),\ s_n = \langle \overline{o}, \overline{h}, \cdot, \cdot \rangle} Pr(\pi = s_0 \ldots s_n).$$

In the following example, we calculate the information leakage from `h` to the public domain in program `P1`.

***Example 2: Information leakage in `P1`.*** Assume that initially the attacker only knows the bit length of `h` and thus the probability distribution of `h` becomes uniform, i.e., $Pr(h) = 1/4$ for all four possible values of `h`. Then, the initial uncertainty is computed as $\mathcal{H}(h) = -\sum_{\overline{h}=0,1,2,3} (1/4) \log_2 (1/4) = 2$. As explained earlier, in order to calculate the remaining uncertainty, we need to compute the joint probabilities $Pr(h, o)$. Using the joint probabilities, the public output occurrence probabilities $Pr(o)$ are computed, and then the posterior probabilities $Pr(h|o)$ are calculated. These details are given in Figure 2. Therefore, we would have $\mathcal{H}(h \mid o = \langle 0, 0\rangle) = \mathcal{H}(h \mid o = \langle 1, 0\rangle) = \mathcal{H}(h \mid o = \langle 1, 1\rangle) = 1$. These yield the remaining uncertainty $\mathcal{H}(h \mid o)$ to be equal to 1. Thus, the amount of leakage is calculated as $\mathcal{L} = \mathcal{H}(h) - \mathcal{H}(h \mid o) = 2 - 1 = 1\ bit$. This is in compliance with the intuition that the attacker infers the least significant bit of the secret.

Figure 3 shows the detailed steps of computing $Pr(h, o)$ for the Markov chain $\mathcal{M}$. The algorithm uses a higher-order map function $ohMap : \overline{o} \mapsto (\overline{h} \mapsto Pr(h = \overline{h}, o = \overline{o}))$ to store the joint probabilities. It traverses the Markov chain $\mathcal{M}$ by a depth-first recursive function, called EXPLOREPATHS($\cdot$), and extracts all paths. It then calculates $Pr(h, o)$.

***Time complexity.*** The costs of computing the information leakage are dominated by the costs of computing the joint probabilities in the algorithm shown in Figure 3. The core of the algorithm is to find all paths of $\mathcal{M}$ using depth-first exploration. $\mathcal{M}$ is a DAG and the number of all possible paths of a DAG can be exponential in the number of its states. Therefore, computing the leakage of $\mathcal{M}$ takes $O(2^n)$ time in the worst case, where $n$ is the number of states of $\mathcal{M}$. It should be noted that this is the expected time complexity for model checking algorithms, as they analyze the whole state space [12]. Furthermore, the method is used for a limited number of times to analyze the security of a program.

*Input*: finite MC $\mathcal{M}$
*Output*: a map containing the joint probabilities $Pr(h, o)$

Let $ohMap$ be an empty higher-order map function from $\overline{o}$ to $\overline{h}$ to $Pr(h = \overline{h}, o = \overline{o})$;
// *i.e.* $ohMap : \overline{o} \mapsto (\overline{h} \mapsto Pr(h = \overline{h}, o = \overline{o}))$
Let $\pi$ be an empty list of states for storing a path;
**for** $s_0$ **in** $Init(\mathcal{M})$ **do**
    EXPLOREPATHS($s_0$, $\pi$, $ohMap$);
**return** $ohMap$;

**function** EXPLOREPATHS($s$, $\pi$, $ohMap$)
    // *add state $s$ to the current path from the initial state*
    $\pi$.add($s$);
    // *found a path stored in $\pi$*
    **if** $s$ is a terminating state **then**
        // *assume $s = \langle \overline{o}, \overline{h}, \cdot, \cdot \rangle$*
        // *define $hMap$ as $Pr(h, o = \overline{o})$*
        **if** $\overline{o}$ not in $ohMap$ **then**
            Let $hMap$ be an empty map from $\overline{h}$ to $Pr(h = \overline{h}, o = \overline{o})$;
        **else**
            $hMap = ohMap.get(\overline{o})$;
        **if** $\overline{h}$ not in $hMap$ **then**
            $prob = Pr(\pi)$;
        **else**
            $prob = Pr(\pi) + hMap.get(\overline{h})$;
        $hMap.put(\overline{h}, prob)$; // *Update $hMap$*
        $ohMap.put(\overline{o}, hMap)$; // *Update $ohMap$*
    **else**
        **for** $s'$ **in** $Post(s)$ **do**
            EXPLOREPATHS($s'$, $\pi$, $ohMap$);
    // *done exploring from $s$, so remove it from $\pi$*
    $\pi$.pop();
    **return** ;

Figure 3. Computing the joint probabilities $Pr(h, o)$.

## IV. IMPLEMENTATION AND CASE STUDY

In this section, we describe an implementation of our proposed algorithm, employing the PRISM model checker. Next, as a case study we study the information leakage in an example protocol.

### A. *PRISM-Leak: An information leakage quantifier*

An efficient implementation of the method requires a model checker to construct the Markov chain of the input program. We have implemented the approach as part of PRISM-

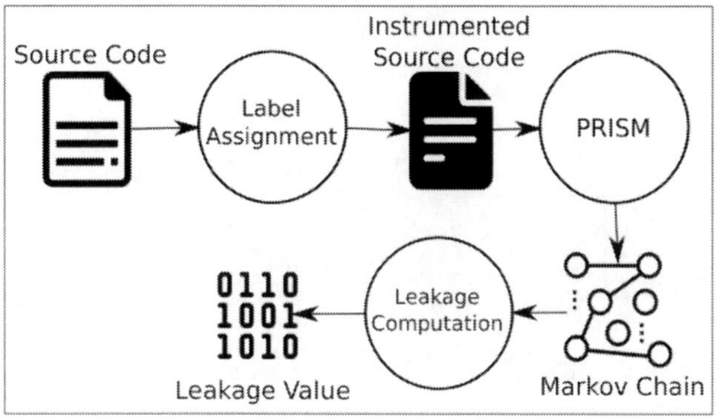


Figure 4. Architecture of PRISM-Leak.

Leak [24]. At a high level, the architecture of PRISM-Leak is depicted in Figure 4. Source code is in the PRISM language and label assignment tags program variables with the public and secret labels. The PRISM model checker builds the Markov chain and stores it via multi-terminal binary decision diagrams. These decision diagrams are efficient symbolic data structures to store states and transitions of Markovian models [27]. PRISM-Leak uses these diagrams to extract the set of reachable states and builds a sparse matrix containing the transitions between the states. Then, it finds the outputs by traversing the model, computes the joint probabilities of the secrets and the public outputs according to the algorithm shown in Figure 3, and employs them to measure the amount of the final leakage.

### B. Case study

In order to evaluate the applicability of the proposed method, we consider the grades protocol [26] as a case study and show how the method computes the leakage of probabilistic programs. In the grades protocol, $k$ students $s_1, \ldots, s_k$ are given secret grades $g_1, \ldots, g_k$, where $0 \leq g_i < m$. The students aim to compute the sum of their grades, without revealing their secret grade to other students. For that, each student $s_i$ produces a random number $r_i$ between 0 and $n = (m-1) \times k+1$ and announces it only to the student $s_{(i-1)\%k}$. Then, the student $s_i$ declares a number $d_i = g_i + r_i - r_{(i+1)\%k}$. The sum of all grades is equivalent to $\left(\sum_i d_i\right) \ \% \ n$. We assume the grades are secret, and the declarations and the sum are public. To evaluate security of the protocol, we consider two cases: 1) the attacker knows the declarations and the sum of the grades, and 2) the attacker only knows the sum. If the amount of leakage is the same for both cases, then the protocol does not leak secret information via the declarations.

Table I reports the amounts of leakage, as well as the number of states and transitions of the Markov chains for the two aforementioned cases. As seen in the table, both leakages are identical and thus, the protocol is secure, i.e., an attacker that knows both the declarations and the sum of the grades gains the same information as an attacker that only knows the sum. PRISM source code of the protocol is available at the Github repository of PRSIM-Leak [24].

## V. Related Work

In this section, we discuss the related work and compare them to ours.

Backes et al. [28] propose an automated method to compute information leakage. They employ the ARMC model checker to extract the equivalence relation of high values which have the same output. They enumerate the size of each equivalence class using the omega-calculator and LATTE (Lattice point Enumeration). They only consider deterministic programs. In this respect, our work covers probabilistic programs, as well.

Chothia et al. [29] propose a framework to quantify the information leakage in every two arbitrary points of a program. They extend their method to consider Java programs by developing LeakWatch [30]. LeakWatch can estimate the leakage using statistical approximation techniques. It also considers intermediate leakages. Our proposed method calculates the exact values and does not consider intermediate leakages.

Klebanov [15] uses symbolic execution besides self-composition to precisely compute the information leakage of deterministic programs. Although his method is precise, it is not automated and requires manual effort. On the other hand our work proposes an automated method.

Biondi et al. [16] develop HyLeak, a tool for measuring the leakage of simple imperative programs. They use a combination of stochastic program simulations and precise methods to calculate an estimated joint probability distribution of secrets and outputs. In contrast, we take a precise approach in calculating the joint probability distribution, which results in exact information leakage values.

Pardo et al. [21] develop PRIVUG, which quantifies the leakage of programs written in Java, Scala, and Python. This tool estimates the leakage and does not compute the exact value.

Salehi et al. [31] utilize an evolutionary algorithm to compute channel capacity of concurrent probabilistic programs. Channel capacity concerns with the maximum amount of leakage that an attacker can learn from a program. They employ their method to compute the leakage values of two anonymity protocols, the dining cryptographers and the single preference protocols.

In addition to the proposed method of this paper, PRISM-Leak contains other methods: 1) a quantitative method [17] which employs a trace-based approach, considering scheduler effect and intermediate leakages, to compute various types of information leakage for concurrent programs; and 2) a qualitative method [32] that checks satisfiability of observational determinism, in order to enforce no-leakage policy. This policy is too restrictive for most applications, as there could be some tolerable amount of leakage in these applications [14].

## VI. Conclusion and Future Work

We have presented an automated method to measure the information leakage of probabilistic programs. The method uses the PRISM model checker to build Markov chain of

TABLE I. LEAKAGES OF THE GRADES PROTOCOL AND THE SUM OF THE GRADES

| $m$ | $k$ | The grades protocol | | | The sum of the grades | | |
|---|---|---|---|---|---|---|---|
| | | $\mathcal{M}_{grades}$ | | Leakage | $\mathcal{M}_{sum}$ | | Leakage |
| | | # states | # transitions | (bits) | # states | # transitions | (bits) |
| 2 | 2 | 196 | 228 | 1.5 (75%) | 16 | 20 | 1.5 |
| | 3 | 3752 | 4256 | 1.81 (60.4%) | 64 | 104 | 1.81 |
| | 4 | 92496 | 102480 | 2.03 (50.8%) | 256 | 528 | 2.03 |
| 3 | 2 | 1179 | 1395 | 2.2 (69.3%) | 36 | 45 | 2.2 |
| | 3 | 66366 | 75600 | 2.53 (53.1%) | 216 | 351 | 2.53 |
| | 4 | 439668 | 597780 | 2.75 (43.3%) | 1296 | 2673 | 2.75 |
| 4 | 2 | 4048 | 4816 | 2.66 (66.4%) | 64 | 80 | 2.66 |
| | 3 | 455104 | 519040 | 2.98 (49.7%) | 512 | 832 | 2.98 |
| | 4 | 3271680 | 6589440 | 3.2 (40%) | 4096 | 8448 | 3.2 |

the programs. The implementation of the method, PRISM-Leak, extracts states and transitions of this Markov chain, finds secrets and outputs, and computes the information leakage. Finally, we have analyzed a case study to show how the proposed method can evaluate the security of probabilistic programs.

As future work, we aim to compare scalability of the proposed method to other leakage quantification methods, some of which are explored in related work. We also aim to incorporate statistical methods to approximate leakage. This can improve the scalability of the method.

In this paper, we only considered terminating programs. As future work, we are planning to work on a method for computing leakage of non-terminating programs. We also aim to extend the proposed method in order to analyze case studies in other application domains, such as cryptographic algorithms.

## REFERENCES


[1] "CWE-200: Exposure of Sensitive Information to an Unauthorized Actor," https://rb.gy/ac6ui0, [retrieved: 10, 2021].

[2] "OWASP Top 10 Privacy Risks," https://rb.gy/vhq4qj, [retrieved: 10, 2021].

[3] A. Sabelfeld and A. C. Myers, "Language-based information-flow security," *IEEE J-SAC*, vol. 21, no. 1, pp. 5–19, 2003.

[4] G. Smith, "Principles of secure information flow analysis," in *Malware Detection. Advances in Information Security, vol 27*. Springer-Verlag, 2007, pp. 291–307.

[5] M. R. Clarkson and F. B. Schneider, "Hyperproperties," *J. Comput. Secur.*, vol. 18, no. 6, pp. 1157–1210, 2010.

[6] D. Schoepe, M. Balliu, B. C. Pierce, and A. Sabelfeld, "Explicit secrecy: A policy for taint tracking," in *EuroS&P*. IEEE, 2016, pp. 15–30.

[7] C. Skalka, S. Amir-Mohammadian, and S. Clark, "Maybe tainted data: Theory and a case study," *J. Comput. Secur.*, vol. 28, no. 3, pp. 295–335, April 2020.

[8] M. S. Alvim, M. E. Andrés, K. Chatzikokolakis, P. Degano, and C. Palamidessi, "Differential privacy: On the trade-off between utility and information leakage," in *FAST*. Springer, 2011, pp. 39–54.

[9] P. Cuff and L. Yu, "Differential privacy as a mutual information constraint," in *CCS*, 2016, pp. 43–54.

[10] F. Biondi and et al., "Scalable approximation of quantitative information flow in programs." in *VMCAI*, 2018, pp. 71–93.

[11] M. Jurado, C. Palamidessi, and G. Smith, "A formal information-theoretic leakage analysis of order-revealing encryption," in *CSF*. IEEE Computer Society, 2021, pp. 1–16.

[12] C. Baier and J.-P. Katoen, *Principles of model checking*. MIT press Cambridge, 2008.

[13] T. M. Cover and J. A. Thomas, *Elements of information theory*. John Wiley & Sons, 2006.

[14] M. S. Alvim and et al., *The Science of Quantitative Information Flow*. Springer, 2020.

[15] V. Klebanov, "Precise quantitative information flow analysis—a symbolic approach," *Theor. Comput. Sci.*, vol. 538, pp. 124–139, 2014.

[16] F. Biondi, Y. Kawamoto, A. Legay, and L.-M. Traonouez, "Hyleak: hybrid analysis tool for information leakage," in *ATVA*. Springer, 2017, pp. 156–163.

[17] A. A. Noroozi, J. Karimpour, and A. Isazadeh, "Information leakage of multi-threaded programs," *Comput. Electr. Eng.*, vol. 78, pp. 400–419, 2019.

[18] R. Chadha, U. Mathur, and S. Schwoon, "Computing information flow using symbolic model-checking," in *FSTTCS*. Schloss Dagstuhl-Leibniz-Zentrum fuer Informatik, 2014, pp. 505–516.

[19] A. Weigl, "Efficient sat-based pre-image enumeration for quantitative information flow in programs," in *DPM*. Springer, 2016, pp. 51–58.

[20] M. S. Alvim and et al., "An axiomatization of information flow measures," *Theor. Comput. Sci.*, vol. 777, pp. 32–54, 2019.

[21] R. Pardo, W. Rafnsson, C. Probst, and A. Wasowski, "Privug: Quantifying leakage using probabilistic programming for privacy risk analysis," *arXiv preprint arXiv:2011.08742*, 2020.

[22] F. Biondi, A. Legay, P. Malacaria, and A. Wasowski, "Quantifying information leakage of randomized protocols," *Theor. Comput. Sci.*, vol. 597, no. C, pp. 62–87, 2015.

[23] S. Amir-Mohammadian, "A semantic framework for direct information flows in hybrid-dynamic systems," in *CPSS-AsiaCCS*. ACM, June 2021, pp. 5–15.

[24] A. A. Noroozi, K. Salehi, J. Karimpour, and A. Isazadeh, "Prism-leak - a tool for computing information leakage of probabilistic programs," https://rb.gy/elgkyi, [retrieved: 10, 2021].

[25] M. Kwiatkowska, G. Norman, and D. Parker, "PRISM 4.0: Verification of probabilistic real-time systems," in *CAV*. Springer, 2011, pp. 585–591.

[26] C.-D. Hong, A. W. Lin, R. Majumdar, and P. Rümmer, "Probabilistic bisimulation for parameterized systems," in *CAV*. Springer, 2019, pp. 455–474.

[27] D. Parker, "Implementation of symbolic model checking for probabilistic systems," Ph.D. dissertation, University of Birmingham, 2002.

[28] M. Backes, B. Köpf, and A. Rybalchenko, "Automatic discovery and quantification of information leaks," in *S&P*. IEEE, 2009, pp. 141–153.

[29] T. Chothia, Y. Kawamoto, C. Novakovic, and D. Parker, "Probabilistic point-to-point information leakage," in *CSF*. IEEE, 2013, pp. 193–205.

[30] T. Chothia, Y. Kawamoto, and C. Novakovic, "Leakwatch: Estimating information leakage from java programs," in *ESORICS*. Springer, 2014, pp. 219–236.

[31] K. Salehi, J. Karimpour, H. Izadkhah, and A. Isazadeh, "Channel capacity of concurrent probabilistic programs," *Entropy*, vol. 21, no. 9, p. 885, 2019.

[32] A. A. Noroozi, K. Salehi, J. Karimpour, and A. Isazadeh, "Secure information flow analysis using the prism model checker," in *ICISS*. Springer, 2019, pp. 154–172.

# Maverick: Detecting Network Configuration and Control Plane Bugs Through Structural Outlierness

Vasudevan Nagendra
*Plume Design Inc.*
Palo Alto, USA
vnagendra@plume.com

Abhishek Pokala
*Stony Brook University*
Stony Brook, USA
apokala@cs.stonybrook.edu

Arani Bhattacharya
*IIIT Delhi*
New Delhi, India
arani@iiitd.ac.in

Samir Das
*Stony Brook University*
Stony Brook, USA
samir@cs.stonybrook.edu

***Abstract*—Proactive detection of network configuration bugs is important to ensure the proper functioning of networks and reducing the issues associated with network outages. In this research, we propose to build a control plane verification tool `MAVERICK` that detects the bugs in the network device configurations by effectively leveraging *structural deviation* i.e., *outliers* in the network configurations. `MAVERICK` automatically infers *signatures* from control plane configurations (e.g., Access Control Lists (ACL), route-maps, route-policies, and so on) and allows administrators to automatically detect bugs in the network configurations with minimal human intervention. The outliers calculated using *signature-based outlier detection* mechanism are further characterized for its severity and ranked or re-prioritized according to their criticality. We consider a wide set of heuristics and domain expertise factors for effectively reducing the false positives. Our evaluation on four medium to large-scale enterprise networks shows that `MAVERICK` can automatically detect the bugs present in the network with ≈86.4% accuracy. Furthermore, with minimal administrator inputs i.e., with a few minutes of signature re-tuning, `MAVERICK` allows the administrators to effectively detect ≈92 – 100% of the bugs present in the network, thereby ranking down less severe bugs and removing false positives.**

***Keywords*— *Network; Control Plane; Verification; Outliers; Machine Learning; Anomaly Detection; Bugs; Severity.***

## I. INTRODUCTION

Network downtime for an enterprise network costs an average of USD $140K – $500K per hour, for which the human error acts as the key contributing factor [1][2]. The fundamental goal of network management and downtime mitigation is *proactive detection* of the control plane and network configuration bugs, and ability to quickly troubleshoot the errors that occurred due to human errors and misconfigurations. Today network administrators either rely on custom *home-made* scripts 'or' model checking-based verification tools for analyzing the network configurations to detect specific types of bugs in the network (e.g., reachability analysis, routing issues, failure impact analysis, and so on) [3][4][5][6]. Such tools provide limited bug detection capability i.e., does not provide comprehensive coverage about the list of bugs present in the network configurations. Therefore, a generic control plane bug detection mechanism that proactively detects a comprehensive list of bugs present in the network with minimal administrator's intervention is key for protecting the networks from downtime and vulnerabilities.

Traditionally, bug detection can be efficiently achieved by defining unique signatures to each of the network properties and matching each of the configuration instances with respective signatures. For example, an ACL that allows web traffic from LAN network to Internet needs to be specified on to a group of network devices along the path of the traffic until the traffic reaches the border gateway of the enterprise network. Therefore, multiple devices should have either same or similar ACL and deviation from the actual ACL definition would be considered a bug. As a similar example, route maps are used for defining the set of route entries that are required to be redistributed to target routing process, requiring the route maps to be specified on to multiple routers.

Manually identifying such signatures (or specifications) in a dynamically changing network infrastructures and effectively using such comprehensive list of signatures for detecting bugs is a daunting task. But, not providing *signatures (i.e., about what specifically needs to be looked for in the network configurations)* results in bugs and errors that either go undetected (with false negatives) or results in false positives that plague the soundness of the bug detection tool. In our observation, there are legions of bugs that remain undetected even with networks "vetted" by verification tools, because of a lack of capability that allows the signature to be specified and used for bug detection.

Therefore, the current network verification tools falls short along following key dimensions: (*i*) proactively detecting control plane bugs (e.g., human errors and configuration mistakes) without (or with minimal) administrator's intervention, (*ii*) ability to effectively incorporate domain expertise in fine-tuning the bug detection, (*iii*) automatically inferring policies or signatures from the network configurations that allows administrators and tools to effectively detect configuration bugs, while providing comprehensive bug detection coverage, (*iv*) generalize findings, i.e., signatures or policies inferred from one network and apply it to other networks or organizations, and (*v*) finally, surfacing the bugs that are critical allowing administrators to channelize their energy in addressing critical bugs rather than wasting time on false negatives.

To address the above challenges, we propose `MAVERICK`, an agile network verification tool that exploits structural deviations (i.e., *Outlierness*) among the network configurations for detecting the bugs. *Outlierness* is the deviation of the network configurations from its general population or most popular values. The key enabler of `MAVERICK` is its ability to automatically infer signatures from the network configurations, which are used for efficiently detecting bugs present in the network, without false negatives. `MAVERICK` also incorporates inputs from the administrators allowing the tool to fine-tune its detection precision. In addition, `MAVERICK` also proposes the need for generalization by which the signatures that are developed for an network can be used with other networks.

We improve the accuracy of our bug detection mechanism and efficiently re-prioritize the bugs to surface them to administrators on the basis of their severity. We calculate severity of the bugs using following key metrics, such as feature importance (i.e., network structural properties such as ACLs, route-maps, IPSec tunnel configurations and so on), feature dependency, the locality of the configuration on specific node, outlierness score from the similarity with signatures, and customized page ranking used for ranking bugs. These metrics allow `MAVERICK` to effectively prioritize bugs on the basis of their severity, pushing false positives or less critical bugs to the bottom of the list. We prove the efficacy of MAVERICK by showing that it provides a mean precision of 86.4% without administrator input, and 92 – 100% using a few minutes of administrator input on a four medium to large-scale enterprise networks.

In summary, our paper makes following key contributions:

- We provide background and illustrate the limitations of existing techniques and motivate the need for signature-based bug detection mechanisms based on outliers (§II).
- We highlight the techniques we used to automatically infer the signatures for various properties of network configurations using their *structural outlierness* for detecting the bugs. We then discuss about simple severity and ranking mechanism that we devised to reprioritize the bugs and reduce the false positives (§III)
- We discuss about the high level system design and key building blocks of MAVERICK (§IV).
- We evaluate the efficacy of MAVERICK with four different medium – large scale campus and enterprise networks with ≈220 – 450 network nodes (e.g., routers, firewalls, switches, proxies, and gateway nodes) (§V).

## II. BACKGROUND & MOTIVATION

Today, majority of the network administrators still rely on plain-text configuration templates, command-line utilities, and wide variety of vendor-supplied programming specifications or user-interfaces for programming their networks [7][8][9] [10]. This results in administrators unintentionally introducing bugs in the network configurations resulting in network outages or leaving the network vulnerable to attacks [11][12].

We understand that for programming the network and creating policies requires same set of rules to be specified on wide range of devices that are present with in a network. Consider for example, an ACL that is specified to allow TCP traffic that is destined to WAN network 100.100.100.0/24 on port 1400 requires a group of same ACLs to be specified on multiple routers or firewalls along multiple paths in which the traffic traverses. Similarly, route-map entries, NAT rules, and route-filters specific to this ACL are also required to be specified on these routers along the paths in which the traffic traverses. In general, administrators either use sample templates or use CLI to configure multiple routers, which may result in human introduced errors.

**Router_1 (Key-value Properties):**

```
{
DNS Servers: ['4.4.4.4']
NTP Servers: ['0.pool.ntp.org' ,
'1.pool.ntp.org']
TACACS Servers: ['10.10.10.15']
Logging Servers: ['10.10.10.22']
}
```

(a) Network Server Properties.

**Router_1 (Named Structure Property):**

```
{
'action': 'PERMIT',
'matchCondition=dstIps=ipWildcard':
[('100.100.100.0/0', 24)],
'matchCondition=ipProtocols': ['6']
'matchCondition=tptDstPort': [('1400')]
}
```

(b) IP ACL.

Figure 1: Illustrating *key-value* properties (e.g., Network Server values) and *named-structure* properties (e.g., IP ACL) in network configurations.

We broadly classify overall network configurations into two property classes (Figure 1): (*i*) *Key-value properties*, and (*ii*) *Named-structure properties*. As illustrated in Figure 1a, *key-value* property is a simple key:value/s pair that represents a discrete and independent network configuration (e.g., NTP Server configured for Router_1 in Figure 1a). While the *named-structure* properties are structures with multiple key:value pairs nested as a complex discrete entity required to configure the network.

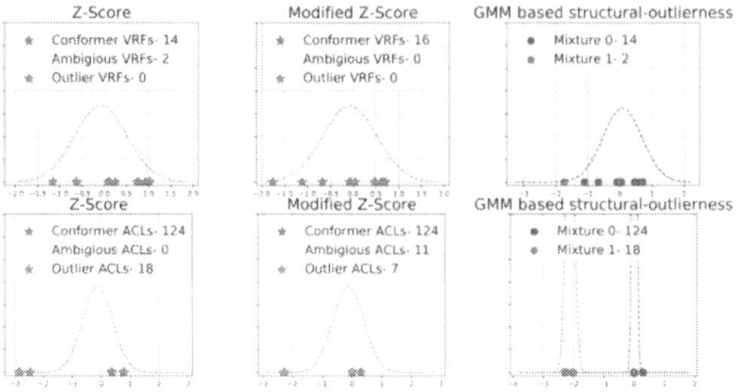


Figure 2: Bug detection using statistical approaches (z-score, modified z-score, GMM) for VRFs, ACLs of network (DS-1).

### A. *Problems with existing approaches*

For effectively detecting the bugs present in the network configurations, existing approaches aim to supplement the manual effort of network administrators by flagging probable network configuration and data plane bugs [13][14], which broadly fall into two categories: (*a*) Statistical approach, and (*b*) logical or rule-based approach.

**Statistical techniques.** Statistical approaches such as z-score, modified z-score and Gaussian Mixture Model (GMM) aim to identify outliers in the configurations, and flag them as probable bugs [15][16][17][18] as illustrated in Figure 2. While we note that the outlying configurations have a much higher probability of being bugs, that in itself is not sufficient to detect real bugs and highlight its severity. The key disadvantages of such statistical approaches are as follows:

- *High mis-classification rate*: Since many of the configurations lie at the boundary of the threshold used to classify as bugs, a large number of either false positives (i.e., incorrectly flagged as bugs) or false negatives (i.e., incorrectly flagged as valid) are identified. Correctly identifying the actual bugs from these lists again requires a lot of manual effort on the part of the administrator.
- *Flagging intentional configuration changes*: Administrators might intentionally change configurations in specific ways to handle an uncommon use case. However, statistical techniques identify even such changes as configuration bugs.
- *Critical bugs vs false positives*: In general, not all network configuration bugs are equally critical. Some bugs require immediate attention from administrators, whereas other bugs can be fixed slowly. However, we lack mechanism to identify the bugs that are critical in nature.

**Logical or rule-based techniques.** This approach is to let users specify grammar rules, any violation of such grammar rules is flagged as a configuration bug [4][19][20][21]. However, this approach too suffers from a number of drawbacks:

- *Requirement of low-level vendor-specific rules*: We see different vendors using different syntax to specify network configurations which introduces an additional level of complexity in specifying these rules. It requires administrators to specify complex low-level grammar rules. Thus, this is usually a cumbersome and technically involved process, that is also prone to mistakes.
- *Lack of coverage*: Even for proficient administrators, it is challenging to anticipate all the types of invalid configurations and proactively fix them. Thus, many configuration bugs may pass through without getting identified.

Therefore, it is becoming increasingly difficult to proactively detect the network configuration bugs before deploying them on to the production networks. In Section III, we present the overview of MAVERICK system that addresses the challenges discussed here.

## III. MAVERICK OVERVIEW

We present the overview of MAVERICK control plane network verification engine that is a tangible step toward addressing the limitations discussed above (§II-A). Figure 3 provides an overview of the MAVERICK system architecture, with the following two key capabilities: (*i*) *signature-based outlier detection* engine, and (*ii*) *severity & ranking* engine. These capabilities allow administrators to proactively detect control plane bugs and fine-tune them to reduce the false positives, while reducing their time vested in triaging critical bugs rather than spending time on false-positives.

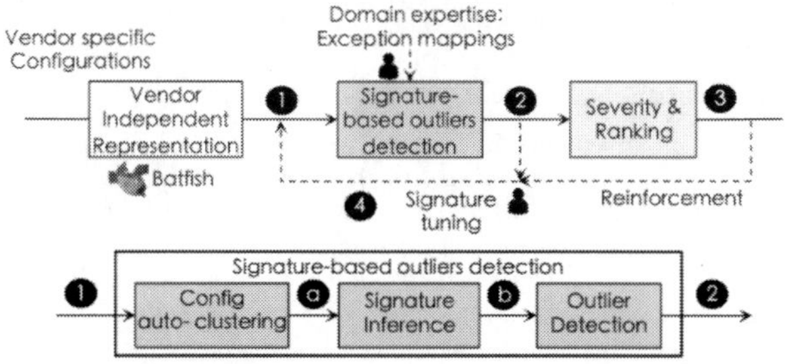


Figure 3: MAVERICK System Architecture.

**Signature-based outlier detection**. This module digests the network configurations provided in vendor-specific format and translates them to *vendor-independent* specification for detecting the outliers in the network configurations (❶). We leverage the specification mechanism used in batfish network verification tool [4]) for representing the configurations in vendor-independent format. We calculate the *structural outlierness* among the network configurations (i.e., represented in vendor-independent format) for effectively detecting bugs in the networks. We define, *structural outlierness* as the deviation of a network property (i.e., key-value property or named-structure) from its group or cluster of configurations (i.e., most popular entries of the cluster) that are programmed onto multiple nodes to achieve the same functionality (discussed in §II) (ⓐ).

For the derived most popular entries within a group or cluster, we apply domain expertise (i.e., captured as *exception mappings*) for automatically inferring the signatures (ⓑ). We supply such automatically inferred signatures to administrator for inspection and fine-tuning these signatures for detecting bugs in the network configurations (❷). Though administrator's intervention is optional in our case, we use *human-in-loop* for reducing false positives (❹). These signatures we inferred could be used to detect bugs in the network configurations before applying them to the network (*Signature-based outlier detection*). The capabilities discussed above are performed by following three key modules of *signature-based outlier detection* engine (see §IV): (*a*) *Config auto-clustering* module, (*b*) *signature-inference* engine, and (*c*) *Outlier detection* engine.

**Severity & ranking**. For the bugs that are detected from the *signature-based outlier detection* module, we apply the severity and ranking mechanism that we developed to re-prioritize the bugs for identifying their severity. Deriving severity of each bug helps to reduce the administrator's effort and time in handling false positives (❸). We use following three key metrics for calculating the severity for ranking the outliers (see §IV-B): (*a*) *Similarity and outlierness scores*, (*b*) Well connected-ness of nodes, (*c*) *Feature-dependency*.

**Design goal.** Our goal is to mitigate the problems in existing enterprise and campus networks by reducing the amount of effort involved in detecting bugs, automatically inferring signatures that acts as reference to verify the network configurations for its sanity and bugs, while increasing the network coverage (for detecting generic bugs). Unlike, existing techniques which requires network configurations to be manually grouped for building the templates [15], MAVERICK automatically clusters the configurations into separate groups for building the signatures. However, a key drawback of such signature inference is that it falsely flags configurations that network administrators have designed for customized use cases. To mitigate this problem, we allow administrators to re-tune inferred signatures. Since there can be multiple valid signatures, this also automatically allows more customized configurations.

We recognize that even with multiple signatures, it is possible to false classify multiple configurations as bugs. However, not all configuration bugs are equally important in a network. Based on the estimated severity score, we assign priority to each of the identified bugs and rank them accordingly. This allows the administrators to focus on the most important bugs, while letting the less important ones remain for longer time.

## IV. HIGH LEVEL SYSTEM DESIGN

In this section, we discuss the network verification mechanism that we developed to address the limitations discussed in §II-A. As shown in Figure 3, MAVERICK supports following key functional components to address these limitations: (*i*) Signature-based outlier detection, and (*ii*) Severity and ranking mechanism.

### A. Signature-based Outlier Detection

We use the specification language discussed in the Batfish [4] to translate the network configurations from vendor-specific languages (e.g., Cisco's IOS, Juniper's JunOS) to vendor-independent (VI) representation, which avoids the need for designing parsers for each of the vendor-specific language in MAVERICK. We extract network configurations i.e., *named structure properties* (e.g., ACL's, route-maps, route-policies), and *network server properties* (e.g., DNS server, NTP server, Authentication servers), and configurations on all the network devices and encode such categorical data into binary encoded format i.e., using Multi-label binarizer [22], which allows us to apply statistical and Machine Learning (ML) techniques on the network configuration data.

The key challenge in bug detection is the ability of administrator to craft the specification or signature that allows the tool to detect the bugs and errors. Therefore, automatically generating (i.e., inferring) the signatures is the key step towards effective detection of bugs in the network configurations. MAVERICK's signature-based outlier detection engine supports following three key capabilities for automatically detecting the bugs present in the network configurations represented in vendor independent format.

**Configuration auto-clustering.** As a first step, we run clustering on each of the named structures (such as ACLs, router-filters, route-maps) independently, to group them on the basis of their categories and properties. For example, a network with thousands of ACLs are clustered into group of tens or groups of hundred on the basis of their similarity i.e., for automatically inferring signatures from each of the ACL groups, which is required to compute its signature. As manually grouping thousands of ACLs into groups on the basis of their name or other properties is a challenging and tedious process, we use simple K-means a ML-based technique to cluster the named structures. The clustered named structures are then used for signature inference. To obtain the right value of K, we use Elbow [23], and Silhouette [24] methods to regress on different values of K to decide the optimum. We heuristically choose a lower limit of K (i.e., regressed from the above three techniques) equal from the number of unique set of names used to configure different named structures. Therefore, clustering reduces the number of signatures inferred, thereby reducing the amount of manual effort involved with administrator in verifying the signatures to re-tune them for increasing the precision of signature-based outlier detection.

**Signature inference & generalization.** The signature inference engine automatically infers and builds the signatures from the clustered

**Algorithm 1** Signature Inference Algorithm.

$F \leftarrow generateVI()$
$P \leftarrow$getNamedStructProps($F$)
$P \leftarrow$encode($P$)
$K \leftarrow$ elbow($P$)
$C \leftarrow$ clusters using K-Means of $P$
Let $F(c, p)$ be the value-frequency pair $\forall c \in C, p \in P$.
Compute threshold $T(c, p)$ from $F(c, p)$, $\forall c \in C, p \in P$.
Let $\epsilon$ be the margin of uncertainty
**for** $c \in C$ **do**
    **for** $p \in P$ **do**
        **for** $(k, v) \in F(c, p)$ **do**
            **if** $v > T(c, p) + \epsilon$ **then**
                Mark $p$ as bug
            **else if** $v > T(c, p)$ & $v < T(c, p) + \epsilon$ **then**
                Mark $p$ as probable bug
            **else**
                Mark $p$ as normal property

named structures. The signature inference engine composes all the named part of the cluster to frame a single signature. We use following grammar in our signature for effectively capturing and generalizing the signatures, which includes following operators: '*', '!' '=' '[]', '{}', 'OR', 'AND', ¡IP-Subnet¿ (i.e., IP specific to that subnet will be considered as legitimate in the signature).

As shown in Figure 4, the signature of a named structure includes set of key-value pairs (i.e., complex nested). The Key is property name and the values are array of tuples. The tuples captures one of the values of property and its weight, where as weight represents the frequency of occurrences or the density of the value for that property with in that cluster.

```
IP_ACL_1 (Signature): {
action: {PERMIT: 45},
matchCondition=Class: {temp1: 36, temp2: 1, temp3:8},
matchCondition=headerspace=ipProtocols: {TCP: 36, UDP: 9],
matchCondition=headerSpace=tcpFlagsMatchConditions: {True: 1},
...
srcPorts: [51102-51102: 37, 51102-51103: 5 51102-51104: 3]
}
```

Figure 4: Signature Inferred by MAVERICK for IP ACL with the popularity weights are shown above. Only part of the signature is shown for brevity.

Also, the ability of these techniques to effectively accommodate the domain expertise and inputs from administrators allows them to effectively detect bugs present in the network. The signature-mappings enforces constraints on the property's key:value pairs that are part of the signature. The signature-mapping which is provided as the domain knowledge from the administrator restricts the signature inference engine to treat specific key:value pairs differently. For example, the inference engine can discard any specific key and value associated with it from being part of the signature. For example, we do not want our bug detection engine to consider the configuration patch added by administrator to specific issue or corner as outliers. This allows us to *white-list*, create *exception*, or *black-list* specific keys to the signature inference engine about the way it should consider the respective key:value pairs.

**Re-tuning outlier detection.** Signatures auto-generated using ML-based techniques could be further fine-tuned by administrator by supplying the domain knowledge as *signature-mappings* or manual inspection. On the contrary, for simple server properties (e.g., DNS servers, TACACS server properties) the names used on different nodes are required to be same, which simplifies our task of grouping configurations for clustering to detect outliers. Hence, they could be simply grouped together for calculating the outliers.

To verify if a named structure is an outlier, we compare the properties of this named structure with the respective properties of the cluster signature. If all the properties in the named structure that is compared with the signature matches, then the named structure is considered as valid and bug otherwise. We also calculate their similarity scores $S_i$ and outlier scores $O_i$, to determine the amount by which a named structure matches with the signature.

$$S_i = \frac{\sum_{i=1}^{n} W_i}{\sum_{j=1}^{s} W_j}, O_i = 1 - S_i, \forall i = 1, \ldots, n; \forall j = 1, \ldots, s, \quad (1)$$

where $n$ is total number of properties in the signature, $s$ is total number of signatures, and $W_i$ represents the weight associated with each of the property in the signature.

### B. *Severity and Ranking*

This list of outliers that is generated as outcome of the signature-based outliers engine contains the outlier definition, the named structure it belongs to, and it's outlier score. The outlier score is an indication of how strongly our engine believes a particular outlier to be a bug and its value is between 0 and 1. But an entry with a very high score could mean that it is a single separate configuration and does not belong to any signature. Our severity and ranking mechanism takes this into consideration for effectively calculating the severity. To rank these outliers, we devise different metrics and assign each outlier a metric score. Then, using a particular combination of these metric scores, we calculate the final score of each outlier and rank them based on this score. MAVERICK uses following three different metrics to calculate the severity and ranking of the outliers:

($i$) *Similarity and outlierness scores* that we derived from the outcome of signature-based outlier engine is used as one factor in deciding the severity of the final bug outcome.

($ii$) *Well-connectedness* of nodes: We use the page-rank algorithm to establish the importance of each node with the general idea being that a possible bug in a more important or well-connected node would be more severe than a bug that has fewer connections.

($iii$) *Feature-Dependency Score*: This metric tells us the importance of the features that the named structure is a part of. The general idea is that the importance of named-structure is network-specific and therefore, dynamically evaluating these scores helps provide a much finer and network-specific bug severity analysis. Consider for example, when a ACL rule marked as outlier will results in impacting the NAT rules, route-filters and VRFs associated with it. Hence, outliers in features that has higher dependency with other features will result in high severe bugs. The final outcome of the severity and ranking module results in generating bugs that result in lesser in FPs and FNs (see TABLE I) and effectively ranked according to its severity (Figure 5).

Finally, the *human-in-the-loop* correlation score helps re-tune the signature and reduces false-positives. Once the network administrator flags a certain outlier as a bug or a FP, all the corresponding outliers in the population (i.e., cluster in our case) show an increase or a decrease in their severity score respectively. This metric allows the administrator to manually inspect numerous bugs of a specific type from a very large network with relative ease.

## V. PROTOTYPE EVALUATION

**Dataset.** We evaluate the performance of MAVERICK over a total of four networks using their network configuration. Of the four networks, three are of medium size network of 157, 132 and 221 nodes (e.g., switches, routers, firewalls, etc.,) and large network of 454 nodes. Medium networks has around 5000 – 10000 properties, while large scale network has around 60000 properties. The properties consist of ACLs, Route Filters, VRFs and Routing Policies with

TABLE I: FINAL RANKED BUG OUTCOME MAVERICK TOOL IN ACCORDANCE WITH ITS SEVERITY.

| Outlier | Signature Definition | Conformer Nodes | Outlier Definition | Outlier Nodes | Outlier Properties | Outlierness Value | Severity Score |
|---|---|---|---|---|---|---|---|
| outlier:Route_Filter_List_0 | {'action': [['PERMIT', 16]], 'ipWildcard':[['100.100.100.0/23', '*', 9], ... ['25-25', '*', 10]]} | ['rt1-dc1', 'rt2-dc1', ... rt91-dc1] | {'action': 'PERMIT', 'ipWildcard': '100.100.0.0/16', 'lengthRange': '16-20'} | ['rt19-dc1', 'rt28-dc1'] | [['lengthRange', '16-20']] | 0.978 | 1.177 |

ACLs predominant in the large network, whereas RouteFilters are predominant in the medium sized networks.

**Performance.** We first compare the performance of MAVERICK in terms of precision and recall for comparison with baseline techniques for medium scale enterprise network dataset (DS-3) (see TABLE II)

The baseline techniques include Z-score, modified Z-score, GMM, and MAVERICK using signature-based outliers. We make two major observations: ($i$) We note that MAVERICK's outlier detection performs better than Z-score, modified Z-score and GMM in terms of both precision and recall. However, the precision is still only around 0.86, which has further scope of improvement. This is primarily due to presence of false positives, as a large number of outliers are detected using the inferred signatures. ($ii$) Manual retuning of signatures can then further increase the precision to 0.92, thus increasing by additional 7 – 8% compared to just outlier-based detection. Careful retuning of ≈97 clusters/signatures detected by MAVERICK for DS-3 required less than 2 hours for manual inspection. This shows that manual retuning of signatures can further improve the precision.

TABLE II: EFFICACY OF MAVERICK FOR MEDIUM SCALE ENTERPRISE NETWORK DATASET (DS-3).

| Approach | TP | FP | FN | Precision | Recall |
|---|---|---|---|---|---|
| Z-score | 392 | 1031 | 240 | 0.275 | 0.620 |
| Modified Z-score | 417 | 692 | 132 | 0.386 | 0.760 |
| GMM | 298 | 608 | 220 | 0.329 | 0.575 |
| Maverick (Outliers) | 472 | 74 | 32 | 0.864 | 0.937 |
| Maverick (Retuning) | 498 | 32 | 8 | 0.92 | 0.984 |

**Severity score.** We now look at how severity score can change the sequence of bugs shown to administrators (Figure 5). We plot the bugs reported in the sequence of their outlier score, along with their severity scores for one of the medium-sized network. We note that the sequence of bugs shown to the administrators changes considerably, with P16 rising up to the most severe rank, followed by P15 and P13. On the other hand, P6 reduces to the least severe rank, followed by P5. This shows that using severity score alters the sequence of bugs shown to the users, and can lead to less important bugs being given less priority even if they have high outlier scores.

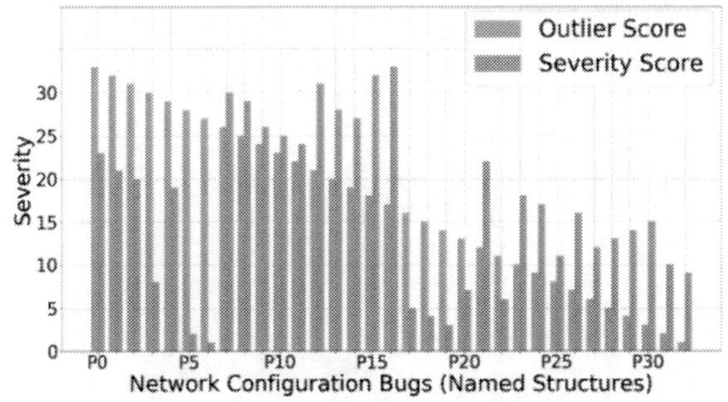


Figure 5: Bugs discovered by MAVERICK with and without severity applied.

**Correlation of outliers with real network issues.** To further observe the type of bugs MAVERICK discovers, we utilize a sankey diagram to show how outliers in different properties correspond to different types of bugs (Figure 6) in one of the medium-sized network (DS-3). Correlation of bugs discovered by MAVERICK with real-world network problems. The left layer corresponds to the type of property in which outlier is detected. The middle layer corresponds to the type of signature that is violated. The right layer is the type of real-world network problem. A higher thickness of flow denotes a higher number of bugs corresponding to a specific signature in the middle layer of vertices and then to types of network problems in the last layer. We observe that most of the bugs arise due to problems in IP access lists, followed by routing policy, route filter list and VNF's. We also observe that the most common type of network problem is undefined references, but each type of outlier roughly has equal probability of leading to an undefined reference.

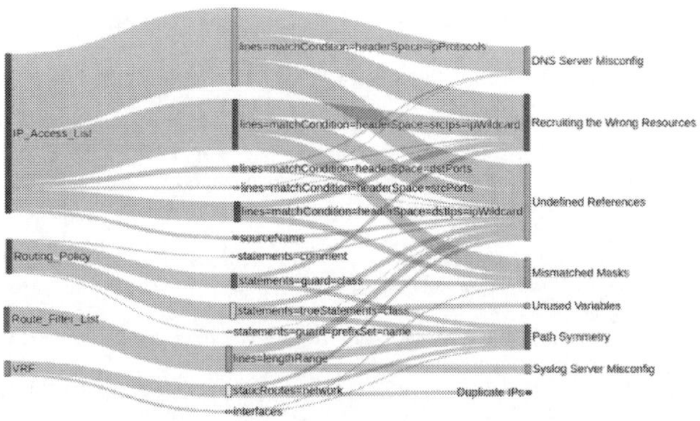


Figure 6: Correlation of bugs discovered by MAVERICK.

## VI. CONCLUSION

This paper presented a novel signature inference framework for detecting the control plane bugs based on structural deviations (i.e., outliers or bugs), while their severity is estimated and bugs are ranked accordingly. The key strength of this work lies in its ability to automatically infer the signatures from raw network configurations without much administrator's intervention and generalize these inferred signatures for transportability. We combine disparate metrics to rank the severity of the detected outliers. We evaluated our approach using four different datasets of campus networks and achieved high bug detection of up to 92% with supply of domain expertise in the form of signature-mappings. While our approach was simple, with inferred signatures we were able to discover numerous bugs, including those that would be impossible to discover with existing network validation tools.

We made our tool and overall framework that supports wide range of statistical and ML algorithms along with signature-based outlier analysis tool as open source to stimulate additional research specifically in enhancing the network verification, and control and data plane bug detection mechanism [25].

## ACKNOWLEDGEMENTS

This work was done by Vasudevan Nagendra, Abhishek Pokala, and Arani Bhattacharya when at WINGS Lab, Computer Science department, Stony Brook University. This work was partially supported by NSF grant CNS-1642965.

## REFERENCES


[1] The Cost of Downtime. https://blogs.gartner.com/andrew-lerner/2014/07/16/the-cost-of-downtime/, July 2014.

[2] The Ugly Truth about Downtime Costs and How to Calculate Your Own. https://www.itondemand.com/2018/05/29/costs-of-downtime/, May 2018.

[3] A. Gember-Jacobson, R. Viswanathan, A. Akella and R. Mahajan. Fast control plane analysis using an abstract representation. In *Proceedings of the 2016 ACM SIGCOMM Conference*, pages 300–313. ACM, 2016.

[4] A. Fogel, S. Fung, L. Pedrosa, M. Sullivan, R. Govindan, R. Mahajan, and T. Millstein. A general approach to network configuration analysis. In *12th {USENIX} Symposium on Networked Systems Design and Implementation ({NSDI} 15)*, pages 469–483, 2015.

[5] A. Panda, K. Argyraki, and M. Sagiv, M. Schapira, and S. Shenker. New directions for network verification. In *1st Summit on Advances in Programming Languages (SNAPL 2015)*. Schloss Dagstuhl-Leibniz-Zentrum fuer Informatik, 2015.

[6] A. Khurshid, X. Zou, W. Zhou, M. Caesar, and B. Godfrey. Veriflow: Verifying network-wide invariants in real time. In *Presented as part of the 10th {USENIX} Symposium on Networked Systems Design and Implementation ({NSDI} 13)*, pages 15–27, 2013.

[7] Use templates to define a common device configuration. *Product Documentation*, 2017.

[8] Managing Multiple Networks with Configuration Templates. *Product Documentation*, 2018.

[9] Google Cloud Networking Incident #19009. *Google Cloud Networking Incidents*, 2019.

[10] 451 Research: Enterprise Network Automation Gets Competitive. *Technical Report*, 2020.

[11] A. Bednarz. Top reasons for network downtime: Network outages linked to human error, incompatible changes, greater complexity. *Technical Report*, 2018.

[12] A. Patrizio. The biggest risk to uptime? Your staff: Human error is the chief cause of downtime, a new study finds. Imagine that. *Technical Report*, 2019.

[13] T. Xu, and Y. Zhou. Systems approaches to tackling configuration errors: A survey. *ACM Comput. Surv.*, 47(4), July 2015.

[14] Y. Li, X. Yin, Z. Wang, J. Yao, X. Shi, J. Wu, H. Zhang and Q. Wang. A survey on network verification and testing with formal methods: Approaches and challenges. *IEEE Communications Surveys Tutorials*, 21(1):940–969, 2019.

[15] S. Kakarla, T. Alan, R. Beckett, K. Jayaraman, T. Millstein, Y. Tamir and G. Varghese. Finding Network Misconfigurations by Automatic Template Inference. In *17th USENIX Symposium on Networked Systems Design and Implementation (NSDI 20)*, pages 999–1013, Santa Clara, CA, February 2020. USENIX Association.

[16] C. Christian, S. Vaton, and M. Pagano. A new statistical approach to network anomaly detection. In *2008 International Symposium on Performance Evaluation of Computer and Telecommunication Systems)*, pages 441 – 447, 2008.

[17] booktitle=International Static Analysis Symposium T. Kremenek, and D. Engler. Z-ranking: Using statistical analysis to counter the impact of static analysis approximations. pages 295–315. Springer, 2003.

[18] T. Kremenek, K. Ashcraft, J. Yang, and D. Engler. Correlation exploitation in error ranking. In *ACM SIGSOFT Software Engineering Notes*, volume 29, pages 83–93. ACM, 2004.

[19] R. Beckett, A. Gupta, R. Mahajan, and D. Walker. A general approach to network configuration verification. In *Proceedings of the Conference of the ACM Special Interest Group on Data Communication*, pages 155–168, 2017.

[20] Z. Yin, X. Ma, J. Zheng, Y. Zhou, L. Bairavasundaram, and S. Pasupathy. An empirical study on configuration errors in commercial and open source systems. In *Proceedings of the Twenty-Third ACM Symposium on Operating Systems Principles*, SOSP '11, page 159–172, New York, NY, USA, 2011. Association for Computing Machinery.

[21] T. Xu, J. Zhang, P. Huang, J. Zheng, T. Sheng, D. Yuan, Y. Zhou, and S. Pasupathy. Do not blame users for misconfigurations. In *Proceedings of the Twenty-Fourth ACM Symposium on Operating Systems Principles*, SOSP '13, page 244–259, New York, NY, USA, 2013. Association for Computing Machinery.

[22] A. Mallidi. Encoding categorical data in machine learning. *Technical Article*, 2019.

[23] P. Bholowalia and A. Kumar. Ebk-means: A clustering technique based on elbow method and k-means in wsn. *International Journal of Computer Applications*, 105:17–24, 2014.

[24] Silhouette (clustering). https://en.wikipedia.org/wiki/Silhouette_(clustering), July 2021.

[25] Maverick: Detection of Control plane and configuration bugs using outlier analysis. https://github.com/vasu018/outlier-analyzers/, May 2021.

# Cost-benefit Analysis Toward Designing Efficient Education Programs for Household Security

N'guessan Yves-Roland Douha[1], Bernard Ousmane Sane[2], Masahiro Sasabe[1], Doudou Fall[1], Yuzo Taenaka[1], and Youki Kadobayashi[1]
[1]Division of Information Science, Nara Institute of Science and Technology, Ikoma, Japan
email: {douha.nguessan_yves-roland.dn6, sasabe, doudou-f, yuzo, youki-k}@is.naist.jp
[2]Faculty of Science and Technology, University Cheikh Anta Diop, Dakar, Senegal
email:bernardousmane.sane@ucad.edu.sn

***Abstract*—The human factor is still a crucial issue in the security chain. People who will live in a smart home might be exposed to many cyber threats due to the remaining lack of Internet of Things (IoT) device security. Cybersecurity awareness training could help households to become more resilient to face cyberattacks. However, the financial costs of training programs and the significant amount of time needed to notice security countermeasures could refrain many smart-home users from engaging in cybersecurity education. In this paper, we propose a game-theoretic approach to analyze the security investment cost-benefit of households. Our numerical results show that the increase of quality of services accessible in a smart home and the security rewards for noticing security countermeasures compared to the potential impacts of cyberattacks will increase the payoffs of households and reinforce the security behaviors. Our results also emphasize the urgent need to address human security toward a more resilient smart home.**

***Keywords-Cost-benefit analysis; game theory; household security awareness; smart-home security.***

## I. INTRODUCTION

Human factor is a recognized issue in information security and many researchers have proposed security awareness and training as a solution [1]–[3]. With the recent advancement of technologies such as ubiquitous systems and human-computer interaction, user security awareness issues are back on the table. Households, especially those who are interested in smart homes, a branch of ubiquitous computing that incorporates smartness into dwellings for a better quality of life [4], might face additional security challenges such as lack of device management, insecure software/firmware, and poor physical security [5]. A recent survey on cybersecurity education shows that adults are worried about cyber threats and the safety and security of children [6]. Given that user awareness of security countermeasures directly influence information systems misuses [7], cybersecurity awareness education could be an effective solution to empower households, including children [8] and senior citizens [9], with knowledge and skills to reduce the success rate of cyberattacks exploiting human vulnerabilities in homes.

However, a critical obstacle to adopting those cybersecurity education programs is the financial costs and resources [10]. For example, regarding employees' training, companies seek to minimize their budget regarding costs that are not tight to their operations. Furthermore, individuals are willing to take cybersecurity awareness training only if their employers sponsor them [6]. Similarly, we assume that the financial costs of cybersecurity training could be challenging for households.

Cost-benefit studies are important to understand the potential value of investing in cybersecurity education programs. Existing security cost-benefit analysis include the work of Zeng [11] who focuses on digital right management products. The author uses the stochastic Petri nets to simulate and predict the impact of the deployment of these digital systems on normal business processes. Furthermore, Zhang et al. [12] propose a new theoretical framework for conducting a cost-benefit analysis of cybersecurity awareness training programs to evaluate different costs and benefits on a company's optimal degree of security. Regarding household security awareness training, we need to identify the minimum investment of time and money that will encourage households to engage in cybersecurity education programs.

To the best of our knowledge, prior research have not addressed households' needs for cybersecurity training. The purpose of the present work is to address this research gap using a game-theoretic approach. We choose this approach to analyze the impacts of households' decision-making of investing in security training and identify the payoffs of each decision.

We summarize the research contributions below.

- We provide a game-theoretical approach to analyze the cost-effectiveness of households' investments in cybersecurity awareness education.
- We investigate the pure and mixed Nash equilibria of the proposed game.
- We propose graphical representations to analyze investment costs and households' payoffs.

We structure the remainder of this paper as follows. Section II presents the related work. Section III introduces the proposed game model, presents the normal-form game, and analyzes the pure and mixed equilibria. Section IV presents the numerical results. Section V discusses the findings of the paper. Section VI concludes the work.

## II. RELATED WORK

This section describes the related work that uses a game-theoretic approach to analyze security investment cost-benefits.

Generally speaking, IT security investment reflects decision-making resulting from an analysis of potential costs and benefits. Thus one might consider decision theory as essential support for this purpose. However, Cavusoglu et al. [13] show that game-theoretic approaches are more suitable than traditional decision-theoretic risk management techniques regarding IT security investment, especially when considering that attackers are strategic. Furthermore, they find that in a game including two players: a firm and an attacker, the firm maximizes its payoff in a sequential game when the firm is the leader and the attacker is the follower. This result shows that it is possible to use a game-theoretic approach to address the research problem of our work. Sun et al. [14] propose a game model to address information security problems in the mobile electronic commerce industry chain. They introduce a penalty parameter that affects organizations that do not invest in IT security. The results indicate that reducing investment costs is essential to promote information security investments. Otherwise, the regulation of a penalty parameter might help to encourage those investments. In the present paper, we propose a reward parameter for users who take cybersecurity training and notice security countermeasures. Qian et al. [15] propose a game model based on information sharing and security investment between strategies for the two firms. The Nash equilibrium analysis shows that firms share no information when they make decisions individually. Furthermore, Zuo et al. [16] use a game-theoretic approach and Nash equilibrium to analyze information security cost investment to improve network security. The existing research and game models do not address security cost-benefits issues regarding households awareness education, which are the main focus of this paper.

In the literature, the studies on user cybersecurity awareness-based cost-benefit analysis are limited. Furthermore, the related work on security investment cost-benefit analysis only consider corporate areas, which are different from households' reality to some extent. In this new era of the Internet of Things (IoT), households' devices and data are valuable to attackers. We need to address issues, such as cost-benefit, related to households' cybersecurity education to avoid large-scale cyberattacks and ensure people's safety and security.

## III. Proposed Game Model

This section introduces and analyzes our game model through four subsections. Subsection A describes the system. Subsection B defines the parameters of the game. Subsection C presents the normal-form game. Subsection D investigates the pure and mixed Nash equilibria of the proposed game.

### A. System

We consider a smart home comprising three types of households: adults ($User_1$), children ($User_2$), and senior citizens ($User_3$). This house is composed of many IoT devices that are convenient for every household. For example, $User_1$ could use IP cameras and smart door locks to ensure the house's physical security. $User_2$ could use a smart TV and smart speakers for advertisement. $User_3$ could use a smart pill dispenser or smartwatch for healthcare.

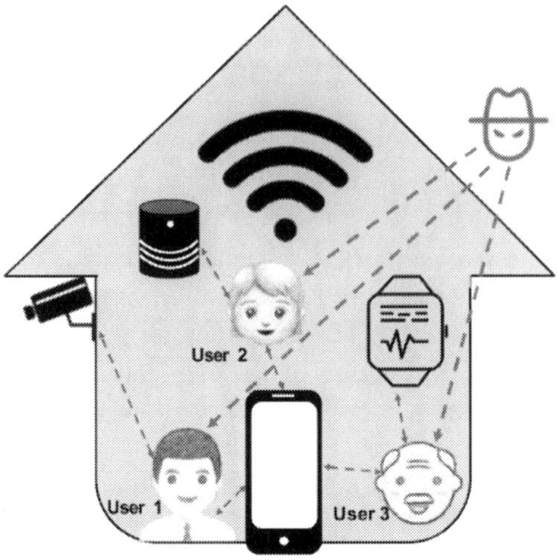


Fig. 1. Illustration of the proposed model.

As illustrated in Figure 1, an attacker could gain interests in compromising that house for various motives, such as accessing private information, using IoT-based home devices to execute Distributed Denial-of-Service (DDoS) attacks, the absence of resistance such as a dedicated cybersecurity team. Furthermore, attackers could discern that households might notice part of security countermeasures, such as changing default passwords, using multi-factor authentication, or recognizing and avoiding phishing links, which could give them various entry points. These attacks could be effective by targeting $User_1$, $User_2$, or $User_3$.

### B. Game Modeling

Let $T_i$ and $\bar{T}_i$, respectively, be the events $User_i$ has got cybersecurity awareness training, and $User_i$ has not got cybersecurity awareness training with $1 \leq i \leq 3$.

Let A be the event that an attacker compromises a user. We consider $P(A/T_i)$ the probability of an attacker to compromise $User_i$ given that $User_i$ has got cybersecurity awareness training, and $P(A/\bar{T}_i)$ the probability of an attacker to compromise $User_i$ given that $User_i$ has not got cybersecurity awareness training.

We assume that

$$P(A/T_1) = P(A/T_2) = P(A/T_3). \quad (1)$$

$$P(A/\bar{T}_1) = P(A/\bar{T}_2) = P(A/\bar{T}_3). \quad (2)$$

We have (1) and (2) because how users could react to an ongoing cyberattack depends more on their level of cybersecurity awareness than on their age.

Let S and $\bar{S}$, respectively, be the events that a user notices security countermeasures, and a user notices part of security countermeasures. We consider $P(A/T_i \cap S)$ the probability of an attacker compromising $User_i$ given that $User_i$ has got cybersecurity awareness training and notices security countermeasures, and $P(A/T_i \cap \bar{S})$ the probability of an attacker compromising $User_i$ given that $User_i$ has got cybersecurity awareness training and notices part of security countermeasures. Like (1) and (2), we assume that

$$P(A/T_1 \cap S) = P(A/T_2 \cap S) = P(A/T_3 \cap S). \quad (3)$$

$$P(A/T_1 \cap \bar{S}) = P(A/T_2 \cap \bar{S}) = P(A/T_3 \cap \bar{S}). \quad (4)$$

We assume that, for a given $User_i$ with $1 \leq i \leq 3$,

$$P(A/T_i \cap S) < P(A/T_i \cap \bar{S}) < P(A/\bar{T}_i). \quad (5)$$

We have (5) because $User_i$ is more secure in the event $T_i \cap S$ than in $T_i \cap \bar{S}$ and more secure in the event $T_i \cap \bar{S}$ than in $\bar{T}_i$. We also assume that

$$0 < P(T_3 \cap S) \leq P(T_2 \cap S) \leq P(T_1 \cap S) \leq 1. \quad (6)$$

$$0 < P(T_1 \cap \bar{S}) \leq P(T_2 \cap \bar{S}) \leq P(T_3 \cap \bar{S}) \leq 1. \quad (7)$$

Furthermore, we have (6) and (7) because many challenges, such as those with cognitive or physical aspects, could regularly hinder senior citizens from noticing security countermeasures. Furthermore, we consider that the basis of knowledge of adults is greater than those of children. Considering every user faces the same potential threats, children might not notice various countermeasures out of ignorance because their cybersecurity-training content might be less intensive than those of adults.

Moreover, we consider the following $User_i$'s costs: $c_{mi}$ the monetary costs related to the event $T$, $c_{ti}$ the time costs related to the event $S$, and $c_{t'i}$ the time costs related to the event $\bar{S}$. We have

$$0 \leq c_{m1} \leq c_{m2} \leq c_{m3}. \quad (8)$$

$$0 \leq c_{t3} \leq c_{t2} \leq c_{t1}. \quad (9)$$

$$0 \leq c_{t'i} < c_{ti}. \quad (10)$$

We have (8) because $User_2$ and $User_3$ might require specific cybersecurity awareness training, which could be more expensive than the training of $User_1$. Furthermore, we consider that it is harder to provide training materials and resources to get $User_3$ than $User_2$ involved. Therefore, the training cost of $User_3$ is more than the training cost of $User_2$, which is more than that of $User_1$. We have (9) because we assume that $User_1$ might invest much more time than $User_2$ and $User_3$ to notice security countermeasures. Furthermore, the effect of age $User_3$'s on memory makes us consider that this user might spend less time noticing security countermeasures than $User_2$. We have (10) because $User_i$ spends much more time in the event $S$ than in the event $\bar{S}$.

We also consider $\delta$ ($\delta > 0$) the costs of a cyberattack on a smart home which could involve interruption costs of smart-home services (e.g., home automation, electric power, healthcare, entertainment, the Internet). Note that $\delta$ applies to every user. Furthermore, we consider $\theta$ ($\theta > 0$) the costs associated with security breaches following an exploit through a user's device. This cost is assigned to the compromised user only. We assume that $\delta > \theta$. Note that $\theta = 0$ for a user who is not attacked and for a user who notices security countermeasures. We assume that

$$\theta P(A/T_i \cap \bar{S}) + \delta \geq c_{mi} + c_{ti} > c_{mi} + c_{t'i}. \quad (11)$$

$\theta$ is different from $\lambda$ ($\lambda \geq 0$), which is the cost associated with privacy incidents related to households. $\lambda$ depends on households' income and social status. We decide to assign this cost to $User_1$ only because being in charge of home safety and security. While $\theta$ could relate to the quality of life (e.g., unavailability of services, a decrease in the sense of privacy and self-esteem), $\lambda$ could relate to money (e.g., ransom requests). Finally, we consider $\varphi$ ($\varphi > 0$), the parameter that quantifies all the comforts and benefits a user could enjoy when living in a smart home. $\varphi$ has the same value for every user. We also consider $R$ the reward for noticing security countermeasures. Note that $R = 0$ for users who notice part of security countermeasures.

### C. Normal-Form Game

We describe strategy sets of each player as matrices. Table I, Table II, and Table III, respectively, present the normal-form games of an attacker targeting $User_1$, $User_2$, and $User_3$. In these tables, each cell from Line 7 - Column 4 represents the payoffs of each player. In each cell, the first line shows $User_1$'s payoffs, the second line shows $User_2$'s payoffs, the third line shows $User_3$'s payoffs, and the fourth line shows the attacker's payoffs. As an illustration, we explain the payoffs of $User_1$ and the attacker described in Table I.

When $User_1$ chooses the events $T$ and $S$, $User_1$'s payoff is $\varphi - c_{m1} - c_{t1} + R$ and the attacker's payoff is 0. Note that in our model the attack fails (attacker's payoff = 0) if the target is a user who takes cybersecurity awareness training and notices security countermeasures. When $User_1$ chooses the events $T$ and $\bar{S}$, $User_1$'s payoff is $\varphi - c_{m1} - c_{t'1} - \theta P(A/T_1 \cap \bar{S}) - \delta - \lambda$ and the attacker's payoff is $\theta P(A/T_1 \cap \bar{S}) + \delta + \lambda$. When $User_1$ chooses the event $\bar{T}$, $User_1$'s payoff is $\varphi - \theta P(A/\bar{T}_1) - \delta - \lambda$ and the attacker's payoff is $\theta P(A/\bar{T}_1) + \delta + \lambda$. Note that when the targeted user chooses the events $\bar{S}$ or $\bar{T}$, the attack affects the other users through the parameter $\delta$. For example in Table I, the payoffs of $User_2$ and $User_3$ are respectively $\varphi - c_{m2} - c_{t2} + R - \delta$ and $\varphi - c_{m3} - c_{t3} + R - \delta$ when both users choose the event $S$ and $User_1$, the target of the attacker, chooses the event $\bar{S}$.

### D. Game Analysis

We aim to understand the rational decision-making of every player: users and the attacker from the perspective of Nash equilibrium. We analyze the best actions of players based on their payoffs. According to the Nash equilibrium, every rational player chooses an action that maximizes his or her payoff.

*1) Pure Strategy Nash Equilibrium:* It refers to a game in which every player's mixed strategy in a mixed strategy Nash equilibrium assigns probability 1 to a single action [17]. In pure strategy Nash equilibrium, a player plays his or her best

TABLE I
NORMAL FORM: AN ATTACKER TARGETS USER 1.

| Attacker targets User 1 | | | User 3 | | | | | | | | |
|---|---|---|---|---|---|---|---|---|---|---|---|
| | | | $T$ | | | | | | $\bar{T}$ | | |
| | | | S | | | $\bar{S}$ | | | | | |
| | | | User 2 | | | User 2 | | | User 2 | | |
| | | | $T$ | | $\bar{T}$ | T | | $\bar{T}$ | $T$ | | $\bar{T}$ |
| | | | $S$ | $\bar{S}$ | | $S$ | $\bar{S}$ | | $S$ | $\bar{S}$ | |
| User 1 | $T$ | S | $\varphi - c_{m1} - c_{t1} + R$;<br>$\varphi - c_{m2} - c_{t2} + R$;<br>$\varphi - c_{m3} - c_{t3} + R$;<br>0 | $\varphi - c_{m1} - c_{t1} + R$;<br>$\varphi - c_{m2} - c_{t2}$;<br>$\varphi - c_{m3} - c_{t3} + R$;<br>0 | $\varphi - c_{m1} - c_{t1} + R$;<br>$\varphi$;<br>$\varphi - c_{m3} - c_{t3} + R$;<br>0 | $\varphi - c_{m1} - c_{t1} + R$;<br>$\varphi - c_{m2} - c_{t2} + R$;<br>$\varphi - c_{m3} - c_{t3}$;<br>0 | $\varphi - c_{m1} - c_{t1} + R$;<br>$\varphi - c_{m2} - c_{t2}$;<br>$\varphi - c_{m3} - c_{t3}$;<br>0 | $\varphi - c_{m1} - c_{t1} + R$;<br>$\varphi$;<br>$\varphi - c_{m3} - c_{t3}$;<br>0 | $\varphi - c_{m1} - c_{t1} + R$;<br>$\varphi - c_{m2} - c_{t2} + R$;<br>$\varphi$;<br>0 | $\varphi - c_{m1} - c_{t1} + R$;<br>$\varphi - c_{m2} - c_{t2}$;<br>$\varphi$;<br>0 | $\varphi - c_{m1} - c_{t1} + R$;<br>$\varphi$;<br>$\varphi$;<br>0 |
| | | $\bar{S}$ | $\varphi - c_{m1} - c_{t1} - \theta P(A/T_1 \cap \bar{S}) - \delta - \lambda$;<br>$\varphi - c_{m2} - c_{t2} + R - \delta$;<br>$\varphi - c_{m3} - c_{t3} + R - \delta$;<br>$\theta P(A/T_1 \cap \bar{S}) + \delta + \lambda$; | $\varphi - c_{m1} - c_{t1} - \theta P(A/T_1 \cap \bar{S}) - \delta - \lambda$ ;<br>$\varphi - c_{m2} - c_{t2} - \delta$;<br>$\varphi - c_{m3} - c_{t3} + R - \delta$;<br>$\theta P(A/T_1 \cap \bar{S}) + \delta + \lambda$; | $\varphi - c_{m1} - c_{t1} - \theta P(A/T_1 \cap \bar{S}) - \delta - \lambda$ ;<br>$\varphi - \delta$;<br>$\varphi - c_{m3} - c_{t3} + R - \delta$;<br>$\theta P(A/T_1 \cap \bar{S}) + \delta + \lambda$; | $\varphi - c_{m1} - c_{t1} - \theta P(A/T_1 \cap \bar{S}) - \delta - \lambda$;<br>$\varphi - c_{m2} - c_{t2} + R - \delta$;<br>$\varphi - c_{m3} - c_{t3} - \delta$;<br>$\theta P(A/T_1 \cap \bar{S}) + \delta + \lambda$; | $\varphi - c_{m1} - c_{t1} - \theta P(A/T_1 \cap \bar{S}) - \delta - \lambda$;<br>$\varphi - c_{m2} - c_{t2} - \delta$;<br>$\varphi - c_{m3} - c_{t3} - \delta$;<br>$\theta P(A/T_1 \cap \bar{S}) + \delta + \lambda$; | $\varphi - c_{m1} - c_{t1} - \theta P(A/T_1 \cap \bar{S}) - \delta - \lambda$;<br>$\varphi - \delta$;<br>$\varphi - c_{m3} - c_{t3} - \delta$;<br>$\theta P(A/T_1 \cap \bar{S}) + \delta + \lambda$; | $\varphi - c_{m1} - c_{t1} - \theta P(A/T_1 \cap \bar{S}) - \delta - \lambda$;<br>$\varphi - c_{m2} - c_{t2} + R - \delta$;<br>$\varphi - \delta$;<br>$\theta P(A/T_1 \cap \bar{S}) + \delta + \lambda$; | $\varphi - c_{m1} - c_{t1} - \theta P(A/T_1 \cap \bar{S}) - \delta - \lambda$;<br>$\varphi - c_{m2} - c_{t2} - \delta$;<br>$\varphi - \delta$;<br>$\theta P(A/T_1 \cap \bar{S}) + \delta + \lambda$; | $\varphi - c_{m1} - c_{t1} - \theta P(A/T_1 \cap \bar{S}) - \delta - \lambda$;<br>$\varphi - \delta$;<br>$\varphi - \delta$;<br>$\theta P(A/T_1 \cap \bar{S}) + \delta + \lambda$; |
| | $\bar{T}$ | | $\varphi - \theta P(A/\bar{T}_1) - \delta - \lambda$;<br>$\varphi - c_{m2} - c_{t2} + R - \delta$;<br>$\varphi - c_{m3} - c_{t3} + R - \delta$;<br>$\theta P(A/\bar{T}_1) + \delta + \lambda$; | $\varphi - \theta P(A/\bar{T}_1) - \delta - \lambda$;<br>$\varphi - c_{m2} - c_{t2} - \delta$;<br>$\varphi - c_{m3} - c_{t3} + R - \delta$;<br>$\theta P(A/\bar{T}_1) + \delta + \lambda$; | $\varphi - \theta P(A/\bar{T}_1) - \delta - \lambda$;<br>$\varphi - \delta$;<br>$\varphi - c_{m3} - c_{t3} + R - \delta$;<br>$\theta P(A/\bar{T}_1) + \delta + \lambda$; | $\varphi - \theta P(A/\bar{T}_1) - \delta - \lambda$;<br>$\varphi - c_{m2} - c_{t2} + R - \delta$;<br>$\varphi - c_{m3} - c_{t3} - \delta$;<br>$\theta P(A/\bar{T}_1) + \delta + \lambda$; | $\varphi - \theta P(A/\bar{T}_1) - \delta - \lambda$;<br>$\varphi - c_{m2} - c_{t2} - \delta$;<br>$\varphi - c_{m3} - c_{t3} - \delta$;<br>$\theta P(A/\bar{T}_1) + \delta + \lambda$; | $\varphi - \theta P(A/\bar{T}_1) - \delta - \lambda$;<br>$\varphi - \delta$;<br>$\varphi - c_{m3} - c_{t3} - \delta$;<br>$\theta P(A/\bar{T}_1) + \delta + \lambda$; | $\varphi - \theta P(A/\bar{T}_1) - \delta - \lambda$;<br>$\varphi - c_{m2} - c_{t2} + R - \delta$;<br>$\varphi - \delta$;<br>$\theta P(A/\bar{T}_1) + \delta + \lambda$; | $\varphi - \theta P(A/\bar{T}_1) - \delta - \lambda$;<br>$\varphi - c_{m2} - c_{t2} - \delta$;<br>$\varphi - \delta$;<br>$\theta P(A/\bar{T}_1) + \delta + \lambda$; | $\varphi - \theta P(A/\bar{T}_1) - \delta - \lambda$;<br>$\varphi - \delta$;<br>$\varphi - \delta$;<br>$\theta P(A/\bar{T}_1) + \delta + \lambda$; |

TABLE II
NORMAL FORM: AN ATTACKER TARGETS USER 2.

| Attacker targets User 2 | | | User 3 | | | | | | User 3 | | |
|---|---|---|---|---|---|---|---|---|---|---|---|
| | | | $T$ | | | | | | $\bar{T}$ | | |
| | | | $S$ | | | $\bar{S}$ | | | | | |
| | | | User 2 | | | User 2 | | | User 2 | | |
| | | | $T$ | | $\bar{T}$ | $T$ | | $\bar{T}$ | $T$ | | $\bar{T}$ |
| | | | $S$ | $\bar{S}$ | | $S$ | $\bar{S}$ | | $S$ | $\bar{S}$ | |
| User 1 | $T$ | $S$ | $\varphi - c_{m1} - c_{t1} + R$;<br>$\varphi - c_{m2} - c_{t2} + R$;<br>$\varphi - c_{m3} - c_{t3} + R$;<br>0 | $\varphi - c_{m1} - c_{t1} + R - \delta - \lambda$;<br>$\varphi - c_{m2} - c_{t'2} - \theta P(A/T_2 \cap \bar{S}) - \delta$;<br>$\varphi - c_{m3} - c_{t3} + R - \delta$;<br>$\theta P(A/T_2 \cap \bar{S}) + \delta + \lambda$ | $\varphi - c_{m1} - c_{t1} + R - \delta - \lambda$;<br>$\varphi - \theta P(A/\bar{T}_2) - \delta$;<br>$\varphi - c_{m3} - c_{t3} + R - \delta$;<br>$\theta P(A/\bar{T}_2) + \delta + \lambda$ | $\varphi - c_{m1} - c_{t1} + R$;<br>$\varphi - c_{m2} - c_{t2} + R$;<br>$\varphi - c_{m3} - c_{t'3}$;<br>0 | $\varphi - c_{m1} - c_{t1} + R - \delta - \lambda$;<br>$\varphi - c_{m2} - c_{t'2} - \theta P(A/T_2 \cap \bar{S}) - \delta$;<br>$\varphi - c_{m3} - c_{t'3} - \delta$;<br>$\theta P(A/T_2 \cap \bar{S}) + \delta + \lambda$ | $\varphi - c_{m1} - c_{t1} + R - \delta - \lambda$;<br>$\varphi - \theta P(A/\bar{T}_2) - \delta$;<br>$\varphi - c_{m3} - c_{t'3} - \delta$;<br>$\theta P(A/\bar{T}_2) + \delta + \lambda$ | $\varphi - c_{m1} - c_{t1} + R$;<br>$\varphi - c_{m2} - c_{t2} + R$;<br>$\varphi$;<br>0 | $\varphi - c_{m1} - c_{t1} + R - \delta - \lambda$;<br>$\varphi - c_{m2} - c_{t'2} - \theta P(A/T_2 \cap \bar{S}) - \delta$;<br>$\varphi - \delta$;<br>$\theta P(A/T_2 \cap \bar{S}) + \delta + \lambda$ | $\varphi - c_{m1} - c_{t1} + R - \delta - \lambda$;<br>$\varphi - \theta P(A/\bar{T}_2) - \delta$;<br>$\varphi - \delta$;<br>$\theta P(A/\bar{T}_2) + \delta + \lambda$ |
| | | $\bar{S}$ | $\varphi - c_{m1} - c_{t'1}$;<br>$\varphi - c_{m2} - c_{t2} + R$;<br>$\varphi - c_{m3} - c_{t3} + R$;<br>0; | $\varphi - c_{m1} - c_{t'1} - \delta - \lambda$ ;<br>$\varphi - c_{m2} - c_{t'2} - \theta P(A/T_2 \cap \bar{S}) - \delta$;<br>$\varphi - c_{m3} - c_{t3} + R - \delta$;<br>$\theta P(A/T_2 \cap \bar{S}) + \delta + \lambda$; | $\varphi - c_{m1} - c_{t'1} - \delta - \lambda$ ;<br>$\varphi - \theta P(A/\bar{T}_2) - \delta$;<br>$\varphi - c_{m3} - c_{t3} + R - \delta$;<br>$\theta P(A/\bar{T}_2) + \delta + \lambda$; | $\varphi - c_{m1} - c_{t'1}$;<br>$\varphi - c_{m2} - c_{t2} + R$;<br>$\varphi - c_{m3} - c_{t'3}$;<br>0; | $\varphi - c_{m1} - c_{t'1} - \delta - \lambda$;<br>$\varphi - c_{m2} - c_{t'2} - \theta P(A/T_2 \cap \bar{S}) - \delta$;<br>$\varphi - c_{m3} - c_{t'3} - \delta$;<br>$\theta P(A/T_2 \cap \bar{S}) + \delta + \lambda$; | $\varphi - c_{m1} - c_{t'1} - \delta - \lambda$;<br>$\varphi - \theta P(A/\bar{T}_2) - \delta$;<br>$\varphi - c_{m3} - c_{t'3} - \delta$;<br>$\theta P(A/\bar{T}_2) + \delta + \lambda$; | $\varphi - c_{m1} - c_{t'1}$;<br>$\varphi - c_{m2} - c_{t2} + R$;<br>$\varphi$;<br>0; | $\varphi - c_{m1} - c_{t'1} - \delta - \lambda$;<br>$\varphi - c_{m2} - c_{t'2} - \theta P(A/T_2 \cap \bar{S}) - \delta$;<br>$\varphi - \delta$;<br>$\theta P(A/T_2 \cap \bar{S}) + \delta + \lambda$; | $\varphi - c_{m1} - c_{t'1} - \delta - \lambda$;<br>$\varphi - \theta P(A/\bar{T}_2) - \delta$;<br>$\varphi - \delta$;<br>$\theta P(A/\bar{T}_2) + \delta + \lambda$; |
| | $\bar{T}$ | | $\varphi$;<br>$\varphi - c_{m2} - c_{t2} + R$;<br>$\varphi - c_{m3} - c_{t3} + R$;<br>0; | $\varphi - \delta - \lambda$;<br>$\varphi - c_{m2} - c_{t'2} - \theta P(A/T_2 \cap \bar{S}) - \delta$;<br>$\varphi - c_{m3} - c_{t3} + R - \delta$;<br>$\theta P(A/T_2 \cap \bar{S}) + \delta + \lambda$; | $\varphi - \delta - \lambda$;<br>$\varphi - \theta P(A/\bar{T}_2) - \delta$ ;<br>$\varphi - c_{m3} - c_{t3} + R - \delta$;<br>$\theta P(A/\bar{T}_2) + \delta + \lambda$; | $\varphi$;<br>$\varphi - c_{m2} - c_{t2} + R$;<br>$\varphi - c_{m3} - c_{t'3}$;<br>0; | $\varphi - \delta - \lambda$;<br>$\varphi - c_{m2} - c_{t'2} - \theta P(A/T_2 \cap \bar{S}) - \delta$;<br>$\varphi - c_{m3} - c_{t'3} - \delta$;<br>$\theta P(A/T_2 \cap \bar{S}) + \delta + \lambda$; | $\varphi - \delta - \lambda$;<br>$\varphi - \theta P(A/\bar{T}_2) - \delta$;<br>$\varphi - c_{m3} - c_{t'3} - \delta$;<br>$\theta P(A/\bar{T}_2) + \delta + \lambda$; | $\varphi$;<br>$\varphi - c_{m2} - c_{t2} + R$;<br>$\varphi$;<br>0; | $\varphi - \delta - \lambda$;<br>$\varphi - c_{m2} - c_{t'2} - \theta P(A/T_2 \cap \bar{S}) - \delta$;<br>$\varphi - \delta$;<br>$\theta P(A/T_2 \cap \bar{S}) + \delta + \lambda$; | $\varphi - \theta - \lambda$;<br>$\varphi - \theta P(A/\bar{T}_2) - \delta$;<br>$\varphi - \delta$;<br>$\theta P(A/\bar{T}_2) + \delta + \lambda$; |

TABLE III
NORMAL FORM: AN ATTACKER TARGETS USER 3.

| Attacker targets User 3 | User 3 | | | | | | | | |
|---|---|---|---|---|---|---|---|---|---|
| | $T$ | | | | | | $\bar{T}$ | | |
| | $S$ | | | $\bar{S}$ | | | | | |
| | User 2 | | | User 2 | | | User 2 | | |
| | $T$ | | $\bar{T}$ | $T$ | | $\bar{T}$ | $T$ | | $\bar{T}$ |
| | $S$ | $\bar{S}$ | | $S$ | $\bar{S}$ | | $S$ | $\bar{S}$ | |
| User 1: $T$, S | $\varphi - c_{m1} - c_{t1} + R$;<br>$\varphi - c_{m2} - c_{t2} + R$;<br>$\varphi - c_{m3} - c_{t3} + R$;<br>0 | $\varphi - c_{m1} - c_{t1} + R$;<br>$\varphi - c_{m2} - c_{t'2}$;<br>$\varphi - c_{m3} - c_{t3} + R$;<br>0 | $\varphi - c_{m1} - c_{t1} + R$;<br>$\varphi$;<br>$\varphi - c_{m3} - c_{t3} + R$;<br>0 | $\varphi - c_{m1} - c_{t1} + R - \delta - \lambda$;<br>$\varphi - c_{m2} - c_{t2} + R - \delta$;<br>$\varphi - c_{m3} - c_{t'3} - \theta P(A/T_3 \cap \bar{S}) - \delta$;<br>$\theta P(A/T_3 \cap \bar{S}) + \delta + \lambda$ | $\varphi - c_{m1} - c_{t1} + R - \delta - \lambda$;<br>$\varphi - c_{m2} - c_{t'2} - \delta$;<br>$\varphi - c_{m3} - c_{t'3} - \theta P(A/T_3 \cap \bar{S}) - \delta$;<br>$\theta P(A/T_3 \cap \bar{S}) + \delta + \lambda$ | $\varphi - c_{m1} - c_{t1} + R - \delta - \lambda$;<br>$\varphi - \delta$;<br>$\varphi - c_{m3} - c_{t'3} - \theta P(A/T_3 \cap \bar{S}) - \delta$;<br>$\theta P(A/T_3 \cap \bar{S}) + \delta + \lambda$ | $\varphi - c_{m1} - c_{t1} + R - \delta - \lambda$;<br>$\varphi - c_{m2} - c_{t2} + R - \delta$;<br>$\varphi - \theta P(A/\bar{T}_3) - \delta$;<br>$\theta P(A/\bar{T}_3) + \delta + \lambda$ | $\varphi - c_{m1} - c_{t1} + R - \delta - \lambda$;<br>$\varphi - c_{m2} - c_{t'2} - \delta$;<br>$\varphi - \theta P(A/\bar{T}_3) - \delta$;<br>$\theta P(A/\bar{T}_3) + \delta + \lambda$ | $\varphi - c_{m1} - c_{t1} + R - \delta - \lambda$;<br>$\varphi - \delta$;<br>$\varphi - \theta P(A/\bar{T}_3) - \delta$;<br>$\theta P(A/\bar{T}_3) + \delta + \lambda$ |
| User 1: $T$, $\bar{S}$ | $\varphi - c_{m1} - c_{t'1}$;<br>$\varphi - c_{m2} - c_{t2} + R$;<br>$\varphi - c_{m3} - c_{t3} + R$;<br>0; | $\varphi - c_{m1} - c_{t'1}$;<br>$\varphi - c_{m2} - c_{t'2}$;<br>$\varphi - c_{m3} - c_{t3} + R$;<br>0; | $\varphi - c_{m1} - c_{t'1}$ ;<br>$\varphi$;<br>$\varphi - c_{m3} - c_{t3} + R$;<br>0; | $\varphi - c_{m1} - c_{t'1} - \delta - \lambda$;<br>$\varphi - c_{m2} - c_{t2} + R - \delta$;<br>$\varphi - c_{m3} - c_{t'3} - \theta P(A/T_3 \cap \bar{S}) - \delta$;<br>$\theta P(A/T_3 \cap \bar{S}) + \delta + \lambda$; | $\varphi - c_{m1} - c_{t'1} - \delta - \lambda$;<br>$\varphi - c_{m2} - c_{t'2} - \delta$;<br>$\varphi - c_{m3} - c_{t'3} - \theta P(A/T_3 \cap \bar{S}) - \delta$;<br>$\theta P(A/T_3 \cap \bar{S}) + \delta + \lambda$; | $\varphi - c_{m1} - c_{t'1} - \delta - \lambda$;<br>$\varphi - \delta$;<br>$\varphi - c_{m3} - c_{t'3} - \theta P(A/T_3 \cap \bar{S}) - \delta$;<br>$\theta P(A/T_3 \cap \bar{S}) + \delta + \lambda$; | $\varphi - c_{m1} - c_{t'1} - \delta - \lambda$;<br>$\varphi - c_{m2} - c_{t2} + R - \delta$;<br>$\varphi - \theta P(A/\bar{T}_3) - \delta$;<br>$\theta P(A/\bar{T}_3) + \delta + \lambda$; | $\varphi - c_{m1} - c_{t'1} - \delta - \lambda$;<br>$\varphi - c_{m2} - c_{t'2} - \delta$;<br>$\varphi - \theta P(A/\bar{T}_3) - \delta$ ;<br>$\theta P(A/\bar{T}_3) + \delta + \lambda$; | $\varphi - c_{m1} - c_{t'1} - \delta - \lambda$;<br>$\varphi - \delta$;<br>$\varphi - \theta P(A/\bar{T}_3) - \delta$;<br>$\theta P(A/\bar{T}_3) + \delta + \lambda$; |
| User 1: $\bar{T}$ | $\varphi$;<br>$\varphi - c_{m2} - c_{t2} + R$;<br>$\varphi - c_{m3} - c_{t3} + R$;<br>0; | $\varphi$;<br>$\varphi - c_{m2} - c_{t'2}$;<br>$\varphi - c_{m3} - c_{t3} + R$;<br>0; | $\varphi$;<br>$\varphi$;<br>$\varphi - c_{m3} - c_{t3} + R$;<br>0; | $\varphi - \delta - \lambda$;<br>$\varphi - c_{m2} - c_{t2} + R - \delta$;<br>$\varphi - c_{m3} - c_{t'3} - \theta P(A/T_3 \cap \bar{S}) - \delta$;<br>$\theta P(A/T_3 \cap \bar{S}) + \delta + \lambda$; | $\varphi - \delta - \lambda$;<br>$\varphi - c_{m2} - c_{t'2} - \delta$;<br>$\varphi - c_{m3} - c_{t'3} - \theta P(A/T_3 \cap \bar{S}) - \delta$;<br>$\theta P(A/T_3 \cap \bar{S}) + \delta + \lambda$; | $\varphi - \delta - \lambda$;<br>$\varphi - \delta$;<br>$\varphi - c_{m3} - c_{t'3} - \theta P(A/T_3 \cap \bar{S}) - \delta$;<br>$\theta P(A/T_3 \cap \bar{S}) + \delta + \lambda$; | $\varphi - \delta - \lambda$;<br>$\varphi - c_{m2} - c_{t2} + R - \delta$;<br>$\varphi - \theta P(A/\bar{T}_3) - \delta$;<br>$\theta P(A/\bar{T}_3) + \delta + \lambda$; | $\varphi - \delta - \lambda$;<br>$\varphi - c_{m2} - c_{t'2} - \delta$;<br>$\varphi - \theta P(A/\bar{T}_3) - \delta$;<br>$\theta P(A/\bar{T}_3) + \delta + \lambda$; | $\varphi - \delta - \lambda$;<br>$\varphi - \delta$;<br>$\varphi - \theta P(A/\bar{T}_3) - \delta$;<br>$\theta P(A/\bar{T}_3) + \delta + \lambda$; |

strategy; the rational player would never change his or her strategy to get a lower payoff than that of the best strategy.

**Theorem 1.** *When every user notices security countermeasures, the proposed game admits a pure strategy Nash equilibrium related to the strategic profile (S, S, S, A).*

*Proof.* The proposed game generates nine strategic profiles when users choose the same actions and 72 otherwise. We study each of these two types of strategic profiles. Let $U_{att(User_i)}$ be the utility of the attacker when targeting $User_i$.

- Strategic profiles (Type 1): Users play the same actions.

*Case 1.1: Every user has not got cybersecurity awareness training.*

$$U_{att(User_i)}(\bar{T}, \bar{T}, \bar{T}, A) = \theta P(A/\bar{T}_i) + \delta + \lambda$$

From (2), there is equality between the attacker's payoffs. The attacker cannot increase his or her payoff. However, $User_i$ can increase his or her payoff from "$\varphi - \theta P(A/\bar{T}_i) - \delta - \lambda$" to "$\varphi - c_{mi} - c_{ti} + R$" by choosing to play $S$ instead of $\bar{T}$ because (5) and (11) show that $-(\theta P(A/\bar{T}_i) + \delta) < -(c_{mi} + c_{ti})$. Therefore, the strategic profile ($\bar{T}, \bar{T}, \bar{T}$, A) is not a pure strategy Nash equilibrium.

*Case 1.2: Every user notices part of security countermeasures.*

$$U_{att(User_i)}(\bar{S}, \bar{S}, \bar{S}, A) = \theta P(A/T_i \cap \bar{S}) + \delta + \lambda$$

From (4), there is equality between the attacker's payoffs whoever his or her target is. The attacker cannot increase his or her payoff. However, $User_i$ can increase his or her payoff from "$\varphi - c_{mi} - c_{t'i} - \theta P(A/\bar{T}_i \cap \bar{S}) - \delta - \lambda$" to "$\varphi - c_{mi} - c_{ti} + R$" by choosing to play $S$ instead of $\bar{S}$ because (11) shows that $-(\theta P(A/\bar{T}_i \cap \bar{S}) + \delta) < -(c_{mi} + c_{t'i})$. Therefore, the strategic profile ($\bar{S}, \bar{S}, \bar{S}$, A) is not a pure strategy Nash equilibrium.

*Case 1.3: Every user notices security countermeasures.*

$$U_{att(User_i)}(S, S, S, A) = 0$$

The attacker gets the same payoff whoever his or her target is. Furthermore, users get the maximum payoff (i.e., "$\varphi - c_{mi} - c_{ti} + R$") when they play "$S$". Therefore, the strategic profile (S, S, S, A) is a pure strategy Nash equilibrium.

- Strategic profiles (Type 2): Every user does not play the same action.

*Case 2.1: One or two users notices security countermeasures.*

The attacker's payoff is zero when targeting a user who notices security countermeasures. The attacker can increase his or her payoff by targeting a user who notices part of security countermeasures. Therefore, the related strategic profiles, such as (S, $\bar{S}$, $\bar{T}$, A), (S, S, $\bar{T}$, A), and (S, S, $\bar{S}$, A), are not pure strategy Nash equilibria.

*Case 2.2: One or two users notices part of security countermeasures and the other user(s) has (have) not got cybersecurity awareness training.*

The attacker's payoff is $\theta P(A/T_i \cap \bar{S}) + \delta + \lambda$ or $\theta P(A/\bar{T}_i) + \delta + \lambda$. From (5), $P(A/T_i \cap \bar{S}) < P(A/\bar{T}_i)$; then the attacker can increase his or her payoff by targeting a user who has not got cybersecurity awareness training. Therefore, the related strategic profiles, such as ($\bar{S}, \bar{T}, \bar{T}$, A), ($\bar{T}, \bar{T}, \bar{S}$, A), and ($\bar{S}, \bar{S}, \bar{T}$, A), are not pure strategy Nash equilibria. □

*2) Mixed Strategy Nash Equilibrium:* It refers to a game in which every player plays a mixed strategy (i.e., a probability distribution over the pure strategies) and cannot improve his or her payoff under the mixed-strategy profile.

We consider the following parameters.

- $u_i$: The probability of $User_i$ taking cybersecurity awareness training, and $1 - u_i$ the probability of $User_i$ not taking the training.
- $u_{si}$: The probability of $User_i$ noticing security countermeasures, and $1 - u_{si}$ the probability of noticing part of security countermeasures.

$$0 \leq u_i, u_{si} \leq 1. \tag{12}$$

Note that $u_i$, $1 - u_i$, $u_{si}$, and $1 - u_{si}$, respectively, refer to as $P(T_i)$, $P(\bar{T}_i)$, $P(T_i \cap S)$, and $P(T_i \cap \bar{S})$ with $1 \leq i \leq 3$.

We consider $a_1$, $a_2$, and $a_3$, respectively, the probabilities associated with the attacker targeting $User_1$, $User_2$, and $User_3$.

$$0 \leq a_1, a_2, a_3 \leq 1. \tag{13}$$

$$a_1 + a_2 + a_3 = 1. \tag{14}$$

We assume that every player (i.e., attacker and users) randomizes his or her strategy.

***2.1) User 1 plays a mixed strategy***

The utility ($U_1$) of $User_1$ is the same when noticing security countermeasures ($S$), noticing part of security countermeasures ($\bar{S}$), or not taking cybersecurity awareness training ($\bar{T}$).

We have

$$U_1(S) = U_1(\bar{S}) = U_1(\bar{T}) \tag{15}$$

where

$$\begin{aligned} U_1(S) =& (\delta + \lambda)(a_2 u_2 u_{s2} + a_3 u_3 u_{s3} - a_2 - a_3) + \\ & R + \varphi - c_{m1} - c_{t1} \\ U_1(\bar{S}) =& - a_1 \theta P(A/T_1 \cap \bar{S}) + (\delta + \lambda)(a_2 u_2 u_{s2} + a_3 u_3 u_{s3}) \\ & + \varphi - \delta - \lambda - c_{m1} - c_{t'1} \\ U_1(\bar{T}) =& - a_1 \theta P(A/\bar{T}_1) + (\delta + \lambda)(a_2 u_2 u_{s2} + a_3 u_3 u_{s3}) \\ & + \varphi - \delta - \lambda \end{aligned}$$

From (14), we have $a_2 + a_3 = 1 - a_1$ then

If $U_1(S) = U_1(\bar{S})$ then

$$a_1 = \frac{-R + c_{t1} - c_{t'1}}{\theta P(A/T_1 \cap \bar{S}) + \delta + \lambda} \tag{16}$$

If $U_1(S) = U_1(\bar{T})$ then

$$a_1 = \frac{-R + c_{m1} + c_{t1}}{\theta P(A/\bar{T}_1) + \delta + \lambda} \tag{17}$$

If $U_1(\bar{S}) = U_1(\bar{T})$ then

$$a_1 = \frac{-(c_{m1} + c_{t'1})}{\theta(P(A/T_1 \cap \bar{S}) - P(A/\bar{T}_1))} \tag{18}$$

***2.2) User j plays a mixed strategy***

Similarly, regarding User $j$, with $2 \leq j \leq 3$, we obtain

If $U_j(S) = U_j(\bar{S})$ then

$$a_j = \frac{-R + c_{tj} - c_{t'j}}{\theta P(A/T_j \cap \bar{S}) + \delta} \tag{19}$$

If $U_j(S) = U_j(\bar{T})$ then

$$a_j = \frac{-R + c_{mj} + c_{tj}}{\theta P(A/\bar{T}_j) + \delta} \tag{20}$$

If $U_j(\bar{S}) = U_j(\bar{T})$ then

$$a_j = \frac{-(c_{mj} + c_{t'j})}{\theta(P(A/T_j \cap \bar{S}) - P(A/\bar{T}_j))} \tag{21}$$

***2.3) The attacker plays a mixed strategy***

The utility ($U_{att}$) of the attacker is the same when targeting $User_1$, $User_2$, or $User_3$.

$$U_{att(User_1)} = U_{att(User_2)} = U_{att(User_3)} \tag{22}$$

Using Equations (2) and (4), for $1 \leq i \leq 3$, we obtain

$$\begin{aligned} U_{att(User_i)} =& u_i \theta P(A/T_i \cap \bar{S})(1 - u_{si}) + \theta P(A/\bar{T}_i)(1 - u_i) \\ & - u_i u_{si}(\delta + \lambda) + \delta + \lambda \end{aligned}$$

The strategy profile at mixed strategy Nash equilibrium is $\{u_1 u_{s1} S + u_1(1 - u_{s1})\bar{S} + (1 - u_1)\bar{T}; u_2 u_{s2} S + u_2(1 - u_{s2})\bar{S} + (1 - u_2)\bar{T}; u_3 u_{s3} S + u_3(1 - u_{s3})\bar{S} + (1 - u_3)\bar{T}; a_1 A_1 + a_2 A_2 + a_3 A_3\}$.

**Theorem 2.** *The proposed game admits many mixed strategy Nash equilibria, especially when $\lambda = 0$, $User_i$ chooses to randomize to play $S$ and $\bar{S}$ with $c_{ti} - c_{t'i} > R$, or chooses to play $S$ and $\bar{T}$ with $c_{mi} + c_{ti} > R$, or chooses to randomize to play $\bar{S}$ and $\bar{T}$.*

*Proof.* Equations (16) and (19) show that, for $1 \leq i \leq 3$, $a_i > 0$ only if $c_{ti} - c_{t'i} > R$. Similarly, Equations (17) and (20) show that $a_i > 0$ only if $c_{mi} + c_{ti} > R$. Therefore, under these conditions, the proposed game may reach mixed strategy Nash equilibria when $User_i$ chooses randomly the events $S$ and $\bar{S}$ or the events $S$ and $\bar{T}$. Equations (18) and (21) show that $a_i > 0$ because (5) states that $P(A/T_i \cap \bar{S}) < P(A/\bar{T}_i)$. Therefore, the proposed game may reach a mixed strategy Nash equilibrium when $User_i$ plays randomly the events $\bar{S}$ and $\bar{T}$. □

## IV. NUMERICAL RESULTS

This section presents the numerical results of the proposed game using the equations obtained in Section III-D. We analyze the payoffs of households and attackers from the perspective of security costs and rewards for noticing security countermeasures. We further consider a more realistic cost covering scenario where $User_1$ pays the monetary cost of cybersecurity training of $User_2$ and $User_3$. In this scenario, we refer to $User_i$ as $Actual\ User\ i$ ($1 \leq i \leq 3$).

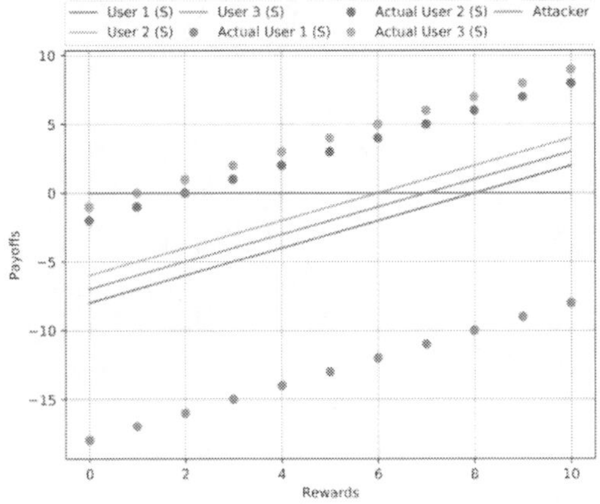


Fig. 2. Illustration of players' payoffs based on users' rewards for noticing security countermeasures with $\varphi < min(c_{m1} + c_{t1}, c_{m2} + c_{t2}, c_{m3} + c_{t3})$.

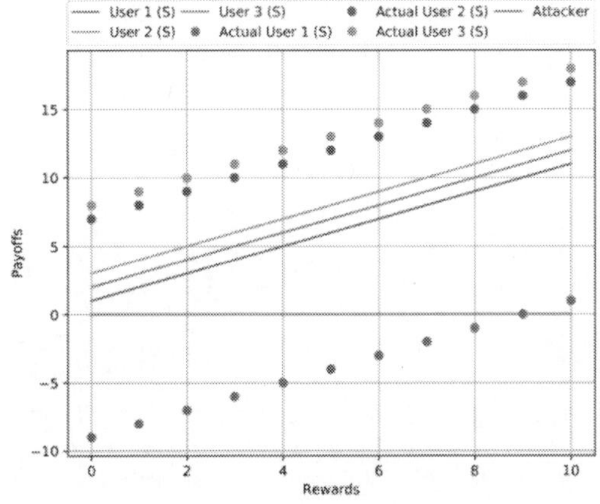


Fig. 3. Illustration of players' payoffs based on users' rewards for noticing security countermeasures with $\varphi > max(c_{m1} + c_{t1}, c_{m2} + c_{t2}, c_{m3} + c_{t3})$.

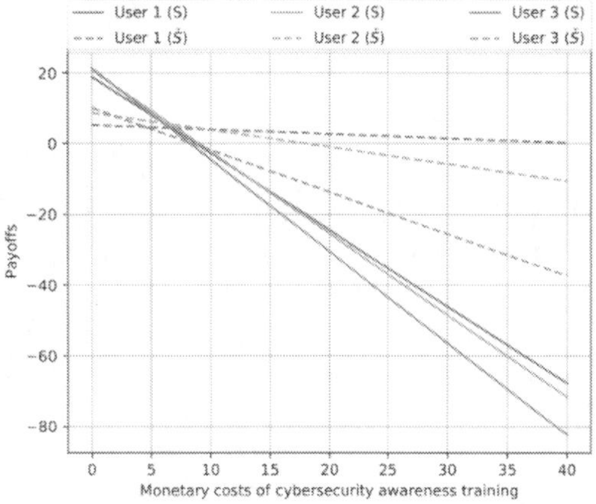


Fig. 4. Illustration of users' payoffs based on security investment costs when $\varphi > (\theta + \delta) > R$.

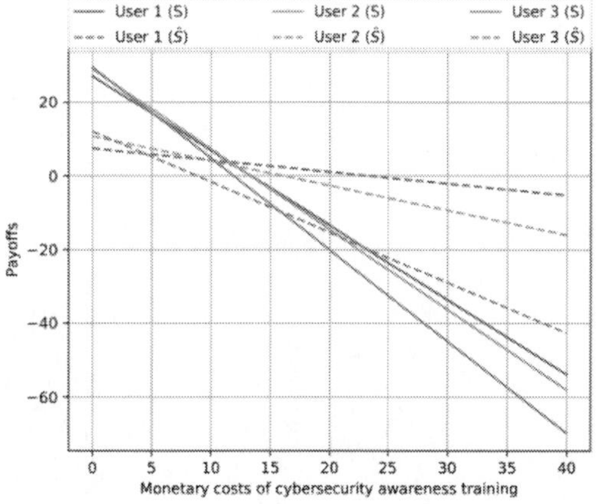


Fig. 5. Illustration of users' payoffs based on security investment costs when $\varphi > R > (\theta + \delta)$.

Our results are essentially based on the following parameters: $\varphi$, $\theta$, $R$, $c_{mi}$, $c_{ti}$, $c_{t'i}$, $P(T_i)$, $P(T_i \cap S)$, $P(A/\bar{T_i})$, and $P(A/T_i \cap \bar{S})$ $(1 \leq i \leq 3)$. We proposed, respectively, two scenarios related to the pure strategy Nash equilibrium and nine scenarios related to the mixed strategy Nash equilibria to examine the potential impacts of rewards for noticing security countermeasures, security costs, and the likelihood of the event $T_1 \cap S$ on the players' payoffs.

In the first two scenarios, the graph results are based on each player's payoff regarding the strategic profile (S, S, S, A). We set $c_{m1} = 3; c_{m2} = 4; c_{m3} = 6; c_{t1} = 6; c_{t2} = 3; c_{t3} = 2$. We choose $\varphi = 1$ in the first scenario and $\varphi = 10$ in the second. Figure 2 presents the results of the first scenario. We can see that when the comfort and benefit of living in a smart home are less considerable than security costs (money and time) to be invested, User 1, User 2, and User 3 will be satisfied with taking security training and noticing security countermeasures only if the security rewards are extremely significant and greater than the security costs invested ($R > 8$). Furthermore "Actual User 2" and "Actual User 3" could be satisfied with a very few security reward ($R > 2$) while "Actual User 1", will never be satisfied whatever the security rewards because his or her payoff remains negative. Figure 3 presents the results of the second scenario. It shows that when User 1, User 2, and User 3 estimate that the comfort and benefit of living in a smart home are more significant than the security costs to be spent, they are more likely to invest and notice security countermeasures whatever the reward. Same goes for "Actual User 2" and "Actual User 3" who are keen to notice security countermeasures. However, "Actual User 1" will be satisfied only if the security rewards are extremely significant ($R > 9$). As it might be seen, in both scenarios, the results show a linear relationship between households' payoffs and the security rewards. Furthermore, the attacker's payoff is null, which reveals that the attacks would fail in such situations.

The graph results of the other scenarios are based on the players' payoffs in the mixed strategy Nash equilibria. We set $0 \leq c_{m1} < 40$; $c_{m2} = 1.25 * c_{m1}$; $c_{m3} = 1.75 * c_{m1}$; $c_{t1} = 6$;

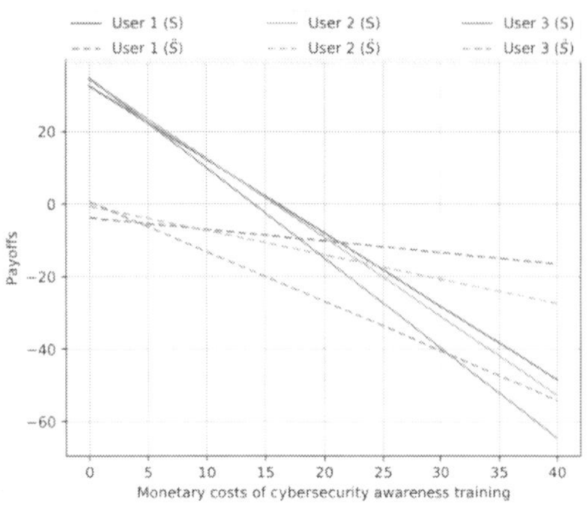


Fig. 6. Illustration of users' payoffs based on security investment costs when $R > \varphi > (\theta + \delta)$.

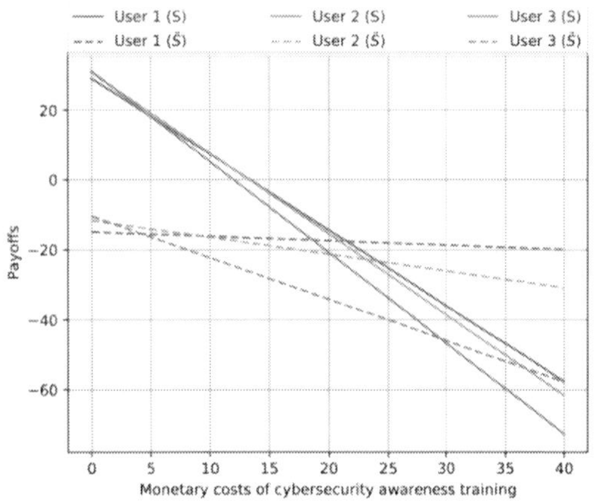


Fig. 7. Illustration of users' payoffs based on security investment costs when $R > (\theta + \delta) > \varphi$.

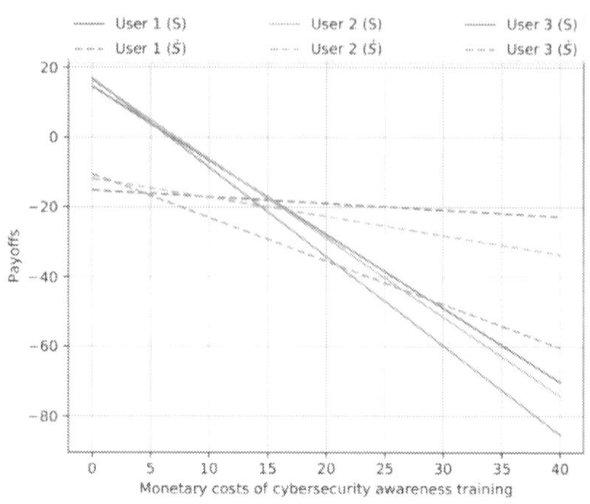


Fig. 8. Illustration of users' payoffs based on security investment costs when $(\theta + \delta) > R > \varphi$.

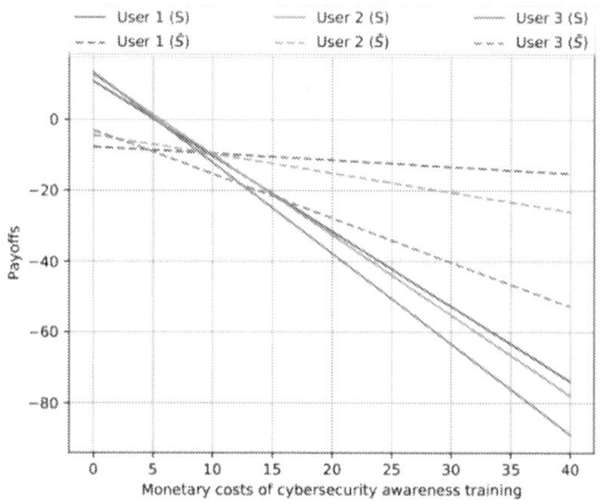


Fig. 9. Illustration of users' payoffs based on security investment costs when $(\theta + \delta) > \varphi > R$.

$c_{t2} = 3$; $c_{t3} = 2$; $c_{t'1} = 4$; $c_{t'2} = 2$; $c_{t'3} = 1$; $P(T_3 \cap S) = 0.5$; $P(T_2 \cap S) = 0.6$; $P(T_1 \cap S) = 0.7$; $P(A/T_i \cap \bar{S}) = 0.4$; $P(A/\bar{T}_i) = 0.9$ $(1 \leq i \leq 3)$.

Scenario 3 [$\varphi > (\theta + \delta) > R$]: We choose $\varphi = 18; \theta = 3; \delta = 7; R = 5$. Figure 4 presents the expected payoffs of households depending on the security costs in money of cybersecurity awareness training. We can see that the maximin strategy (the best of a set of worst possible security investment strategies) of households is reached when User 1 plays $\bar{S}$ and User 3 plays $S$ with $c_{m1} = 6.56$ and *payoff* $= 4.39 > 0$.

Scenario 4 [$\varphi > R > (\theta + \delta)$]: We choose $\varphi = 18; \theta = 2; \delta = 3; R = 10$. Figure 5 shows that the maximin strategy of households is reached when User 1 plays $\bar{S}$ and User 3 plays $S$ with $c_{m1} = 10.24$ and *payoff* $= 4.16 > 0$.

Scenario 5 [$R > \varphi > (\theta + \delta)$]: We choose $\varphi = 10; \theta = 2; \delta = 3; R = 18$. As presented in Figure 6, the maximin strategy of households is reached when User 1 plays $\bar{S}$ and User 3 plays $S$ with $c_{m1} = 17.82$ and *payoff* $= -9.47$.

Scenario 6 [$R > (\theta + \delta) > \varphi$]: We choose $\varphi = 5; \theta = 3; \delta = 7; R = 18$. Figure 7 shows that the maximin strategy of households is reached when User 1 plays $\bar{S}$ and User 3 plays $S$ with $c_{m1} = 18.63$ and *payoff* $= -17.19 < 0$.

Scenario 7 [$(\theta + \delta) > R > \varphi$]: We choose $\varphi = 5; \theta = 6; \delta = 12; R = 10$. Figure 8 shows that the maximin strategy of households is reached when User 1 and User 3 play $\bar{S}$ with $c_{m1} = 13.58$ and *payoff* $= -17.77 < 0$.

Scenario 8 [$(\theta + \delta) > \varphi > R$]: We choose $\varphi = 10; \theta = 6; \delta = 12; R = 5$. As presented in Figure 9, the maximin strategy of households is reached when User 1 plays $\bar{S}$ and User 3 plays $S$ with $c_{m1} = 8.91$ and *payoff* $= -9.41 < 0$.

Scenario 9 [$\varphi > (\theta + \delta) > R$]: We choose $\varphi = 18; \theta = 3; \delta = 7; R = 5$. The previous results demonstrate that *Scenario 3* is the best option for households to minimize the monetary costs and get better payoffs. However, Figure 10 shows that *Scenario 3* may not suit actual users when only "Actual User 1" is accountable for the monetary costs. We can see that the maximin strategy of actual users is reached when "Actual User 1" plays $\bar{S}$ or $S$ with $c_{m1} = 6.71$ and

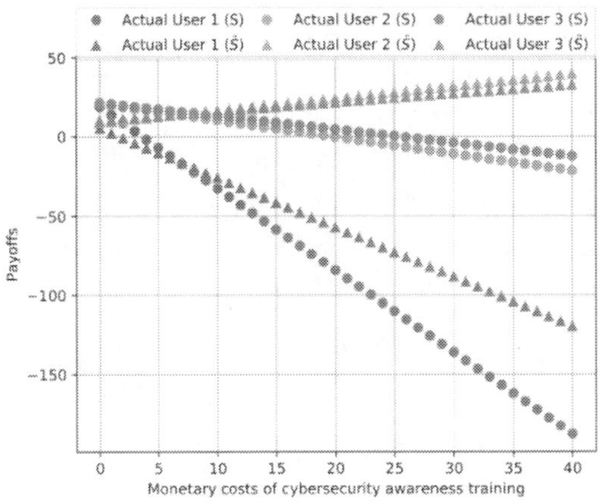


Fig. 10. Illustration of actual users' payoffs based on security investment costs when $\varphi > (\theta + \delta) > R$.

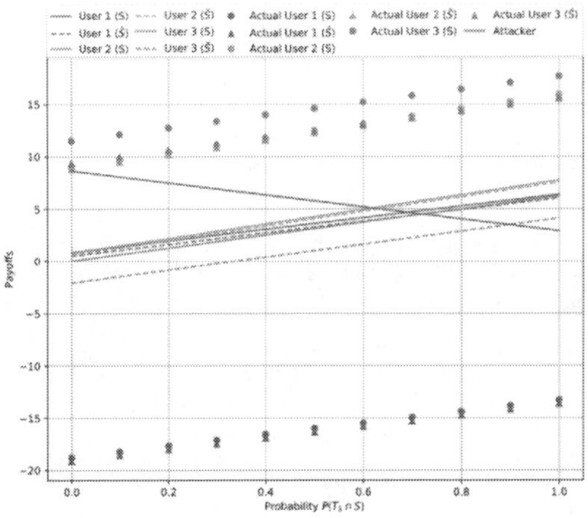

Fig. 11. Illustration of players' payoffs based on $P(T_1 \cap S)$ when $\varphi > (\theta + \delta) > R$ and $c_{m1} = 6.56$.

*payoff* $= -15.80 < 0$.

Scenario 10 [$\varphi > (\theta + \delta) > R$]: We choose $\varphi = 18; \theta = 3; \delta = 7; R = 5$. We analyze the payoffs of users and the attacker based on the probability $P(T_1 \cap S)$ regarding to the best maximin strategy ($c_{m1} = 6.56$). Figure 11 shows that the attacker payoff decreases linearly from 8.65 to 2.91. The payoffs of User 1, User 2, and User 3 increase linearly in the range of $-2.09$ to 7.75. Furthermore, the payoff of "Actual User 2" and "Actual User 3" increase linearly in the range of 7.49 to 17.29. We note that the payoffs of "Actual User 1" increases linearly from $-19.16$ to $-13.28$. Even with $P(T_1 \cap S) = 1$, the payoffs of "Actual User 1" remain negative.

Scenario 11 [$\varphi > (\theta + \delta) > R$]: We choose $\varphi = 18; \theta = 3; \delta = 7; R = 5; c_{m1} = 0$. Figure 12 shows that the attacker payoff decreases linearly from 8.65 to 2.91. Users' payoffs are all positive even though they decrease linearly. Furthermore, User 1 payoff $\geq$ attacker payoff when $P(T_1 \cap S) \geq 0.55$. We can also notice that the payoffs of User $i$ and "Actual User $i$"

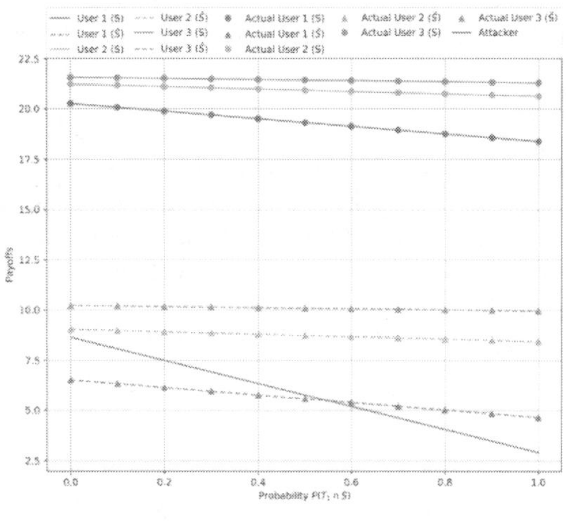

Fig. 12. Illustration of players' payoffs based on $P(T_1 \cap S)$ when $\varphi > (\theta + \delta) > R$ and $c_{m1} = 0$.

are similar (with $1 \leq i \leq 3$).

## V. Discussion

The analysis of the numerical results indicates that security investments and the reward for noticing security countermeasures may influence households to engage in cybersecurity awareness education. The numerical results related to the pure strategy Nash equilibrium show that households would take the cybersecurity awareness training and notice security countermeasures under two conditions. First, the smart home should provide original values and vital comfort, and the other is that the security rewards should be very significant. Thus, investigating and providing new frameworks for security rewards in smart homes is a research area that needs to be explored and addressed.

Regarding the results of mixed strategies, we can see that *Scenario 3* is the best option for households because they can minimize the security investment costs and get a positive payoff. However, as shown in Figure 10, if a rational adult (e.g., "Actual User 1") has to pay the monetary costs for every user, then minimizing the security investment costs would provide a negative payoff. Furthermore, Figure 11 shows that even though a rational adult notices security countermeasures (with $P(T_1 \cap S) = 1$), his payoff will remain negative. Therefore "Actual User 1" will not be satisfied with the security investment done, which may impact his decision to keep noticing security countermeasures and affect the security behaviors of the other users. To address this issue, we encourage government to support households by subsidizing the cybersecurity training costs. As presented in Figure 12, when the training costs are zero, the payoff of every user is positive. Thus, households will be more likely to notice security countermeasures. Note that the decrease of users' payoff could shed light on the need to encourage households constantly on the importance of noticing security behaviors.

It is worth noting that the results of this paper rely on the effectiveness of cybersecurity awareness programs. We have assumed that those programs provide the required information to households to be aware of and deal with most known cyberattacks. Therefore, one limitation of this study is due to the existence of unknown cyberattacks that will not be teaching in the cybersecurity awareness programs. Furthermore, we have made some assumptions such as those of Equations (1), (2), (3), and (4) which may not be realistic. Additional research on this matter is recommended. Moreover, this study provides many insights regarding the future of cybersecurity education programs. The numerical results show the importance of the parameters $\varphi$ and $R$. It would be highly appropriate for households to access tailored-service in smart homes. Thus, the comfort and benefit of living in such houses will encourage users to invest in cybersecurity to preserve their quality of life at home. Furthermore, providing households with tangible security rewards could also engage them in cybersecurity education programs. Our work also highlights the importance of developing specific and efficient programs for each category of households: children, adults, and senior citizens. Finally, we encourage public cybersecurity policy towards households security to provide free cybersecurity awareness training. Once the monetary costs are addressed, another challenge will be to reduce the time costs and make cybersecurity easier to learn and more intuitive for households.

## VI. Conclusion and Future Work

In this paper, we proposed a game-theoretic approach to analyze cybersecurity awareness cost-benefit toward designing efficient education programs for households security. The goal is to encourage home users to engage in cybersecurity awareness education by identifying the minimum security investment cost that satisfies households and compare households' payoffs and the attacker's payoffs given a cyberattack. We provide a normal-form game with four players: three home users, including a senior citizen, an adult, and a child, and one attacker. We determine the conditions to reach the pure and mixed Nash equilibria of the proposed game. The numerical results show that the quality of services provided in a smart home, the security rewards of taking cybersecurity awareness training and noticing security countermeasures, and the potential impacts of cyberattacks may affect the payoffs of households and the attacker. Our research finds that the increase of quality of services accessible in a smart home may motivate households to engage in cybersecurity awareness education. Furthermore, providing security rewards to households may help them raise and maintain a high level of security awareness.

Future work may extend the present study to more than three users and many attackers. More importantly, we will propose an evolutionary game-theoretic approach to study the evolution of real users' behaviors in the proposed game and provide more realistic results. We will also seek to provide a survey research to confirm the findings of this paper. This work may also encourage a deeper investigation into cybersecurity education programs to provide more efficient frameworks for households, including children, adults, and senior citizens. Furthermore, our work may inspire smart-home providers to develop high-quality, tailored services for households. Finally, future work may also investigate the reduction of time costs and the design of security rewards in smart homes.

## Acknowledgment

Part of this study was funded by the ICS-CoE Core Human Resources Development Program.

## References

[1] S. Hansche, "Designing a security awareness program: Part 1," *Information systems security*, vol. 9, no. 6, pp. 1–9, 2001.

[2] S. Furnell, M. Gennatou, and P. Haskell-Dowland, "A prototype tool for information security awareness and training," *Logistics Information Management*, vol. 15, pp. 352–357, 12 2002.

[3] D. Ki-Aries and S. Faily, "Persona-centred information security awareness," *Computers & Security*, vol. 70, pp. 663–674, 2017.

[4] M. R. Alam, M. B. I. Reaz, and M. A. M. Ali, "A review of smart homes—past, present, and future," *IEEE Transactions on Systems, Man, and Cybernetics, Part C (Applications and Reviews)*, vol. 42, no. 6, pp. 1190–1203, 2012.

[5] OWASP, "Internet of Things Top Ten," 2014.

[6] J. Ricci, F. Breitinger, and I. Baggili, "Survey results on adults and cybersecurity education," *Education and Information Technologies*, vol. 24, no. 1, pp. 231–249, 2019.

[7] J. D'Arcy, A. Hovav, and D. Galletta, "User awareness of security countermeasures and its impact on information systems misuse: A deterrence approach," *Information systems research*, vol. 20, no. 1, pp. 79–98, 2009.

[8] A. A. Al Shamsi, "Effectiveness of Cyber Security Awareness Program for young children: A Case Study in UAE," *International Journal of Information Technology and Language Studies*, vol. 3, no. 2, 2019.

[9] C. G. Blackwood-Brown, "An Empirical Assessment of Senior Citizens' Cybersecurity Awareness, Computer Self-Efficacy, Perceived Risk of Identity Theft, Attitude, and Motivation to Acquire Cybersecurity Skills," Ph.D. dissertation, Nova Southeastern University, 2018.

[10] H. Aldawood and G. Skinner, "Challenges of implementing training and awareness programs targeting cyber security social engineering," in *2019 Cybersecurity and Cyberforensics Conference (CCC)*. IEEE, 2019, pp. 111–117.

[11] W. Zeng, "A methodology for cost-benefit analysis of information security technologies," *Concurrency and Computation: Practice and Experience*, vol. 31, no. 7, p. e5004, 2019.

[12] Z. J. Zhang, W. He, W. Li, and M. Abdous, "Cybersecurity awareness training programs: a cost–benefit analysis framework," *Industrial Management & Data Systems*, vol. 121, pp. 613–636, 2021.

[13] H. Cavusoglu, S. Raghunathan, and W. T. Yue, "Decision-theoretic and game-theoretic approaches to it security investment," *Journal of Management Information Systems*, vol. 25, no. 2, pp. 281–304, 2008.

[14] W. Sun, X. Kong, D. He, and X. You, "Information security problem research based on game theory," in *2008 International Symposium on Electronic Commerce and Security*, 2008, pp. 554–557.

[15] X. Qian, X. Liu, J. Pei, and P. M. Pardalos, "A new game of information sharing and security investment between two allied firms," *International Journal of Production Research*, vol. 56, no. 12, pp. 4069–4086, 2018.

[16] Z. Zuo, Y. Fang, L. Liu, F. Fang, and X. Hu, "Research on information security cost based on game-theory," in *2013 IEEE 8th Conference on Industrial Electronics and Applications (ICIEA)*. IEEE, 2013, pp. 1435–1436.

[17] M. J. Osborne, *An introduction to game theory*. Oxford university press New York, 2004, vol. 3, no. 3.

# Cryptanalysis of RSA with Moduli N=p^r q Based on Coppersmith Method: A survey

Simeng Yuan, Wei Yu, Kunpeng Wang, Xiuxiu Li
*State Key Laboratory of Information Security, Institute of Information Engineering, CAS*
*School of Cyber Security, University of Chinese Academy of Sciences*
Beijing, China
emails: yuansimeng@iie.ac.cn, yuwei_1_yw@163.com, wangkunpeng@iie.ac.cn, lixiuxiu@iie.ac.cn

***Abstract*—This paper briefly summarizes the Coppersmith method, its extension strategy and lattice construction techniques. Then we describe several attacks on Rivest-Shamir-Adleman cryptosystem with moduli $N = p^r q$ based on Coppersmith method, including small exponent attacks, partial key exposure attacks, and factoring RSA moduli with partial known. A survey of recent progress for these three kinds of attacks, and general methods on how these attacks work are given.**

***Keywords*—*Coppersmith method; Takagi RSA; prime power RSA.***

## I. Introduction

RSA is one of the most widely used public key cryptosystems today. In the environment with limited resources, it may be slow for encryption and decryption, due to the modular operation of large integers. In order to speed up the operation, many RSA fast variants have been produced. One of the most important variants is the scheme proposed by Takagi [30] with moduli $N = p^r q$. Compared with the standard RSA scheme, Takagi RSA is more efficient in key generation and decryption. Another fast variant with moduli $N = p^r q$ is the prime power RSA. For Takagi RSA, the public exponent $e$ and the secret exponent $d$ satisfy

$$ed \equiv 1 \bmod (p-1)(q-1),$$

and for the prime power RSA, $e$ and $d$ satisfy

$$ed \equiv 1 \bmod p^{r-1}(p-1)(q-1).$$

These fast variants are usually used in smart cards and programs with higher speed.

With the development of lattice theory, the famous algorithm proposed by Lenstra, Lenstra and Lovász (LLL algorithm), and lattice basis reduction technique has become an important tool for cryptanalysis of RSA and its variants. In 1996, Coppersmith proposed so called Coppersmith algorithm to find small roots of single variable modular equation [7] or the double variable integer equation [6]. The core idea of this algorithm is to convert the modular equation or integer equation with large norm into integer equations with small norm by lattice basis reduction algorithm such as LLL algorithm, and the roots of the original equation can be found over integers. In the above process, the construction of the lattice basis is the most critical part. Howgrave-Graham [16] simplified the work of [7], and put forward a more straightforward lattice basis construction method, which can be generalized to the case of multivariable modular equation. Since then, a large number of scholars have used this lattice analysis method to analyze the security of RSA. The method has also continued to be extended, and gradually form the current Coppersmith method. In 2006, Jochemsz and May [19] proposed a general strategy for multivariate modular equations and integer equations. They gave a method to obtain a triangular matrix when one constructs lattice basis. In the case of multivariable equations, the methods mentioned above are based on a heuristic assumption that the reduced basis output by LLL algorithm is algebraically independent.

In order to get a better lattice, there are many lattice basis construction techniques, of which the two most widely used techniques are substitution technique and unraveled linearization technique. Substitution technique was first used by Durfee and Nguyen [10]. According to the RSA equation $ed = 1 + k(p-1)(q-1)$, they constructed a three variable modular equation $f(x, y, z) = x(N + 1 + y + z) + 2 \pmod e$ with roots $(x_0, y_0, z_0) = (k, -p, -q)$. Knowing $N = pq$, they replaced all occurrences of the monomial $yz$ with $N$, when constructing the lattice. By this substitution technique, they reduced the number of variables and optimized the result of lattice analysis. Unraveled linearization technique was first proposed by Herrmann and May [14]. By exploiting the implicit algebraic relationships in equations, the construction of lattice can be simplified and the result of lattice analysis can be improved.

In this paper, we focus on RSA with moduli $N = p^r q$, and survey the applications of Coppersmith method in the cryptanalysis of it.

The remainder of this paper is organized as follows. In Section II, we describe the theory and steps of Coppersmith method, and summarize Jochemsz-May strategy and unraveled linearization. The general methods of small exponent attacks on RSA with moduli $N = p^r q$ are given in Section III. We conclude the partial key exposure attacks in Section IV, and the methods of factoring RSA moduli with partial known in Section V. Section VI gives the development suggestions.

## II. Coppersmith Method

Before describing the Coppersmith method, we first revise the concept of lattices and LLL algorithm. Let $\boldsymbol{b_1}, \ldots, \boldsymbol{b_n} \in$

$\mathbb{Z}^\omega$ be linearly independent row vectors. The set of all integer linear combinations of $\boldsymbol{b_1}, \ldots, \boldsymbol{b_n}$ compose lattice, which is written as

$$L(\boldsymbol{b_1}, \ldots, \boldsymbol{b_n}) = \left\{ \sum_{j=1}^{n} x_j \boldsymbol{b_j} : x_j \in \mathbb{Z} \right\}.$$

We write $n$ the rank of the lattice and $\omega$ the dimension of the lattice. The matrix $B \in \mathbb{Z}^{n \times \omega}$ consisting of $\boldsymbol{b_1}, \ldots, \boldsymbol{b_n}$ is a basis matrix of lattice $L$. We call these lattices full-rank when $n = \omega$. The determinant of $L$ is denoted as $\det(L) = \sqrt{\det(BB^T)}$. In order to find short vectors on lattices, Lenstra, Lenstra and Lovász proposed the LLL algorithm [20].

**Lemma 1 (LLL).** $L$ is a $\omega$-dimensional lattice, and the LLL algorithm can output a reduced basis vectors $\boldsymbol{v_1}, \ldots, \boldsymbol{v_\omega}$ satisfying

$$\|\boldsymbol{v_i}\| \leq 2^{\frac{\omega(\omega-1)}{4(\omega-i+1)}} \det(L)^{\frac{1}{\omega-i+1}}, \text{ for } 1 \leq i \leq \omega.$$

The time complexity of LLL algorithm is polynomial in $\omega$ and the bitsize of input.

### A. Coppersmith Method

Coppersmith [7] described the method to get small root of modular equations based on LLL algorithm. Then, the sufficient condition for Coppersmith method was given by Howgrave-Graham [16].

**Lemma 2 (Howgrave-Graham).** Let $g(x_1, \ldots, x_n) \in \mathbb{Z}[x_1, \ldots, x_n]$ be a polynomial, which has at most $\delta$ monomials. Let $p$, $m$ be positive integers. Suppose that

1.$g(\widetilde{x}_1, \ldots, \widetilde{x}_n) \equiv 0 \pmod{p^m}$, where $|\widetilde{x}_1| < X_1, \ldots, |\widetilde{x}_n| < X_n$,

2.$\|g(x_1X_1, \ldots, x_nX_n)\| < \frac{p^m}{\sqrt{\delta}}$.

Then, $g(\widetilde{x}_1, \ldots, \widetilde{x}_n) = 0$ holds over integers.

Therefore, the modular equation can be converted into $n$ integer equations, if these $n$ short vectors output by LLL algorithm satisfy Lemma 2, that is

$$\|\boldsymbol{v_i}\| \leq 2^{\frac{\omega(\omega-1)}{4(\omega-i+1)}} \det(L)^{\frac{1}{\omega-i+1}} < \frac{p^m}{\sqrt{\delta}}, \text{ for } 1 \leq i \leq \omega.$$

Ignoring the small items, the condition becomes $\det(L) < p^{m\omega}$. One can use Gröbner base or a resultant of these $n$ integer equations to find all roots.

Next, we will illustrate the general steps of Coppersmith method. Take the solution of univariate modular equation for example. Let $f(x)$ be a univariate modular polynomial of degree $\delta$

$$f(x) = x^\delta + a_{\delta-1}x^{\delta-1} + \ldots + a_1x + a_0 \pmod{p}.$$

The root of $f(x_0) \equiv 0 \pmod{p}$, is bound by $X$. And the steps of Coppersmith method are as follows.

- Construct $\omega$ shift polynomials $g_1(x), \ldots, g_\omega(x)$, which have the same small roots $x_0$ modulo $p^m$, and $m, t$ is positive integers (which can be optimized). Shift polynomials can be constructed in the following way
  $g_i(x) = x^ip^{m-j}f^j(x)$ for $i = 0, \ldots, \delta - 1, j = 0, \ldots, m-1$,
  $g_{\delta+i}(x) = x^if^m(x)$ for $i = 0, \ldots, t-1$.
- Use the coefficient vectors of $g_i(xX)$ and $g_{\delta+i}(xX)$ to construct a lattice basis.
- Apply LLL algorithm to the lattice basis, and we get a short vector $\boldsymbol{v}$, corresponding a polynomial $v(x)$. Since the vectors on the lattice are integer linear combination of the lattice basis vectors, the polynomials $v(x)$ is integer linear combination of $g_i(x)$ and $g_{\delta+i}(x)$, with the same small roots $x_0$ modulo $p^m$.
- If $\boldsymbol{v}$ is short enough to satisfy Lemma 2, the modular equation can be converted to an integer equation. And we can solve it over integers

For the case of multivariate modular equation $f(x_1, \ldots, x_n) \equiv 0 \bmod p$, the steps are similar. Notice that the dimension of the lattice should be larger than the number of variables, which means $\omega > n$. And the shift polynomials can be defined as

$$g_{i_1,\ldots,i_n}(x_1, \ldots, x_n) := x_1^{i_1}, \ldots, x_n^{i_n}p^{m-j}f^j$$

The parameters $i_1, \ldots, i_n$ and $j$ are selected based on different cases.

The most time-consuming part of Coppersmith method is LLL algorithm, and it works in polynomial time. Therefore, Coppersmith method also works in polynomial time.

### B. Jochemsz-May Strategy

In order to optimize the bound of desired roots, Jochemsz and May [19] proposed a general strategy for constructing full rank lattices and gave the methods to solve modular equations and integer equations with arbitrary variables. Jochemsz-May strategy is the best method for finding small roots of integer equations at present. Next, we will describe Jochemsz-May strategy to solve small roots of multivariate integer equations.

Let $f(x_1, \ldots, x_n) = \sum f_{i_1,\ldots,i_n}x_1^{i_1} \cdots x_n^{i_n}$ be a monic polynomial with roots $(\widetilde{x}_1, \ldots, \widetilde{x}_n)$ which are bound by $(X_1, \ldots X_n)$. First, we give some notations. Denote $l_j$ as the maximum exponent of $x_j$ in $f(x_1, \ldots, x_n)$. Take an integer $W$ as large as possible satisfying that $W \leq \|f(x_1, \ldots, x_n)\|_\infty$. Define an integer $R := WX_1^{l_1(m-1)+t}\prod_{j=2}^{k}X_j^{l_j(m-1)}$ ($m$ and $t = O(m)$ are positive integers, which will be optimized later). Then, we define two sets

$$S := \bigcup_{0 \leq j \leq t} \{x_1^{i_1+j}x_2^{i_2} \cdots x_k^{i_k} \,|\, x_1^{i_1}x_2^{i_2} \cdots x_k^{i_k} \text{ is a monomial of } f^{m-1}\}$$

$$M := \{\text{monomial of } x_1^{i_1} \cdots x_k^{i_k} \cdot f \mid x_1^{i_1} \cdots x_k^{i_k} \in S\}$$

The next steps are similar to the original Coppersmith method. 1) Construct a set of shift polynomials with the same roots $(\widetilde{x}_1, \ldots, \widetilde{x}_n)$ modulo $R$. 2) Construct lattice by the coefficient vectors of the shift polynomials. 3) Apply LLL algorithm to get $n$ short vectors. 4) Obtain $n$ integer equations corresponding these $n$ short vectors, and solve these integer equations. The selection of shift polynomials is different from the original Coppersmith method.

$$g : x_1^{i_1} \cdots x_k^{i_k} \cdot f \cdot X_1^{l_1(m-1)+t-i_1} \prod_{j=2}^{k} X_j^{l_j(m-1)-i_j},$$
$$\text{for } x_1^{i_1} \cdots x_k^{i_k} \in S$$

$$g' : x_1^{i_1} \cdots x_k^{i_k} \cdot R, \text{ for } x_1^{i_1} \cdots x_k^{i_k} \in M \backslash S$$

And the condition to get all small roots becomes

$$\prod_{j=1}^{k} X_j^{s_j} < W^{|S|} \text{ for } s_j = \sum_{x_1^{i_1} \ldots x_k^{i_k} \in M \backslash S} i_j$$

### C. Unraveled linearization

Herrmann and May [14], combining the method of linearization and Coppersmith method, introduced a new technique called unraveled linearization.

Recall the work of Boneh and Durfee [3]. They transformed the RSA moduli factorization problem into solving the small inverse problem. Specifically, they obtained an equation $ed + k(N+1-p-q) = 1$ from RSA equation $ed \equiv 1 \bmod \varphi(N)$. Let $A = (N+1)$ and $s = (-p-q)$. Then, they got $k(A+s) = 1 \bmod e$, where $k, s$ are unknown. The RSA system can be completely broken by solving small roots of the modular equation

$$f(x, y) = 1 + x(A+y) = 0 \bmod e.$$

Let $e = N^{\alpha}, d = N^{\beta}$. The small roots $(x_0, y_0) = (-k, s)$ satisfy

$$|x_0| = |k| = \frac{ed-1}{\varphi(N)} < \frac{ed}{\frac{1}{2}N} = 2N^{\alpha+\beta-1} = X,$$
$$|y_0| = |-s| = p + q < 2N^{\frac{1}{2}} = Y.$$

For a fixed integer $m$, Boneh and Durfee constructed two sets of shift polynomials, such that the roots are the same as $(x_0, y_0)$ modulo $e^m$.

$$g_{i,j}(x, y) = x^i e^{m-j} f^j \text{ for } i = 0, \ldots, m-j,\ j = 0, \ldots, m$$
$$h_{i,j}(x, y) = y^i e^{m-j} f^j \text{ for } i = 1, \ldots, t,\ j = 0, \ldots, m$$

Next, we use a example to illustrate the construction of lattice basis in [3]. Let $m = 2, t = 1$, and the lattice basis matrix consisting of the coefficient vectors of $g_{i,j}(xX, yY)$ and $h_{i,j}(xX, yY)$ is as Figure 1.

According to Coppersmith method, the equation can be solved under the condition $\det(L) < e^{m\omega}$ ($\omega$ is dimension of the lattice). The elements on the diagonal should be as small as possible to make this condition easier to meet. On average, the diagonal elements less than $e^m$ are helpful. We call the shift polynomials helpful if the diagonal elements introduced by them are less than $e^m$. For the sake of better lattice and superior result, Boneh and Durfee [3] excluded the unhelpful polynomials $ye^2$ and $yef$. Consequently, the lattice basis matrix was no longer triangular, and it is difficult to derive the determinant formula for general $m$ and $t$. They

| | $1$ | $x$ | $x^2$ | $xy$ | $x^2y$ | $x^2y^2$ | $y$ | $xy^2$ | $x^2y^3$ |
|---|---|---|---|---|---|---|---|---|---|
| $g_{0,0} = e^2$ | $e^2$ | | | | | | | | |
| $g_{1,0} = xe^2$ | | $e^2X$ | | | | | | | |
| $g_{2,0} = x^2e^2$ | | | $e^2X^2$ | | | | | | |
| $g_{0,1} = ef$ | $e$ | $eAX$ | | $eXY$ | | | | | |
| $g_{1,1} = xef$ | | $eX$ | $eAX^2$ | | $eX^2Y$ | | | | |
| $g_{0,2} = f^2$ | $1$ | $2AX$ | $A^2X^2$ | $2XY$ | $2AX^2Y$ | $X^2Y^2$ | | | |
| $h_{1,0} = ye^2$ | | | | | | | $e^2Y$ | | |
| $h_{1,1} = yef$ | | | | $eAXY$ | | | $eY$ | $eXY^2$ | |
| $h_{1,2} = yf^2$ | | | | $2AXY$ | $A^2X^2Y$ | $2AX^2Y^2$ | $Y$ | $2XY^2$ | $X^2Y^3$ |

Figure 1. Lattice basis for $m = 2, t = 1$.

introduced a technique called geometric progressive matrix to solve this problem.Their result shows that one can factor the modulus $N$ in polynomial time, when $d < N^{0.292}$. So far, no other attack improve this bound.

Herrmann and May applied the unraveled linearization technique [15], and got the same result as [3]. They replaced $xy + 1$ by $u$, and changed the original polynomial $f(x, y) = 1 + x(A+y) = 0 \pmod{e}$ into a linear polynomial $\hat{f}(x, u) = u + Ax = 0 \pmod{e}$. They used the new polynomial $\hat{f}(x, u)$ to construct shift polynomials in the similar way. They replaced $xy$ by $u - 1$, $x^2y$ by $ux - x$, and $uxy$ by $u^2 - u$. Then, for $m = 2, t = 1$, the lattice basis matrix is as Figure 2.

| | $1$ | $x$ | $x^2$ | $u$ | $ux$ | $u^2$ | $y$ | $uy$ | $u^2y$ |
|---|---|---|---|---|---|---|---|---|---|
| $g_{0,0} = e^2$ | $e^2$ | | | | | | | | |
| $g_{1,0} = xe^2$ | | $e^2X$ | | | | | | | |
| $g_{2,0} = x^2e^2$ | | | $e^2X^2$ | | | | | | |
| $g_{0,1} = ef$ | | $eAX$ | | $eU$ | | | | | |
| $g_{1,1} = xef$ | | | $eAX^2$ | | $eUX$ | | | | |
| $g_{0,2} = f^2$ | | | $A^2X^2$ | | $2AUX$ | $U^2$ | | | |
| $h_{1,0} = ye^2$ | | | | | | | $e^2Y$ | | |
| $h_{1,1} = yef$ | $-eA$ | | | $eAU$ | | | | $eUY$ | |
| $h_{1,2} = yf^2$ | | $-A^2X$ | | $-2AU$ | $A^2UX$ | $2AU^2$ | | | $U^2Y$ |

Figure 2. Lattice basis for $m = 2, t = 1$.

It is also a triangular matrix after removing the unhelpful polynomials $ye^2$ and $ye\hat{f}$, because $y\hat{f}^2$ only introduces one monomial $u^2y$.

Although Herrmann and May [15] did not improve the bound $d < N^{0.292}$, they simplified the calculation of determinant by unraveled linearization technique.

### D. Factor RSA Moduli by Coppersmith Method

Coppersmith method is a kind of method to solve the small roots of modular equations or integer equations, which can be construted from RSA equations. Due to special parameter selection (small private key exponent $d$) or partial information (partial private key $d$ or partial $p$) exposured, the roots have upper bound and we just need to find all the roots in a relatively small range. Therefore, RSA is broken by Coppersmith method.

Next, we will discuss how to construct the equations and use Coppersmith method to solve them in three specific cases including private key exponent $d$ small, partial private key $d$ known and partial information of $p$ known. Suppose that the size of $p$ and $q$ are the same. Let $e = N^{\alpha}, d = N^{\beta}$. For partial key exposure attacks, we write known partial of $d$ as $\tilde{d}$. When most significant bits (MSBs) are known, write unknown bits as $d_0 = d - \tilde{d}$ such that $|d_0| < N^{\delta}$. For known least significant bits (LSBs) of the private exponent, denote $d_1$ as unknown bits, and $d = d_1 M + \tilde{d}$, where $M = 2^{\lfloor(\beta-\delta)\log N\rfloor}$.

## III. Small Exponent Attacks

Wiener [33] proposed an attack on RSA with small decryption exponent. Their algorithm was based on continued fraction, and they proved that $d$ can be recovered in polynomial time under the condition $d < N^{0.25}$. Boneh and Durfee [3] improved Wiener's bound to $d < N^{0.292}$ based on Coppersmith method. Next, we mainly discuss the small decryption exponent attack on RSA with moduli $N = p^r q$.

### A. Attack on Takagi RSA

Recall the equation of Takagi RSA

$$ed \equiv 1 \bmod (p-1)(q-1).$$

There is an integer $k$ satisfying

$$ed - k\,(p-1)\,(q-1) = 1$$

where $k, p, q$ and $d$ are unknown. Then, we construct a three-variable modular polynomial

$$f\,(x, y, z) = x\,(y-1)\,(z-1) + 1 = 0 \pmod{e}.$$

The roots $(x_0, y_0, z_0) = (k, p, q)$ of the equation have upper bounds

$$|x_0| = |k| = \frac{ed-1}{(p-1)(q-1)} < \frac{2ed}{pq} < N^{\alpha+\beta-\frac{2}{(r+1)}} = X,$$
$$|y_0| = |p| < 2N^{1/(r+1)} = Y,$$
$$|z_0| = |q| < 2N^{1/(r+1)} = Z.$$

Then, we use the Coppersmith method to find the small roots. Due to the additional algebraic relations $N = p^r q$, we use substitution technique (replace each occurrence of $y^r z$ by $N$ to construct the lattice) to optimize the lattice basis. Unraveled linearization technique can also be used to remove unhelpful polynomials and construct triangular matrices which are easier to analyze.

Itoh et al. [18] proved that $d$ can be recovered in polynomial time when $d \le N^{\frac{2-\sqrt{2}}{r+1}}$. Their result is based on geometric progressive matrix. The attack on standard RSA described by Boneh and Durfee [3] is a special case of $r = 1$. Takayasu and Kunihiro [32] obtained the same results based on unraveled linearization technique. They use linearization $u_1 = 1 + xy$ and $u_2 = 1 + xz$ to remove the unhelpful polynomials and construct a triangular matrix which simplify the calculation.

### B. Attack on Prime Power RSA

Recall the equation of prime power RSA

$$ed \equiv 1 \bmod p^{r-1}(p-1)(q-1).$$

There is an integer $k$ satisfying

$$ed - kp^{r-1}\,(p-1)\,(q-1) = 1$$

where $k$, $p$, $q$ and $d$ are unknown. A three-variable modular polynomial is obtained

$$f\,(x, y, z) = 1 + xy^{r-1}(y-1)(z-1) = 0 \pmod{e}.$$

The roots $(x_0, y_0, z_0) = (k, p, q)$ are bound by $X = N^{\alpha+\beta-1}, Y = Z = 2N^{1/(r+1)}$.

In the similar way, we use Coppersmith method to find the roots of the modular equation and factor $N$.

Takagi [30] applied Wiener's attack on prime power RSA and proved that one can recover $d$ in polynomial time under the condition $d \le N^{\frac{1}{2(r+1)}}$. Later, May [25] gave two small exponent attacks using Coppersmith method. The first attack works when $d \le N^{\frac{r}{(r+1)^2}}$ for $r \ge 2$, based on the result of [5]. The second attack works when $d \le N^{1-\frac{4r}{(r+1)^2}}$ for $r \ge 2$, based on solving univariate modular equation. Sarkar [27] studied the case of $r = 2$, and showed that $N$ can be factored in polynomial time when $d < N^{0.395}$. It improves the bound $d < N^{0.22}$ in [25]. Lu et al. [24] put forward three algorithms for solving three types of linear equations. The first one is multivariate linear equation modulo an unknown divisor $p^v$ for a known composite integer $N$ ($N \equiv 0 \bmod p^u, u \ge 1$). As an application of the algorithm, they proved that one can factor $N$ when $d < N^{\frac{r(r-1)}{(r+1)^2}}$, which improves the work of [25]. Sarkar [28] further extended the result of [27]. They studied the case of $2 < r < 8$, and improved previous works when $r = 3, 4$.

Similar to modular equation, one can obtain integer equations

$$f\,(x_1, x_2, x_3, x_4) = 1 - ex_1 + x_2(x_3-1)(x_4-1).$$

from Takagi RSA, and

$$f\,(x_1, x_2, x_3, x_4) = 1 - ex_1 + x_2 x_3^{r-1}(x_3-1)(x_4-1).$$

from prime power RSA.

Then, we can follow the steps of Jochemsz-May strategy to solve small roots of the integer equations. Takayasu and Kunihiro analyzed the case of solving integer equation base on Jochemsz-May strategy. Their results [32] show that using modular equation and unraveled linearization technique can analyze a wider range than using integer equation and Jochemsz-May strategy. Therefore, the modular equation combined with unraveled linearization can usually obtain better results.

### C. Attack on RSA with Modulus $N = p^r q^s$

Lim et al. [21] proposed a RSA scheme with modulus $N = p^r q^s$. They showed that the scheme is even more efficient. Lu et al. [22] extended small exponent attack to RSA with moduli $N = p^r q^s$. They analyzed both variants satisfying $ed \equiv 1 \bmod (p-1)(q-1)$ and $ed \equiv 1 \bmod p^{r-1}(p-1)(q-1)$. For the first variant, they used the same modular equation as the attack on Takagi RSA. Note that they replaced $y^r z^s$ with $N$ instead of $y^r z$. Finally, they proved that $N$ can be factored in polynomial time when $d \leq N^{\frac{7-2\sqrt{7}}{3(r+s)}}$. For the second variant, they used an univariable modulus equation. They took $d$ as the variable and obtained a modular equation

$$f(x) = (E - x) \bmod p^{r-1} q^{s-1}$$

where $E$ is the inverse of $e$ modulo $N$. Finally, they proved that $N$ can be factored in polynomial time when $d < N^{1-(3r+s)(r+s)^{-2}}$.

## IV. Partial Key Exposure Attacks

In 1998, Boneh, Durfee and Frankel [4] studied partial private key exposure attack on RSA with moduli $N = pq$. They pointed out that if one knows a quarter bit of the private, it is enough to recover the whole private key, when the encryption exponent is small. More private key bits are required for recovering private key with a larger encryption exponent. However, their attacks only work when $e < N^{0.5}$. Subsequently, Blömer and May [2] improved the result of [4], expanding the range of $e$ from $N^{0.5}$ to $N^{0.725}$. When the LSBs are known, they proposed an algorithm with better result $e < N^{0.875}$. Soon afterwards, Ernst et al. [11] proposed some attacks for known MSBs or LSBs of the private exponent. Their work first considers the case of full size $e$. Aono [1] proposed an optimized method for lattice construction, and use it to attack RSA with small $d$ and known LSBs of $d$. The method is theoretically more effective than the previous partial private key exposure attack. Later, Takayasu and Kunihiro [31] combined unraveled linearization technique and improved previous works. They gave the attacks with known MSBs of $d < N^{0.5625}$ or LSBs of $d < N^{0.368}$. Recently, Suzuki, Takayasu and Kunihiro [29] extended the work of [31] and proposed an attack when both MSBs and LSBs of $d$ are known. At the same time, some scholars have also studied private key exposure attacks of other RSA variants. Next, we mainly discuss private key exposure attacks on RSA with modulus $N = p^r q$.

### A. Attack on Takagi RSA

If we know the MSBs of $d$, and the equation of Takagi RSA is

$$e\left(\widetilde{d} + d_0\right) = 1 + k(p-1)(q-1)$$

where $d_0, k, p, q$ are unknown. A four variable modular polynomial is obtained

$$f(x_1, x_2, x_3, x_4) = ex_1 + x_2(x_3 - 1)(x_4 - 1) + 1$$

The roots $(\widetilde{x}_1, \widetilde{x}_2, \widetilde{x}_3, \widetilde{x}_4) = (-d_0, k, p, q)$ of $f(\widetilde{x}_1, \widetilde{x}_2, \widetilde{x}_3, \widetilde{x}_4) = 0 \pmod{e\widetilde{d}}$ are bound by $X_1 = N^{\delta}, X_2 = 2N^{\alpha+\beta-2/(r+1)}, X_3 = X_4 = 2N^{1/(r+1)}$.

Suppose the LSBs of $d$ are exposured, and the equation of Takagi RSA can be rewritten as

$$e\left(d_1 M + \widetilde{d}\right) = 1 + k(p-1)(q-1).$$

We can construct a three variable modular polynomial

$$f(x, y, z) = x(y-1)(z-1) + \left(1 - e\widetilde{d}\right).$$

The roots $(x_0, y_0, z_0) = (k, p, q)$ of $f(x_0, y_0, z_0) = 0 \pmod{eM}$ are bound by $X = 2N^{\alpha+\beta-2/(r+1)}, Y = Z = 2N^{1/(r+1)}$.

Thus, the problem of recovering $d$ is converted to solving modular equation.

We can also use the integer equation. Assuming we know some bits of $d$ regardless of the MSBs or LSBs. Write known bits as $\widetilde{d}$, and the equation of Takagi RSA is

$$e\left(\widetilde{d} + \left(d - \widetilde{d}\right)\right) = 1 + k(p-1)(q-1).$$

Construct a four variable integer equation

$$f(x_1, x_2, x_3, x_4) = 1 - e\widetilde{d} + eMx_1 + x_2(x_3 - 1)(x_4 - 1) + 1$$

where $M = 1$ for known MSBs, and $M = 2^{\lfloor(\beta-\delta)\log N\rfloor}$ for known LSBs. And the roots $(\widetilde{x}_1, \widetilde{x}_2, \widetilde{x}_3, \widetilde{x}_4) = (-d_0, k, p, q)$ are bound by $X_1 = N^{\delta}, X_2 = 2N^{\alpha+\beta-2/(r+1)}, X_3 = X_4 = 2N^{1/(r+1)}$. Thus, the problem of recovering $d$ is converted to solving integer equation. Then, we can use Jochemsz-May Strategy to find the roots.

In 2014, Huang et al. [17] studied partial key exposure attacks on Takagi RSA. They used the lattice basis structure similar to [18] and gave the attacks with known MSBs, known LSBs and known some bits in the middle of the private exponent known. Their results show that one can factor $N$ in polynomial time giving about $(1 - \frac{\delta}{\beta})$-fraction of MSBs or continuous bits in middle of $d$ when

$$\delta \leq \frac{7}{4(r+1)} - \frac{1}{4}\sqrt{\frac{24(\alpha+\beta)}{r+1} - \frac{39}{(r+1)^2}} - \epsilon.$$

For known LSBs, they proved that one can factor $N$ in polynomial time giving about $(1 - \frac{\delta}{\beta})$-fraction of LSBs of $d$ when

$$\delta \leq \frac{5}{3(r+1)} - \frac{2}{3}\sqrt{\frac{3(\alpha+\beta)}{r+1} - \frac{5}{(r+1)^2}} - \epsilon.$$

Later, Takayasu and Kuniriho [32] used integer equation and modular equation respectively to improve the results in [17] for known MSBs and LSBs.

### B. Attack on Prime Power RSA

For prime power RSA, the method to recover $d$ is analogous to Takagi RSA. In addition, because $p^{r-1}$ is in prime power RSA equation, we get a polynomial modulo $p^{r-1}$. Suppose we know some bits of $d$ regardless of the MSBs or LSBs. Write known bits as $\widetilde{d}$ such that $\left|d - \widetilde{d}\right| < N^{\delta}$, and the equation of prime power RSA can be rewritten as

$$f(x) = eMx + e\widetilde{d} - 1 \pmod{p^{r-1}}$$

where $M = 1$ for known MSBs, and $M = 2^{\lfloor(\beta-\delta)\log N\rfloor}$ for known LSBs. The root $x_0$ is bound by $X = N^{\delta}$. Thus, the problem of recovering $d$ is converted to solving univariate modular equation. We use Coppersmith method to find the root.

May [25] studied partial private key exposure attack on prime power RSA. They extended two small decryption exponent attacks on prime power RSA to partial private key exposure attack, and proved that one can factor $N$ in polynomial time giving about $\min\{1 - \frac{r}{(r+1)^2}, \frac{4r}{(r+1)^2}\}$-fraction of MSBs or LSBs. Later, Esgin et al. [12] extended the small decryption exponent attack on prime power RSA in [27] to partial private key exposure attack. Sarkar [28] gave the partial private key exposure attack when $r < 8$ and $d < N^{\frac{1}{r+1} + \frac{3r-2\sqrt{3r+3}+3}{3(r+1)}}$.

## V. Factoring RSA Moduli with partial Known

In this section, we will describe attacks on RSA when partial bits of moduli $N$ are known by side channel analysis or other ways. As early as 1985, Rivest and Shamir [26] have analyzed this problem. They used the method of integer programming to factor $N = pq$ in the case of two thirds of the consecutive bits of $p$ known. Then, Coppersmith [6] factored $N$ based on the lattice analysis method when half of the consecutive bits of $p$ are known. Herrmann and May [13] first considered the situation that known bits are inconsecutive, and extended the problem to factor $N$ with $n$ blocks bits known. They proved that one could factor $N$ when know 70% of random bits of $p$.

For the RSA scheme with modulus $N = p^r q$, Boneh, Durfee and Howgrave-Graham [5] showed that one can factor $N$ when know $\frac{1}{r+1}$-fraction of the MSBs bits of $p$. Their basic idea is to guess the high bits of $p$, and calculate the entire $p$. Let the high bits of $p$ as known $P$ and the low bits as a variable $x$. Then, we get a univariate modular equation

$$f(x) = (P + x)^r \bmod p^r.$$

The small root can be found by Coppersmith method. Lu et al. [23] extend the problem to the case of $n$ unknown bit blocks rather than a consecutive block. Their results show that the modulus $N$ can be factored when $\frac{\ln(r+1)}{r}$-fraction of random bits of $p$ are known.

Subsequently, Coron et al. [8] extended the attack of [5] to RSA with modulus $N = p^r q^s$. They used

$$\begin{cases} r = u \cdot \alpha + a \\ s = u \cdot \beta + b \end{cases}$$

And skillfully converted $N = p^r q^s$ into $N = P^u Q$, where $P := p^{\alpha} q^{\beta}, Q := p^a q^b$. Next, $N$ can be factored based on [5]. Their results show that when $r$ or $s$ is greater than $(\log p)^3$, $N$ can be factored in polynomial time.

Lu et al. [22] also discussed the security of RSA with modulus $N = p^r q^s$. They studied the case of known LSBs of $p$, and proposed two attacks, modulo $p$ and modulo $pq$. They showed that when know $\min\{\frac{s}{r+s}, \frac{2(r-s)}{r+s}\}$ of the bits of $p$, one can factor $N$ in polynomial time. When $2r > 3s$, the attack modulo $p$ is better than modulo $pq$.

Later, Coron and Zeitoun [9] took advantage of Bézout identity and got a new relationship

$$\alpha \cdot s - \beta \cdot r = 1.$$

They converted $N = p^r q^s$ to $N = P^r q$, where $P := p^{\alpha} q^{\beta}$. Then, the results of [5] was used to factor $N$, which improved the result of [8]. That is, when $r \geq \log p$, $N$ can be factored in polynomial time.

## VI. Conclusion

Coppersmith method is a very important tool in RSA cryptanalysis. We survey the application of Coppersmith method in RSA with modulus $N = p^r q$ from three aspects, including small exponent attack, partial key exposure attack and factoring RSA moduli with partial known. These three types of attacks usually rely on special parameter selection. Therefore, the selection of parameters needs to be more careful to avoid the above attacks.

For the three attacks discussed in this paper, adding more helpful polynomials and eliminate unhelpful polynomials to construct lattice basis are the key to improve the attacks, which means to factor $N$ with less information known. In addition, there are other attacks on RSA with moduli $N = p^r q$, which are mentioned in [34] and [35].

The crux of Coppersmith method is how to transform the problem of solving modular equation or integer equation into a short vector problem on lattices. In other words, the construction of the lattice basis is the most critical step. For now, Jochemsz-May strategy is the best general strategy for solving multivariate integer equation. A triangular matrix can be constructed easily by Jochemsz-May strategy. However, for some special algebraic structures, Jochemsz-May strategy does not always get the best results. We need to exploit the implicit algebraic relationships to construct a better lattice basis. The work of [32] shows that modular equations combined with unraveled technique usually obtain better results than integer equation based on Jochemsz-May Strategy. The construction of a better lattice basis and optimization of the results still have room for improvement.

## References

[1] Y. Aono, "A new lattice construction for partial key exposure attack for RSA," In Public Key Cryptography - PKC 2009, volume 5443 of Lecture Notes in Computer Science, pp. 34–53, Springer, 2009.

[2] J. Blömer and A. May, "New partial key exposure attacks on RSA," In Advances in Cryptology - CRYPTO 2003, 23rd Annual International Cryptology Conference, volume 2729 of Lecture Notes in Computer Science, pp. 27–43, Springer, 2003.

[3] D. Boneh and G. Durfee, "Cryptanalysis of RSA with private key $d$ less than $N^{0.292}$," In Advances in Cryptology - EUROCRYPT 1999, volume 1592 of Lecture Notes in Computer Science, pp. 1–11, Springer, 1999.

[4] D. Boneh, G. Durfee, and Y. Frankel, "An attack on RSA given a small fraction of the private key bits," In Advances in Cryptology - ASIACRYPT 1998, volume 1514 of Lecture Notes in Computer Science, pp. 25–34, Springer, 1998.

[5] D. Boneh, G. Durfee, and N. Howgrave-Graham, "Factoring $N = p^r q$ for large $r$," In Advances in Cryptology - CRYPTO 1999, volume 1666 of Lecture Notes in Computer Science, pp. 326–337, Springer, 1999.

[6] D. Coppersmith, "Finding a small root of a bivariate integer equation; factoring with high bits known," In Advances in Cryptology - EUROCRYPT 1996, volume 1070 of Lecture Notes in Computer Science, pp. 178–189, Springer, 1996.

[7] D. Coppersmith, "Finding a small root of a univariate modular equation," In Advances in Cryptology - EUROCRYPT 1996, volume 1070 of Lecture Notes in Computer Science, pp. 155–165, Springer, 1996.

[8] J. Coron, J. Faugère, G. Renault, and R. Zeitoun, "Factoring $n = p^r q^s$ for large $r$ and $s$," In Topics in Cryptology - CT-RSA 2016, volume 9610 of Lecture Notes in Computer Science, pp. 448–464, Springer, 2016.

[9] J. Coron and R. Zeitoun, "Improved factorization of $n = p^r q^s$," In Topics in Cryptology - CT-RSA 2018, volume 10808 of Lecture Notes in Computer Science, pp. 65–79, Springer, 2018.

[10] G. Durfee and P. Q. Nguyen, "Cryptanalysis of the RSA schemes with short secret exponent from asiacrypt'99," In Advances in Cryptology - ASIACRYPT 2000, volume 1976 of Lecture Notes in Computer Science, pp. 14–29, Springer, 2000.

[11] M. Ernst, E. Jochemsz, A. May, and B. de Weger, "Partial key exposure attacks on RSA up to full size exponents," In Advances in Cryptology - EUROCRYPT 2005, volume 3494 of Lecture Notes in Computer Science, pp. 371–386, Springer, 2005.

[12] M. F. Esgin, M. S. Kiraz, and O. Uzunkol, "A new partial key exposure attack on multi-power RSA," In Algebraic Informatics - CAI 2015, volume 9270 of Lecture Notes in Computer Science, pp. 103–114, Springer, 2015.

[13] M. Herrmann and A. May, "Solving linear equations modulo divisors: On factoring given any bits," In Advances in Cryptology - ASIACRYPT 2008, volume 5350 of Lecture Notes in Computer Science, pp. 406– 424, Springer, 2008.

[14] M. Herrmann and A. May, "Attacking power generators using unravelled linearization: When do we output too much?" In Advances in Cryptology - ASIACRYPT 2009, volume 5912 of Lecture Notes in Computer Science, pp. 487–504, Springer, 2009.

[15] M. Herrmann and A. May, "Maximizing small root bounds by linearization and applications to small secret exponent RSA," In Public Key Cryptography - PKC 2010, volume 6056 of Lecture Notes in Computer Science, pp. 53–69, Springer, 2010.

[16] N. Howgrave-Graham, "Finding small roots of univariate modular equations revisited," In Cryptography and Coding 1997, volume 1355 of Lecture Notes in Computer Science, pp. 131–142, Springer, 1997.

[17] Z. Huang, L. Hu, J. Xu, L. Peng, and Y. Xie, "Partial key exposure attacks on takagi's variant of RSA," In Applied Cryptography and Network Security - ACNS 2014, volume 8479 of Lecture Notes in Computer Science, pp. 134–150, Springer, 2014.

[18] K. Itoh, N. Kunihiro, and K. Kurosawa, "Small secret key attack on a variant of RSA (due to takagi)," In Topics in Cryptology - CT-RSA 2008, volume 4964 of Lecture Notes in Computer Science, pp. 387–406, Springer, 2008.

[19] E. Jochemsz and A. May, "A strategy for finding roots of multivariate polynomials with new applications in attacking RSA variants," In Advances in Cryptology - ASIACRYPT 2006, volume 4284 of Lecture Notes in Computer Science, pp. 267–282, Springer, 2006.

[20] A. K. Lenstra, H. W. Lenstra, and L. Lovász, "Factoring polynomials with rational coefficients," Mathematische Annalen, vol. 261(4), pp.515–534, 1982.

[21] S. Lim, S. Kim, I. Yie, and H. Lee, "A generalized takagi-cryptosystem with a modulus of the form $p^r q^s$," In Progress in Cryptology - INDOCRYPT 2000, volume 1977 of Lecture Notes in Computer Science, pp. 283–294, Springer, 2000.

[22] Y. Lu, L. Peng, and S. Sarkar, "Cryptanalysis of an RSA variant with moduli $n = p^r q^l$," J. Math. Cryptol., vol. 11(2), pp. 117-130, 2017.

[23] Y. Lu, R. Zhang, and D. "Lin. Factoring multi-power RSA modulus $N = p^r q$ with partial known bits," In Information Security and Privacy - ACISP 2013, volume 7959 of Lecture Notes in Computer Science, pp. 57–71, Springer, 2013.

[24] Y. Lu, R. Zhang, L. Peng, and D. Lin, "Solving linear equations modulo unknown divisors: Revisited," In Advances in Cryptology - ASIACRYPT 2015, volume 9452 of Lecture Notes in Computer Science, pp. 189– 213, Springer, 2015.

[25] A. May, "Secret exponent attacks on rsa-type schemes with moduli $n = p^r q$," In Public Key Cryptography - PKC 2004, volume 2947 of Lecture Notes in Computer Science, pp. 218–230, Springer, 2004.

[26] R. L. Rivest and A. Shamir, "Efficient factoring based on partial information," In Advances in Cryptology - EUROCRYPT 1985, volume 219 of Lecture Notes in Computer Science, pp. 31–34, Springer, 1985.

[27] S. Sarkar, "Small secret exponent attack on RSA variant with modulus $n = p^r q$," Des. Codes Cryptogr., vol. 73(2), pp. 383–392, 2014.

[28] S. Sarkar, "Revisiting prime power RSA," Discret. Appl. Math., vol. 203, pp. 127– 133, 2016.

[29] K. Suzuki, A. Takayasu, and N. Kunihiro, "Extended partial key exposure attacks on RSA: improvement up to full size decryption exponents," Theor. Comput. Sci., vol. 841, pp. 62–83, 2020.

[30] T. Takagi, "Fast rsa-type cryptosystem modulo $p^k q$," In Advances in Cryptology - CRYPTO 1998, volume 1462 of Lecture Notes in Computer Science, pp. 318–326, Springer, 1998.

[31] A. Takayasu and N. Kunihiro, "Partial key exposure attacks on RSA: achieving the Boneh-Durfee bound," In Selected Areas in Cryptography - SAC 2014, volume 8781 of Lecture Notes in Computer Science, pp. 345–362, Springer, 2014.

[32] A. Takayasu and N. Kunihiro, "How to generalize RSA cryptanalyses," In Public-Key Cryptography - PKC 2016, volume 9615 of Lecture Notes in Computer Science, pp. 67–97, Springer, 2016.

[33] M. J. Wiener, "Cryptanalysis of short RSA secret exponents," IEEE Trans. Inf. Theory, vol. 36(3), pp. 553–558, 1990.

[34] L. Peng, L. Hu, Y. Lu, S. Sarkar, J. Xu, Z. Huang, " Cryptanalysis of Variants of RSA with Multiple Small Secret Exponents," In: Biryukov A., Goyal V. (eds) Progress in Cryptology - INDOCRYPT 2015, volume 9462 of Lecture Notes in Computer Science, pp. 105-123, Springer, 2015.

[35] A. Nitaj and T. Rachidi, "New Attacks on RSA with Moduli $N = p^r q$ ," In: El Hajji S., Nitaj A., Carlet C., Souidi E. (eds) Codes, Cryptology, and Information Security. C2SI 2015. volume 9084 of Lecture Notes in Computer Science, pp. 352-360 Springer, 2015.

# Securing Runtime Memory via MMU Manipulation

Marinos Tsantekidis
*Institute of Computer Science - FORTH*
Heraklion, Greece
E-mail: tsantekid@ics.forth.gr

Vassilis Prevelakis
*AEGIS IT RESEARCH GmbH*
Braunschweig, Germany
E-mail: vp2020@aegisresearch.eu

*Abstract*—**It is often useful for a code component (e.g., a library) to be able to maintain information that is hidden from the rest of the program (e.g., private keys used for signing, or usage counters used for behavioral monitoring of the program). In this paper, we present an extension to a previously developed mechanism for controlling access to libraries, in order to implement a scheme that allows each library to have its own private storage space. When running code outside the address space of a given library, the pages containing the private memory of that library are not mapped into the program's address space, hence are not accessible to the rest of the program. Finally, we present an API that allows library developers to utilize private storage.**

***Keywords—Secure; Run-time; Memory; MMU.***

## I. INTRODUCTION

The advancement of technology is everlasting and non-stop, which leads to modern software systems becoming more and more complex. This results in new challenges and vulnerabilities being discovered every day and users increasingly requiring security considerations and provisions for their applications. At the same time, there is a parallel and oftentimes one-step-ahead increase in attackers' capabilities and effectiveness, especially if there is profit involved in their illicit activities. However, complete security of a program is unfeasible. Conceding that vulnerable code will be included in production software systems, there is a need to either detect these vulnerabilities so that they may be fixed before an adversary can exploit them in a zero-day attack or determine if such a vulnerability is actively being exploited. Our compromise is that by monitoring the behavior of a program we can distinguish such situations, determine whether their cause is security-related and, if so, take appropriate corrective actions. We implement such actions at an abstract level, between the Operating System (OS) and a running application. Our approach is to break up a running application into its main components (essentially the main program and the libraries it uses) by leveraging the Memory Management Unit (MMU) of the Linux kernel and examine the interactions between the individual components. We use two techniques for our analysis, based our previous work [1]–[3], which enables us to intercept all library calls from both the user as well as the kernel side, analyze them and take some form of action (reporting, argument checking, policy enforcement, etc.) before allowing them to continue.

Looking at the subject of software run-time behavior monitoring, analysis and modification from another point of view, we propose to implement the notion of a Trusted Execution Environment (TEE) at the memory space of a user application. A TEE [4] is a secure, integrity-protected processing environment, consisting of memory and storage capabilities [5]. It establishes an isolated execution environment that runs parallel to a standard OS and it protects sensitive code and data from privileged attacks without compromising the native OS. It prevents unauthorized access or modification of executing code and data while they are in use, so that the applications running the code can have high levels of trust in the TEE, because they can ignore threats from the rest of the system. Hardware vendors (e.g., Intel) have already implemented the concept of TEE into their products (e.g., SGX technology). Virtual TEEs (e.g., Open-TEE [6]) allow developers to create trusted applications using the GlobalPlatform TEE specification [7].

In this paper, we present our idea to include the concept of a TEE to our previous work [2] [3], where we program the MMU in such a way so as to map protected private pages into the address space of a running program, that are accessible only by specific functions inside the external libraries that said program uses. Upon interception of a library call, our system - after redirecting the call through the *gate* (already mapped, specially crafted library) - determines if the call can access the information stored securely in the newly-mapped private memory. In this way, we protect sensitive data inside a secure enclosure and we minimize what can access them, as we limit their exposure to only a specific set of legitimate functions found in the *gate* library, imposing serious limitations on what actions can be performed on the protected data, by what part of the program and at which point in execution time.

The remainder of this paper is organized in the following manner: In Section II, we present some important work that has been carried out over the years with respect to defenses against code injection/reuse attacks C[IR]As, as well TEEs - the two aspects of our approach. In Section III, we detail the design of our mechanism. In Section IV, we describe the implementation specifics. In Section V, we evaluate our approach both in terms of performance and memory coverage. We also list two real-life scenarios where our mechanism can be used. In Section VI, we conclude our work.

## II. BACKGROUND AND RELATED WORK

Behavior control techniques have been the subject of research against code reuse attacks [8]–[13] for many years.

The DisARM defense technique [14] protects against both code-injection and code-reuse based buffer overflow attacks by breaking the ability of attackers to manipulate the return address of a function. DisARM uses a fine-grained analysis of the binary to find all critical interactions that manipulate the hardware PC and verifies any change to the PC before the change is applied. For each such critical instruction, a verification block is inserted immediately before the instruction in order to evaluate whether the target address is valid with respect to the current instruction the program is executing.

Kanuparthi et al. [15] propose a hardware-based dynamic integrity checking approach. It permits the instructions to commit before the integrity check is complete, and allows them to make changes to the register file, but not the data cache. The changes made by the instructions are held in the store buffer or in a shadow register file until the check is complete. Then, the values are accordingly written to the L1 data cache or the original register file. The system is rolled back to a known state, if the checker deems the instructions as modified.

In [16], Graziano et al. discuss a new class of Direct Kernel Object Manipulation (DKOM) attacks that they call Evolutionary DKOM (E-DKOM). The goal of this attack is to alter the way some data structures "evolve" over time. It targets the evolution of a data structure in memory, with the goal of tampering with a particular property of the operating system. On the attack side, they are able to temporarily block any process or kernel thread, without leaving any trace that could be identified by existing DKOM detection and protection systems. On the defense side, they present the design and implementation of a hypervisor-based detector that can verify the fairness of the OS scheduler. Their implementation shows that it needs to be customized on a case-by-case basis and that evolutionary attacks are very hard to deal with, requiring more research to mitigate this threat.

Kayaalp et al. [17] examine a signature-based detection of code reuse attacks (CRAs), where the attack is detected by observing the behavior of programs and detecting the gadget execution patterns. They demonstrate a new attack that renders previously proposed signature-based approaches ineffective by introducing delay gadgets, in order to obfuscate the execution patterns of the attack without performing any useful computation. They develop a complete working JOP attack that incorporates delay gadgets. Then, they propose and develop the Signature-based CRA Protection (SCRAP) hardware-based architecture for detecting such stealth JOP attacks. SCRAP recognizes the formal grammar that expresses the attack signatures or the patterns of executed instructions that are indicative of a JOP attack, which are significantly different from those of the regular programs as they execute frequent indirect *jump* (or *call*) instructions to jump from gadget to gadget.

Additionally, with regards to TEEs, Intel's Software Guard Extensions (SGX) [18] is a hardware feature that helps encrypt a portion of memory. This portion - *enclave* - is used by the OS/applications to define private regions of code and data that cannot be accessed by any (potentially running at a higher privilege level) process outside the enclave, thus preserving the confidentiality and integrity of sensitive code and data. However, several attacks have been developed that break the security of SGX. In [19], Schwarz et al. were able to extract a full RSA private key by performing a cache side-channel attack on a co-located SGX enclave. Later on, countermeasures were released against this attack [20] [21]. More recently, the Spectre attack [22] was adapted to target SGX enclaves [23]. Similarly, the Foreshadow attack exploits speculative execution (e.g., Spectre) in order to read the contents of SGX-protected memory [24]. Additionally, it has been proven that a ROP attack can be constructed and launched all from within an enclave [25] [26]. However, a defense against this attack vector was later presented in [27].

## III. DESIGN

The goal of our proposed approach is two-fold. On one hand, since it is based on our previous approach [2] [3], it thwarts control-flow hijacking attacks by segregating a process's executable areas which correspond to its external libraries or the main executable. It, then, imposes strict control over any attempt to invoke such an area, by redirecting all calls through a *gate* library - mapped by a custom Linux kernel, one for each area - where we can implement several checks before allowing a call to move forward (Figure 1).

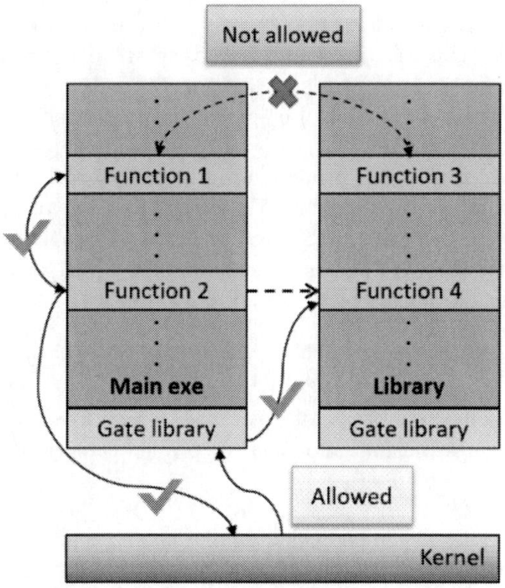


Figure 1. Memory segmentation and access control

On the other hand, it protects sensitive information of an application (e.g., a private signing key) by mapping private secure memory pages for each area at run-time and making them accessible only to specific functions inside the *gate* library and only at specific intervals during execution (Figure 2).

Separation of data used by the libraries from data used by the running application is a significant step of our approach. Originally, the application and library code share their stack and heap spaces, which provides a breeding ground

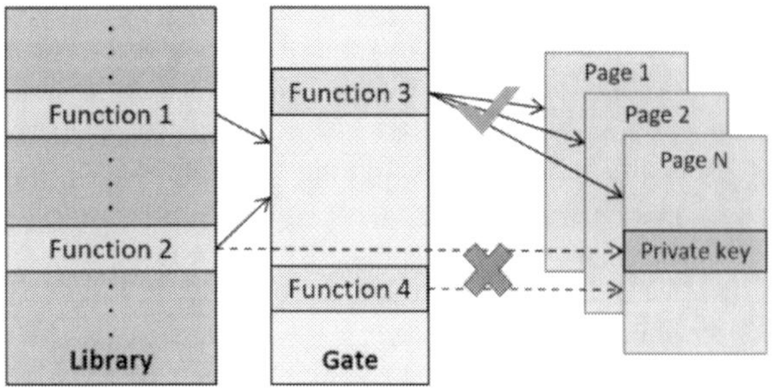


Figure 2. Secure memory mapping

for interfering with the execution of library code. Since we already have a mechanism that allows us to rewrite the page table whenever a library boundary is crossed, we can now extend it by adding private memory for every library. This is memory that is accessible only when running code of a specific library; code outside this library will find the pages associated with the private memory inaccessible. In this way, our *gates* can maintain state (e.g., which library tried to access the gate indicating a possible breach attempt if different from the associated one, how many times a given routine has been called, or the sequence of calls to various library functions). Library code can, thus, take advantage of private memory to protect its own data structures e.g., making them completely inaccessible (no read/write/execute rights) to the rest of the program.

Transparency is, also, of paramount importance. Applications continue to work as originally intended by the developer, but the access control mechanism underneath delivers secure execution of the program. When a call to a separated library is intercepted, our mechanism redirects it through the *gate* library where a decision is made on how it will proceed and if it is allowed to access the information securely stored in the private pages.

## IV. Implementation

Based on our design, there are two aspects to our approach: $(a)$ compartmentalization and $(b)$ private memory mapping.

### A. Compartmentalization

In order to compartmentalize the running application based on its libraries, we separate all the executable Virtual Memory Areas (VMAs) and map a custom *gate* library in the process's memory space, one for each identified VMA. Aiming to adhere to the library-level granularity of our design (i.e., intercept only calls between libraries and not internal ones), after we make all the VMAs non-executable (NX), we then follow the procedure depicted in Figure 3, when transitioning from one library to another. We first check the previous address where we caused a deliberate fault to determine if it corresponds to the same VMA as the current one (meaning same executable/library) (Figure 3 (1)), in which case we leave the VMA as executable (the current VMA needs to be executable by default, in order not to disrupt execution) and store the current faulting address in a custom field in the process (Figure 3 (2)) .

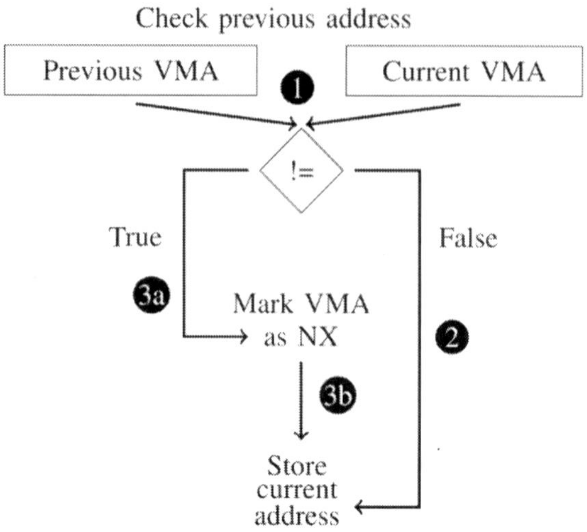


Figure 3. Compartmentilizing an application at library-level granularity

If the previous and current VMAs are different (meaning different executables/libraries by extension), we mark the previous VMA as NX (Figure 3 (3a)), before storing the current faulting address in the custom field (Figure 3 (3b)). At this stage all the addresses of our process are in a non-executable state, but the execution is able to continue since it is in the context of the Page Fault Exception Handler (PFEH) [28] that intervened to rectify our deliberate page fault, which we caused in order to intercept the call. From there it is redirected inside the *gate*, where a security policy can be applied in order to determine whether to allow the call to access the requested information inside the protected memory and to continue to the originally-intended path. When the PFEH intervenes to rectify the next fault, the same procedure is followed from the top.

### B. Private Memory Mapping

Following the separation of the process's memory area into regions, we are now ready to associate private memory pages with each of them. After mapping the *gates*, we introduce protected pages to the process's memory space, where we can save sensitive information that need protection against disclosure, tampering, execution, etc. These pages are only mapped when the CPU executes code within the associated library. When execution is transferred outside the library, the pages get unmapped, thus protecting data stored in them from unauthorized access.

This whole procedure is performed automatically on the kernel side, without requiring access to the source code/binary of the application or linked libraries, thus making our approach completely transparent.

*Application Programming Interface:* In order to facilitate the use of this extended capability, we propose an Application Programming Interface (API) analogous to the one used for shared memory [29]. Listing 1 showcases a sample of our proposed API, where the code has the ability to allocate a private memory space to a specific region.

```
1  ...
2  char *addr;
3  int fd;
4  fd = scrm_open(PAGE_SIZE, <FLAGS>);
5  addr = mmap(NULL, PAGE_SIZE,
6              PROT_READ | PROT_WRITE,
7              MAP_PRIVATE, fd, 0);
8  scrm_assoc(<caller>, fd, addr,
9             addr + PAGE_SIZE);
10 ...
11 scrm_unlink(fd);
12 ...
```

Listing 1. Usage example of Secure API

First, we create a secure memory (scrm) object with specific flags and its size set to that of a page (line 4). Then we map the object into the process's address space (line 5). Following, we associate the object with the caller (a given region) in line 8. Finally, after some processing we return the memory to the system, by unlinking the scrm object.

## V. Evaluation

In order to evaluate the performance overhead incurred by our mechanism, we use the OpenSSL benchmark test of Phoronix Test Suite (PTS). Our test-bed can be seen in Figure 4, as reported by PTS.

Figure 4. System configuration

PTS [30] is an open-source automated benchmarking suite that supports a variety of platforms, including Linux. We use it to run a benchmark test for the OpenSSL library, which is executed five times, for both cases: (a) default MMU, (b) MMU customized with our mechanism. The outcome reports on the performance of RSA 4096-bit signing. Figure 5 summarizes the results of the tests (rounded numbers), while Table I shows the deviation for each run. As is evident, there is only minimal decrease in performance - about 2% on average - when using our custom MMU, which makes our approach very efficient.

TABLE I
DEVIATION FOR EACH RUN OF THE OPENSSL BENCHMARK OF PTS

| | Deviation | |
|---|---|---|
| # | Default MMU | Custom MMU |
| 1 | 0.02% | 0.04% |
| 2 | 0.08% | 1.3% |
| 3 | 0.16% | 1.23% |
| 4 | 0.02% | 1.32% |
| 5 | 0.16% | 1.32% |

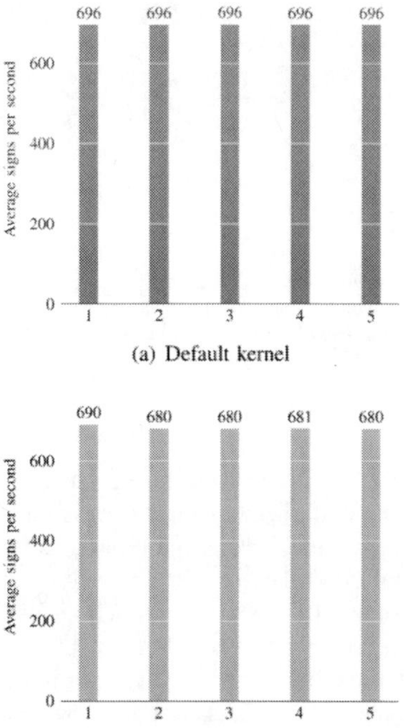


(a) Default kernel

(b) Custom kernel

Figure 5. Performance evaluation of our mechanism using the OpenSSL benchmark of PTS

### A. Memory Coverage Analysis

In order to measure to what degree our mechanism compartmentalizes a program's memory space and by extension confines an attacker's code base that is available at any given point in time for them to mount an attack, we analyze four well-known applications, i.e., NGINX HTTP server, VMware Player, Sublime Text Editor and GNOME MPlayer - with respect to their executable memory areas. We chose these applications for analysis, based on their broad acceptance and usage in their respective domains in a Linux environment.

In Table II, we can see the result of the analysis for the NGINX HTTP server. We only measure the size of the

TABLE II
MEMORY COVERAGE OF LIBRARIES FOR THE NGINX MAIN APPLICATION

| Library | Size (in bytes) | % of total |
|---|---|---|
| nginx (main) | 528384 | 6.84% |
| libnss_files | 45056 | 0.58% |
| libnss_nis | 45056 | 0.58% |
| libnsl | 90112 | 1.17% |
| libnss_compat | 32768 | 0.42% |
| libdl | 2093056 | 27.11% |
| libc | 1835008 | 23.77% |
| libz | 102400 | 1.33% |
| libcrypto | 2207744 | 28.59% |
| libpcre | 450560 | 5.84% |
| libcrypt | 36864 | 0.48% |
| libpthread | 98304 | 1.27% |
| ld | 155648 | 2.02% |
| Total | 7720960 | 100% |

TABLE III
LIBRARIES WITH MAXIMUM COVERAGE FOR THE OTHER THREE APPLICATIONS

| Application | Library | % of total |
|---|---|---|
| VMware Player | libvmwareui | 21.53% |
| Sublime Text Editor | libgtk-3 | 20.63% |
| GNOME MPlayer | libicudata | 34.74% |

executable VMAs, since all others are out of scope. We can see that the biggest memory area corresponds to *libcrypto* and it takes up around 29% of the program's total executable memory. Similarly, based on our analysis of the other three applications (Table III) - details of which we omit for the sake of space, since they are composed of tens of libraries - we can see that at the maximum only a small portion of the address space is available to the attacker at any given moment, which results in them having much lower chances of success when trying to launch a CRA. If we also consider that each of these smaller regions has one or at most a few pages of memory dynamically associated with it, where only it has access and can store sensitive code and data, it becomes even clearer that a rogue (part of an) application will find it extremely difficult to gain access to this information and compromise the system.

### B. Real-life Scenarios

In this section, we present two examples that showcase the applicability of our defense mechanism.

First, let's consider the case of the Dual Elliptic Curve Deterministic Random Bit Generator (Dual_EC_DRBG) backdoor. Dual_EC_DRBG [31] was presented as a cryptographically-secure pseudorandom number generator that used elliptic curve cryptography. Despite the fact that there were several weaknesses publicly identified, one of which being a backdoor that could only be exploited by someone who knew about it (presumably the United States government's National Security Agency), the algorithm was adopted as a standard by several standardization bodies. In such a case, using our mechanism we would not have to wait for a patch/updated version to be released or some other kind of action to be taken by the responsible parties (later the algorithm was withdrawn). Upon detecting a call to one of the Dual_EC_DRBG-related functions, we immediately produce a warning/error informing that this specific generator contains vulnerabilities, and/or prevent the call to continue to the intended function (we can also disable/remove the algorithm from the results when reporting which pseudorandom number generators are available in a library). In this way, our defense acts more as a preventive measure and less as a responsive one after the fact, protecting the user even before an attacker gets a chance to exploit the vulnerabilities. Even in the case of such a widely-adopted algorithm, used by a number of official bodies, our approach would be able to offer sufficient information to the users to make an informed decision.

The second scenario deals with handling a private key. In this case, we leverage the OpenSSL library and specifically its *libcrypto*/*libssl* libraries. When a program needs to sign a piece of data (text, file, etc.), it needs access to a private key. Under our scheme, when a call to a function from these libraries is intercepted, it is redirected inside the *gate*, where we forbid it to access the private key directly. We have already included a secure function in the *gate* - `sec_pkey()`, which is the only one that can access the secure private memory associated with OpenSSL, where the key is stored. There is a number of ways the key can be placed in memory: (*a*) after the program starts, we read the private key from a file with elevated privileges, store it in private memory and then close the file. From then on we revoke access to the file, which means that access to the key is provided only through the *gate* and OpenSSL's private memory, (*b*) the program creates its own private key and places it in memory, or (*c*) the key is initially retrieved from a file and stored in memory *lazily*, i.e., only when there is a call to an OpenSSL function.

`sec_pkey()` retrieves the key, signs the data and returns the result. This way, the rest of the program does not have access to the private key. Inside `sec_pkey()` we can perform a number of checks to verify that only a specific legitimate OpenSSL function requested access to the key and that was only to read it and at an appropriate point in execution time. To determine at which point the execution is, we can store in private memory a finite state automaton/state model of the application, which e.g., we have created by running the application through our custom MMU in learning mode or the developer has provided us with. Inside the *gate*, we also have a relevant function that is responsible for checking the program state `chk_stt()`, that checks several parameters (e.g., depth/size of stack, call origin/destination, number of call parameters, etc.) and their combinations to determine if the current state corresponds to the one saved in the model. This way, we can make sure that execution is at the correct point in time and that nothing has interfered with the execution flow.

## VI. CONCLUSION

In this paper, we present an extension of our previous work in [2] [3] where, after separating the memory of a running process into regions at the granularity of executables/external libraries, it maps private pages for each region that are only accessible from the associated *gate*, leveraging the MMU. Our approach is very efficient and transparent and can be used on binary/legacy applications and existing environments, as well as serve as a complimentary measure of defense alongside already implemented mechanisms. Furthermore, we present two scenarios where our mechanism can protect real-life applications.

## ACKNOWLEDGMENTS

This work is supported by the European Commission through the following H2020 projects: SENTINEL under Grant Agreement No. 101021659, ROXANNE under Grant Agreement No. 833635 and CONCORDIA under Grant Agreement No. 830927.

## REFERENCES


[1] M. Tsantekidis and V. Prevelakis, "Library-Level Policy Enforcement," in *SECURWARE 2017, The Eleventh International Conference on Emerging Security Information, Systems and Technologies*, Rome, Italy, 2017, [Retrieved: 10-2021]. [Online]. Available: http://www.thinkmind.org/index.php?view=article&articleid=securware_2017_2_20_30034

[2] M. Tsantekidis and V. Prevelakis, "Efficient Monitoring of Library Call Invocation," in *Sixth International Conference on Internet of Things: Systems, Management and Security (IOTSMS)*, Granada, Spain, 2019, [Retrieved: 10-2021]. [Online]. Available: https://doi.org/10.1109/IOTSMS48152.2019.8939203

[3] M. Tsantekidis and V. Prevelakis, "MMU-based Access Control for Libraries," in *Proceedings of the 18th International Conference on Security and Cryptography - SECRYPT*, INSTICC. SciTePress, 2021, pp. 686–691, [Retrieved: 10-2021]. [Online]. Available: https://www.scitepress.org/Link.aspx?doi=10.5220/0010536706860691

[4] S. T. Alliance, "Trusted Execution Environment (TEE) 101: A Primer," 2018, [Retrieved: 10-2021]. [Online]. Available: https://www.securetechalliance.org/wp-content/uploads/TEE-101-White-Paper-FINAL2-April-2018.pdf

[5] N. Asokan, J.-E. Ekberg, K. Kostiainen, A. Rajan, C. Rozas, A.-R. Sadeghi, S. Schulz, and C. Wachsmann, "Mobile trusted computing," *Proceedings of the IEEE*, vol. 102, no. 8, pp. 1189–1206, 2014.

[6] L. Limited, "Open Portable Trusted Execution Environment," 2021, [Retrieved: 10-2021]. [Online]. Available: https://www.op-tee.org/

[7] GlobalPlatform, "Trusted Execution Environment (TEE) Committee," 2021, [Retrieved: 10-2021]. [Online]. Available: https://globalplatform.org/technical-committees/trusted-execution-environment-tee-committee/

[8] H. Shacham, "The geometry of innocent flesh on the bone: Return-into-libc without function calls (on the x86)," in *Proceedings of the 14th ACM Conference on Computer and Communications Security*, ser. CCS '07. New York, NY, USA: ACM, 2007, pp. 552–561.

[9] S. Checkoway, L. Davi, A. Dmitrienko, A.-R. Sadeghi, H. Shacham, and M. Winandy, "Return-oriented programming without returns," in *Proceedings of the 17th ACM Conference on Computer and Communications Security*, ser. CCS '10. New York, NY, USA: ACM, 2010, pp. 559–572.

[10] R. Roemer, E. Buchanan, H. Shacham, and S. Savage, "Return-oriented programming: Systems, languages, and applications," *ACM Trans. Inf. Syst. Secur.*, vol. 15, no. 1, pp. 2:1–2:34, Mar. 2012.

[11] T. Bletsch, X. Jiang, V. W. Freeh, and Z. Liang, "Jump-oriented programming: A new class of code-reuse attack," in *Proceedings of the 6th ACM Symposium on Information, Computer and Communications Security*, ser. ASIACCS '11. New York, NY, USA: ACM, 2011, pp. 30–40.

[12] K. Z. Snow, F. Monrose, L. Davi, A. Dmitrienko, C. Liebchen, and A.-R. Sadeghi, "Just-In-Time Code Reuse: On the Effectiveness of Fine-Grained Address Space Layout Randomization," in *Proceedings of the 2013 IEEE Symposium on Security and Privacy*, ser. SP '13. Washington, DC, USA: IEEE Computer Society, 2013, pp. 574–588.

[13] A. Bittau, A. Belay, A. Mashtizadeh, D. Mazières, and D. Boneh, "Hacking Blind," in *2014 IEEE Symposium on Security and Privacy*, May 2014, pp. 227–242.

[14] J. Habibi, A. Panicker, A. Gupta, and E. Bertino, *DisARM: Mitigating Buffer Overflow Attacks on Embedded Devices*. Cham: Springer International Publishing, 2015, pp. 112–129.

[15] A. K. Kanuparthi, R. Karri, G. Ormazabal, and S. K. Addepalli, "A high-performance, low-overhead microarchitecture for secure program execution," in *2012 IEEE 30th International Conference on Computer Design (ICCD)*, Sept 2012, pp. 102–107.

[16] M. Graziano, L. Flore, A. Lanzi, and D. Balzarotti, *Subverting Operating System Properties Through Evolutionary DKOM Attacks*. Cham: Springer International Publishing, 2016, pp. 3–24.

[17] M. Kayaalp, T. Schmitt, J. Nomani, D. Ponomarev, and N. A. Ghazaleh, "Signature-based protection from code reuse attacks," *IEEE Transactions on Computers*, vol. 64, no. 2, pp. 533–546, Feb 2015.

[18] M. Hoekstra, "Intel® SGX for Dummies (Intel® SGX Design Objectives)," 2015, [Retrieved: 10-2021]. [Online]. Available: https://software.intel.com/en-us/blogs/2013/09/26/protecting-application-secrets-with-intel-sgx

[19] M. Schwarz, S. Weiser, D. Gruss, C. Maurice, and S. Mangard, "Malware guard extension: Using sgx to conceal cache attacks," in *Detection of Intrusions and Malware, and Vulnerability Assessment - 14th International Conference, DIMVA 2017*, ser. Lecture Notes in Computer Science (including subseries Lecture Notes in Artificial Intelligence and Lecture Notes in Bioinformatics), vol. 10327 LNCS. Springer-Verlag Italia, 2017, pp. 3–24.

[20] D. Gruss, J. Lettner, F. Schuster, O. Ohrimenko, I. Haller, and M. Costa, "Strong and efficient cache side-channel protection using hardware transactional memory," in *Proceedings of the 26th USENIX Conference on Security Symposium*, ser. SEC'17. USA: USENIX Association, 2017, p. 217–233.

[21] F. Brasser, S. Capkun, A. Dmitrienko, T. Frassetto, K. Kostiainen, U. Müller, and A. Sadeghi, "DR.SGX: hardening SGX enclaves against cache attacks with data location randomization," *CoRR*, vol. abs/1709.09917, 2017.

[22] P. Kocher, J. Horn, A. Fogh, D. Genkin, D. Gruss, W. Haas, M. Hamburg, M. Lipp, S. Mangard, T. Prescher, M. Schwarz, and Y. Yarom, "Spectre attacks: Exploiting speculative execution," in *40th IEEE Symposium on Security and Privacy*, 2019.

[23] D. O'Keeffe, D. Muthukumaran, P.-L. Aublin, F. Kelbert, C. Priebe, J. Lind, H. Zhu, and P. Pietzuch, "Spectre attack against SGX enclave," 2015, [Retrieved: 10-2021]. [Online]. Available: https://github.com/lsds/spectre-attack-sgx

[24] J. Van Bulck, M. Minkin, O. Weisse, D. Genkin, B. Kasikci, F. Piessens, M. Silberstein, T. F. Wenisch, Y. Yarom, and R. Strackx, "Foreshadow: Extracting the keys to the Intel SGX kingdom with transient out-of-order execution," in *Proceedings of the 27th USENIX Security Symposium*. USENIX Association, August 2018.

[25] J. Lee, J. Jang, Y. Jang, N. Kwak, Y. Choi, C. Choi, T. Kim, M. Peinado, and B. B. Kang, "Hacking in darkness: Return-oriented programming against secure enclaves," in *Proceedings of the 26th USENIX Conference on Security Symposium*, ser. SEC'17. USA: USENIX Association, 2017, p. 523–539.

[26] M. Schwarz, S. Weiser, and D. Gruß, "Practical enclave malware with Intel SGX," in *Detection of Intrusions and Malware, and Vulnerability Assessment*, ser. Lecture Notes in Computer Science. Springer International, 2019, pp. 177–196.

[27] S. Weiser, L. Mayr, M. Schwarz, and D. Gruss, "SGXJail: Defeating enclave malware via confinement," in *22nd International Symposium on Research in Attacks, Intrusions and Defenses (RAID 2019)*. USENIX Association, Sep. 2019, pp. 353–366.

[28] D. P. Bovet and M. Cesati, "Page Fault Exception Handler," in *Understanding the Linux Kernel, 3rd Edition*. O'Reilly, 2005, ch. 9.4.

[29] M. Kerrisk, "shm_overview(7) — Linux manual page," 2008, [Retrieved: 10-2021]. [Online]. Available: https://www.man7.org/linux/man-pages/man7/shm_overview.7.html

[30] PTS, "Phoronix Test Suite," [Retrieved: 10-2021]. [Online]. Available: https://www.phoronix-test-suite.com

[31] E. Barker and J. Kelsey, "Recommendation for Random Number Generation Using Deterministic Random Bit Generators," National Institute of Standards and Technology (NIST), Tech. Rep., 2012, [Retrieved: 10-2021]. [Online]. Available: https://nvlpubs.nist.gov/nistpubs/Legacy/SP/nistspecialpublication800-90a.pdf

# Adaptive User Profiling with Online Incremental Machine Learning for Security Information and Event Management

Dilli P. Sharma *, Barjinder Kaur *, Farzaneh Shoeleh *, Masoud Erfani*, Duc-Phong Le †, Arash Habibi Lashkari *, Ali A. Ghorbani *
*Canadian Institute for Cybersecurity, University of New Brunswick, NB, Canada
E-mail: {dilli.sharma, kaur.barjinder, farzaneh.shoeleh, masoud.erfani, a.habibi.l, ghorbani}@unb.ca
† Bank of Canada, Ottawa, Canada, E-mail: dle@bankofcanada.ca

***Abstract*—In the past few years, there has been an exponential growth in network and Internet traffic. This trend will continue to increase due to digitalization and resulting in more interconnectivity among the users. Due to this, more data has started being treated as streaming data. This data distribution, mostly non-stationary, high-speed, and infinite length, contains information regarding user activities. Thus, it is essential to provide an anomaly detection model that can deal with the evolving nature of data, update, adapt, and give system administrators timely action and minimize false alarms. This paper proposes a dynamic and adaptable user profiling for security information and event management system using online incremental machine learning. An anomaly detection-based user profiling technique dynamically learns users' activities and updates their profiles over time. The experiments to detect anomalous activities is performed on datasets generated in realistic scenario based on user's activities and recorded in three different time windows (e.g., 30-minutes, 1-hour, and 2-hour) of a month. The system's efficacy is evaluated with the Isolation Forest *(iForest)* approach to detect anomalies in incremental learning settings for all the datasets. We further compared the performance of our proposed incremental approach with a non-incremental baseline model in terms of the detection of abnormal user activities. The experimental results show that our proposed incremental model outperformed its baseline counterpart model. It can be used more opportunistically to profile users as a component of Security Information and Event Management (SIEM) systems.**

***Index Terms*—Machine learning; anomaly detection; cybersecurity; user profiling; incremental learning**

## I. Introduction

Internet is said to be the core pillar where all the information can be easily and readily available. With the advancement in Internet technologies, more users are getting themselves connected to this technology. The recent study came in January 2021, highlighting the stats that there were 4.66 billion active Internet users worldwide [6]. So, there is an unprecedented amount of data presented from different domains which help users in one way or another. But this has led to an increase in cybercrime either network intrusion or posing a threat by performing different malicious activities from both inside and outside of the organization.

This shows that although solutions are being provided for securing the data, the organizations lack capturing the user experience. A special report published in 2020 measured cybercrime costs to grow by 15 percent per year over the next five years, reaching $10.5 trillion USD annually by 2025, up from $3 trillion USD in 2015 [11]. Due to the easy accessibility of the devices and connectivity over the network, different kinds of applications are run on the machine; the same machine could also be used to browse different websites. Simultaneously, logs are generated that capture profile of a user. Thus, constructing a user profile is one such important concept that has become the need of the hour and needs to be built dynamically using users' activities. This profile based on users' activities collected from different sources will further help organizations to detect anomalous activity, generate alerts, and change policies according to it. An approach proposed by Lashkari et al. [8] creates a new user profile from all the available sources. After gathering users' information based on different profiling criteria, the authors created a security profile of a user. Similarly, a recommendation system is proposed for Google News, where each user's profile is updated and built based on their click history [3]. However, user behavior is unpredictable, i.e., the system needs to be monitored continuously. Also, it has become essential to design a system that can detect significant deviations in data and provide user-oriented service in real-time.

In this work, we propose an anomaly detection-based user profiling that dynamically learns from the user activities and updates the model. Fig. 1 depicts steps of our proposed framework, which we followed in this study to develop this adaptive user profiling model. The steps are defined as follows:

1) The data source is prepared, which included data recorded from three different user activities, i.e., web-browsing, network, and process-based activities.
2) Based on the activities data recorded, three different datasets such as 1Month_30minutes, 1Month_1H, 1Month_2H were prepared, and all the datasets have all the records of three activities.
3) The raw data is further normalized, i.e., preprocessed.
4) Further, features are extracted from three different categories, which are divided into general, network, and

process (application) based; these features are explained in Section V.

5) The selected features were fed into the machine learning approach to perform experiments.
6) Finally, the results are comparatively analyzed and presented with a $'non-incremental'$ approach and our proposed online $'incremental'$ approach.

This proposed adaptive user profiling system updates the data according to the dynamic changing behavior of the user. The **key contributions** of this work are as follows:

- We propose a dynamic and adaptable user profiling with online incremental machine learning for the Security Information and Event Management (SIEM) system.
- Secondly, we have analyzed the results on three different datasets (e.g., 1Month_30min, 1Month_1H, 1Month_2H)
- Finally, we compared the performance of our proposed approach with a baseline non-incremental model.

The rest of the paper is organized as follows: Section II briefly recalls the related works for user profiling. Section III discusses data preprocessing and anomaly detection classifier used in this work. Section IV presents our proposed incremental approach. In Section V, the dataset details, experimental setup and results analysis are presented. Finally, the conclusion and future directions are discussed in Section VI.

## II. Related Work

In the recent past, research has been bent towards analyzing user behavior and building profiles in real-time [23][24]. However, most of the existing studies report their results using either static dataset or did not incrementally update and adapt, i.e., baseline model according to the changes noticed.

In [19] authors presented an adaptive search system based on user profile. The information is collected from browsing history for constructing the user's profile, and the update is performed whenever a change is noticed in browsed web pages. The search results should be adapted to users with different information need.

An insider-threat detection model based on user behavior has been proposed in [7]. The behavior is analyzed from the collected dataset, i.e., user's daily activity summary, e-mail contents topic distribution, and user's weekly e-mail communication history. The abnormal behavior is detected using four different one-class machine learning algorithms Gaussian density estimation (Gauss), Parzen window density estimation (Parzen), Principal Component Analysis (PCA), and K-means clustering. On the same theme of inside-threat detection, the user-profile approach has been utilized to detect anomalous behavior. Singh et al. [17] used an ensemble hybrid machine learning approach using Multi-State Long Short-Term Memory (MSLSTM) and Convolution Neural Networks (CNN) approaches to detect outlier activities from the patterns extracted from spatial-temporal behavior features.

Another study presented an unsupervised user behavior modeling based on session activities. The authors analyzed the activities using LSTM based autoencoder following a two-step process. First, it calculates the reconstruction error using the autoencoder on the non-anomalous dataset, and then it is used to define the threshold to separate the outliers from the normal data points. The identified outliers are then classified as anomalies. The CERT dataset, which is recorded using users' day-to-day activities, includes all the files about system usage, logged time, and date that has been used for research work [14]. A study has been proposed for enterprise organizations with the same dataset where user profiling is built by analyzing log authorization. To evaluate their method, the authors used Random Forest and achieved an accuracy of 97.81% for detecting the anomalous behavior of the user [25].

The authors in [22] proposed a novel Ouda's authentication framework for security purposes. The framework is built by using a user profile that captures the anomalous actions from users' activities. The information representing user activities is collected using their unique identification. Important features are selected that represent anomalous action, preprocessing performed, and results are predicted on a binary-basis, which acts as a base for building user profile. The anomaly detection technique used was implemented based on machine learning clustering algorithms [21] [20].

The anomalous behavior of the user was also detected based on similarity clustering. The authors proposed a model consisting of four components: datalog collector, data log analyzer, profile storage, and behavior detector, which performs different functionality [4]. The User and Entity Behavior Analytics (UEBA) module presented by Madhu Shashanka et al. [15] uses the Singular Values Decomposition (SVD) algorithm to detect anomalous behavior. The module built tracks and simultaneously monitors users' IP addresses and devices. The system was proposed for an enterprise network.

A knowledge-driven user pattern discovery approach was proposed to analyze user behavior in [10]. The authors extracted the patterns using audit logs from distributed medical imaging systems. These patterns help the administrators to identify the users with anomalous behavior, which may threaten the data privacy and system's integrity.

A scalable system for high-throughput real-time analysis of heterogeneous data streams was proposed in [2]. The architecture named RADISH enables the incremental development of models for predictive analytics and anomaly detection as data arrives into the system. The architecture also allows for ingesting and analysis of data on the fly, thereby detecting and responding to anomalous behavior in near real-time.

Shaman et al. [13] proposed a supervised learning-based user profiling approach using Gradient boosting. This work provides a mechanism for user identification and behavior profiling by analyzing the individual uses of each application. The application-level flow sessions were identified based on DNS filtering criteria and timing. However, the scope of this work is limited to the application level.

Most of the existing user profiling work mainly focuses on the static aspect of user behavior analysis. However, user behavior changes dynamically over time. So, the static nature of the model cannot learn and adapt to the changing behavior of the users. In this work, we devise dynamic and adaptable

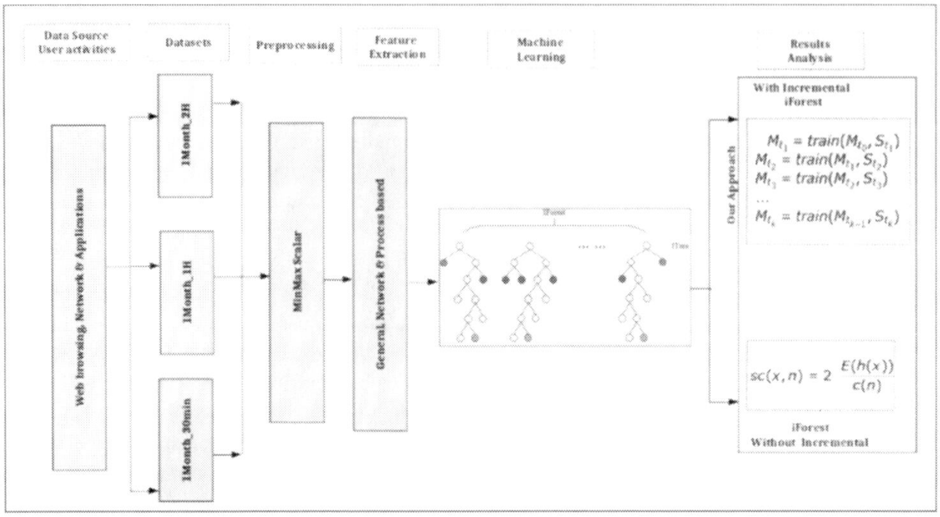


Fig. 1: User profiling framework with the proposed incremental approach.

user profiling using increment learning.

## III. PRELIMINARIES

In this section, we describe data preprocessing and Isolation Forest classifier for detecting abnormal user behaviors.

### A. Data Preprocessing

As datasets contain numerical and nominal values, preprocessing the training and testing dataset is an important step. The goal is to normalize the feature values to the same scale. Our approach considers all the features of the dataset as each feature is equally important. For this we applied the MinMaxScaler object from the sklearn library [18] to rescale the values into the range*[0,1]* [1]. The MinMaxScaler can be defined using (1).

$$Xnr = \frac{F - Min_F}{Max_F - Min_F} \tag{1}$$

where $Max_F$ and $Min_F$ are maximum and minimum values obtained for $F$, which is a feature vector of the features. We replaced the null values with zero. The network data suffer from missing or null values that could also appear as outliers or wrong data, so we have replaced these null values with zero before performing our analysis.

### B. Anomaly Detection using Isolation Forest Classifier

In this work, we have used Isolation Forest (iForest) [9] to detect abnormal user behaviors. It is a popular tree-based, unsupervised outlier detection approach that works on isolating outliers, i.e., anomalies. The quantitative property of iForest is they are fewer and very different from the usual instances.

It works by building an ensemble of *iTrees* from a given dataset. The algorithm takes n random samples of size from a given dataset. For each random sample, the *"iTree"* is built by splitting the sub-sample instances over a split value of a randomly selected feature so that the instances whose corresponding feature value is smaller than the split value go left. The others go right, and the process continues recursively until the tree is entirely built. The split value is selected at random between the minimum and maximum values of the selected feature. This results in a shorter tree path for outliers and is thus easy for detecting [9][12]. The anomalous score $sc$ is calculated as defined in (2).

$$sc(x,n) = 2^{-\frac{E(h(x))}{c(n)}} \tag{2}$$

where $h(x)$ is the path length of sample $x$, and $E(h(x))$ represents the average value of $h(x)$ from *iTrees* collection. The value of $c(n)$ is the average path length of unsuccessful search in a Binary Search Tree with $n$ nodes [9]. Then the instance $x$ is assigned to outlier if the value of $sc$ is close to 1 otherwise considered as normal.

## IV. PROPOSED ONLINE INCREMENTAL LEARNING MODEL

In this section, we present our proposed online incremental learning model. We design an incremental model where a machine evolves incrementally learning from the previously trained model with a new data block. The learning process starts from an initial baseline model. Evolving of a machine using this approach is shown in Fig. 2. Let $M_{t_0}$ denotes an initial baseline model at a time point $t_0$. A sequence of model $\{M_{t_1}, M_{t_2}, M_{t_3}, \ldots, M_{t_k}\}$ is generated from the baseline $M_{t_0}$ with incremental training on stream of data blocks $\{S_{t_1}, S_{t_2}, S_{t_3}, \ldots, S_{t_k}\}$ at time $t_1$, $t_2$ ,$t_3$, and $t_k$, respectively. The model $M_{t_k}$ is evolving from the baseline model $M_{t_0}$ with $k$ total incremental updates using the data stream. This incremental model evolution is derived as follows:

$$\begin{aligned} M_{t_1} &= train(M_{t_0}, S_{t_1}) \\ M_{t_2} &= train(M_{t_1}, S_{t_2}) \\ M_{t_3} &= train(M_{t_2}, S_{t_3}) \\ &\ldots \\ M_{t_k} &= train(M_{t_{k-1}}, S_{t_k}) \end{aligned} \tag{3}$$

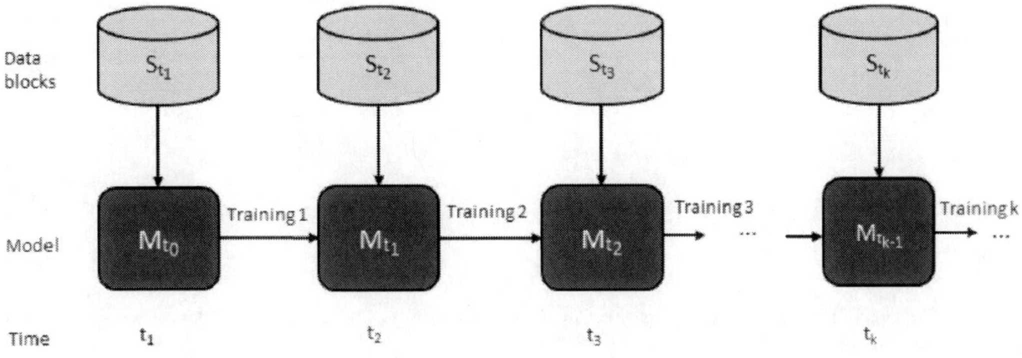


Fig. 2: Evolving a model (machine) with online incremental learning

where, $w = t_k - t_{k-1}$ is a model (re)training time window. This time window can be a fixed constant or variable time period (e.g., 1 day, 3 days, 7 days, etc.) or dynamic (event-driven). The dynamic (re)training time window is an event driven where receiving alerts from security event detectors or predictive analytic determines when the model is to be retrained.

## V. Experimental Setup & Results Analysis

In this section, we present the description of dataset, experimental setup and results analysis.

### A. Dataset Description

We used the dataset collected from four users performing three different activities. The activities include web browsing, network, and application. The users' activities captured has three common properties (*IP, MAC-Address, Activities*) where *IP* represents the users' IP address, and *MAC-Address* represent the machine address using which the user is performing the different activity. On the other hand, *Activities* properties include generating a users' activities: web-browsing, file transferring, and opening an application.

The users' activities have been recorded between 8:00 AM to 5:00 PM. Furthermore, the occurrences of the users' activities have been randomly considered, while it would be possible that the user performed two kinds of activities together. The number of activities for each user has been identified based on predefined averages and standard deviations. Regarding being a normal or abnormal activity, various types have been defined for users' activities.

After generating user scenarios that include their activities, the generated file has been processed by another implemented module that produces the final STIX format. The module reads, analyzes, and identifies the type of activities in the JSON file. Table I presents the details of simulated datasets. The features are extracted from STIX format file which are categorised into *general, network-based, process-based*. Here, the network features include all those features related to network activities of the user, process-based features include the information regarding file transfer, process values, whereas the general feature summarizes the minimum and maximum

TABLE I: SUMMARY OF THE DATASETS.

| Name | Time period | Session duration | Number of instances | Features |
|---|---|---|---|---|
| 1Month_30min | One month | 30 minutes | 2280 | 44 |
| 1Month_1H | One month | 1 hour | 1116 | 44 |
| 1Month_2H | One month | 2 hours | 560 | 44 |

session of a user. More detailed description of the dataset can be found in [16].

### B. Experimental Setup

We used a standard sklearn [18] Application Programming Interface (API) for the experimentation. As described in Section III-B, we trained Isolation Forest (iForest) classifier for the anomaly detection with the three-datasets as presented in Table I. Each dataset is randomly divided into training and testing sets with 90% (training) and 10% (testing). Each training data is further divided into ten blocks, each with a time window of three days. Then, we trained both our incremental iForest model and a baseline iForest model with each data block. The baseline model is retrained with each new data block only, whereas; the proposed model is trained and updated incrementally with each new data block adding more estimators. Below is the description of model fitting and updating incrementally over time using the proposed approach.

**Incremental Training & Updating**: During training, we incrementally trained our model with the new data samples over time. Initially, a model is created using the iForest classifier with some initial number of base estimators in the ensemble ($n\_estimators = 100$) and $warm\_start = True$. A setting of $warm\_start$ to $True$ enables us to continue training to the previously trained model and add more estimators to the ensemble. Before every training, we increment the $n\_estimators$ parameter and update it to the model using the $set\_params()$ method. The trained model is persistently saved/loaded to/from a file on disk. We use joblib [5] API for reading or reconstructing a Python object of the model from a file persisted dump.

The performance of each evolving model (machine) is evaluated with the same test data after each incremental/(re)training. We stored the anomalies detected after each re/training of our proposed and a baseline model. An increase or decrease in the number of anomalies in each iterative (re)training step can help us measure the model's performance.

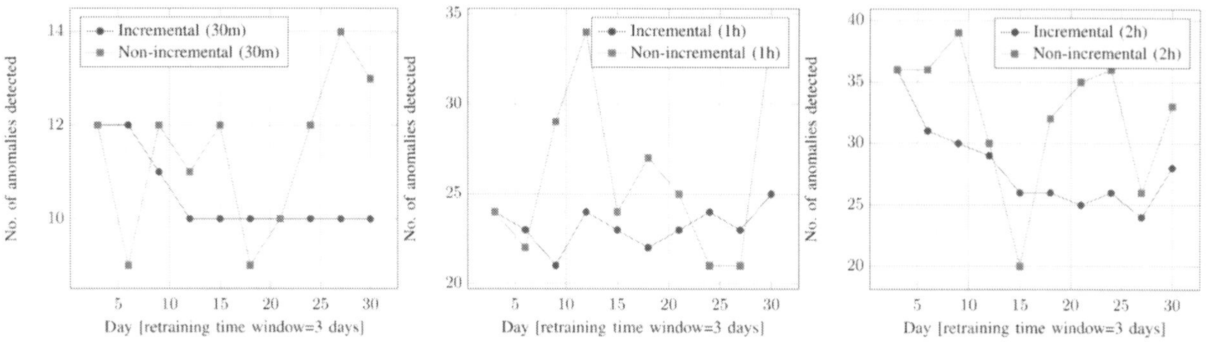


(a) 30min dataset (b) 1hour dataset (c) 2hour dataset

Fig. 3: Comparison of results of our proposed incremental model with a non-incremental model.

The obtained results are comparatively analyzed and discussed in Section V-C.

### C. Results Analysis

Here, we present the results analyzed using our proposed incremental approach where the system dynamically learns and adapts according to changes noticed in user activities. A comparison of results in terms of several anomalous activities detected with the proposed incremental training model and a baseline non-incremental model using three different datasets can be seen in Fig. 3, where the x-axis represented the day of a month when we trained the model and the y-axis represents the number of anomalies detected.

In Fig. 3 (a) we present the results of 1Month_30min dataset. A comparative analysis performed between proposed incremental approach with a baseline non-incremental using iForest model as discussed in Section IV shows that several detected anomalies significantly decreases with increasing the number of incremental training and it converges to a steady after fourth incremental training ( i.e., after 12 days) using the proposed approach. However, in the non-incremental settings, the number of anomalies detected was found to be inconsistent and unpredictable.

Further, we analyzed and compared the results with two datasets, i.e., 1Month_1H and 1Month_2H. The results presented in Fig. 3 (b) and (c) shows that although the detected number of anomalies slightly decreases using the proposed model, there are some fluctuations since the incremental model requires more iterations of training and more data to learn and adapt with user activities data collected in a longer period of time ( i.e., large time window). Also, there are larger changes and fluctuations in Fig. 3 (b) and (c) since training with the new data only poses a concept drift. The results show that the small-time window provides more insight into user activities as large-time windows are more diverse to changes.

An in-depth analysis has been performed using the proposed online incremental approach in terms of whether all the anomalies detected by the $i+1$th model are from the anomalies detected in the previous $i$th model or new anomalies. For this, we analyzed the results obtained after conducting experiments on all three datasets and presented them as a summary in Table II. Each row of the table has three components, first, no. of anomaly detected, second no. of new anomalies anomaly detected, and an arrowhead/hyphen. For example, the first row of the 3rd iteration column has $11(0) \downarrow$ where 11 is a no. of anomaly detected in a 3rd machine, (0) indicates no new anomaly detected in this machine that is all the detected 11 anomalies are from the previous machine (2nd machine), and $\downarrow$ represents detected no. of anomalies are less (decreased) than the previous model. Similarly, $\uparrow$ represents no. of anomalies increases, - (hyphen) means no change. Color 'green' shows a machine is performing well as expected, 'blue' color indicates a machine is good but not desired because the machine detected lower no. of anomalies, but it also detected new anomalies. 'Red' color represents a machine performing not well. Results show that our incremental model perfectly leaned as expected with 1Month_30min datasets since there are neither more anomalies detected nor new anomalies in each consecutive training. However, the non-incremental model has many fluctuations. With all three-datasets, our proposed incremental iForest model shows significantly good performance as compared to the baseline non-incremental iForest model.

## VI. Conclusion

The biggest challenge nowadays is to identify the malicious activities which are increasing due to inter-connectivity among users and the devices. Also, it has been noticed due to this global pandemic, a greater number of users are accessing office networks for communication, transferring files sitting back at home. This has resulted in an upsurge in hidden attacks as malicious users are trying to access the system in one way or another. In this dynamic changing environment where everything is non-stationery and data distribution is changing faster, building a user profile helps in identifying the intentions of these users and taking timely action to prevent further harm. To overcome this issue, the following are the key findings obtained from this study which can help us build a user profiling system that adapts and raise an alert when there is a slight deviation in the system:

- We proposed an online incremental anomaly detection-based user profiling model for SIEM systems. The pro-

TABLE II: SUMMARY OF THE COMPARATIVE PERFORMANCE ANALYSIS OF RESULTS.

| Model | Datasets | # of anomalies, # of new anomalies after each (re)training | | | | | | | | | |
|---|---|---|---|---|---|---|---|---|---|---|---|
| | | 1st | 2nd | 3rd | 4th | 5th | 6th | 7th | 8th | 9th | 10th |
| **Our Incremental using iForest Model** | 1month_30min | 12 | 12 (0) - | 11 (0) ↓ | 10 (0) ↓ | 10 (0) - | 10 (0) - | 10 (0) - | 10 (0) - | 10 (0) - | 10 (0) - |
| | 1month_1h | 24 | 23 (2) ↓ | 21 (0) ↓ | 24 (4) ↑ | 23 (0) ↓ | 22 (0) ↓ | 23 (1) ↑ | 24 (2) ↑ | 23 (0) ↓ | 25 (2) ↑ |
| | 1month_2h | 36 | 31 (1) ↓ | 30 (1) ↓ | 29 (1) ↓ | 26 (0) ↓ | 26 (0) - | 25 (0) ↓ | 26 (1) ↑ | 24 (0) ↓ | 28 (4) ↑ |
| **Non-Incremental using iForest Model** | 1month_30min | 12 | 9 (0) ↓ | 12 (3) ↑ | 11 (0) ↓ | 12 (2) ↑ | 9 (0) ↓ | 10 (1) ↑ | 12 (2) ↑ | 14 (2) ↑ | 13 (0) ↓ |
| | 1month_1h | 24 | 22 (2) ↓ | 29 (11) ↑ | 34 (12) ↑ | 24 (1) ↓ | 27 (7) ↑ | 25 (3) ↓ | 21 (2) ↓ | 21 (6) - | 34 (16) ↑ |
| | 1month_2h | 36 | 26 (1) ↓ | 39 (16) ↑ | 30 (3) ↓ | 20 (1) ↓ | 32 (17) ↑ | 35 (12) ↑ | 36 (7) ↑ | 26 (2) ↓ | 33 (9) ↑ |

posed model dynamically learns from the user activities and updates the model incrementally over time.

- We validated the performance of the proposed incremental approach against the non-incremental model in terms of adaptability of user activities for 3-different datasets.
- The experimental results proved that our proposed incremental model outperformed its counterpart model.
- Our findings suggest that the proposed model should be applied more opportunistically to profile users as a SIEM system component.

## ACKNOWLEDGEMENT

The authors graciously acknowledge the funding support from the NSERC CRD Grant, Tier 1 Canada Research Chair, and IBM to Dr. Ghorbani.

## REFERENCES


[1] I. Apostol, M. Preda, C. Nila, and I. Bica, "IoT Botnet Anomaly Detection Using Unsupervised Deep Learning," *Electronics*, vol. 10, no. 16, p. 1876, 2021.

[2] B. Böse, B. Avasarala, S. Tirthapura, Y.-Y. Chung, and D. Steiner, "Detecting insider threats using radish: A system for real-time anomaly detection in heterogeneous data streams," *IEEE Systems Journal*, vol. 11, no. 2, pp. 471–482, 2017.

[3] A. S. Das, M. Datar, A. Garg, and S. Rajaram, "Google news personalization: scalable online collaborative filtering," in *Proceedings of the 16th international conference on World Wide Web*, 2007, pp. 271–280.

[4] S. Hu, Z. Xiao, Q. Rao, and R. Liao, "An anomaly detection model of user behavior based on similarity clustering," in *2018 IEEE 4th Information Technology and Mechatronics Engineering Conference (ITOEC)*. IEEE, 2018, pp. 835–838.

[5] Joblib, "Joblib: Running Python Functions as Pipeline Jobs," 2021, https://joblib.readthedocs.io/en/latest/, Accessed on 2021-09-10.

[6] J. Johnson, "digital- population-worldwide," 2021, urlhttps://www.statista.com/statistics/617136/digital-population-worldwide/, Accessed on 2018-09-20.

[7] J. Kim, M. Park, H. Kim, S. Cho, and P. Kang, "Insider threat detection based on user behavior modeling and anomaly detection algorithms," *Applied Sciences*, vol. 9, no. 19, p. 4018, 2019.

[8] A. H. Lashkari, M. Chen, and A. A. Ghorbani, "A survey on user profiling model for anomaly detection in cyberspace," *Journal of Cyber Security and Mobility*, pp. 75–112, 2019.

[9] F. T. Liu, K. M. Ting, and Z.-H. Zhou, "Isolation forest," in *2008 eighth ieee international conference on data mining*. IEEE, 2008, pp. 413–422.

[10] W. Ma, K. Sartipi, and D. Bender, "Knowledge-driven user behavior pattern discovery for system security enhancement," *International Journal of Software Engineering and Knowledge Engineering*, vol. 26, no. 03, pp. 379–404, 2016.

[11] S. Morgan, "Cybercrime to cost the world 10.5 trillion annually by 2025," 2021, https://cybersecurityventures.com/hackerpocalypse-cybercrime-report-2016/, Accessed on 2018-09-21.

[12] R. C. Ripan, I. H. Sarker, M. M. Anwar, M. Furhad, F. Rahat, M. M. Hoque, M. Sarfraz *et al.*, "An isolation forest learning based outlier detection approach for effectively classifying cyber anomalies," in *International Conference on Hybrid Intelligent Systems*. Springer, 2020, pp. 270–279.

[13] F. Shaman, B. Ghita, N. Clarke, and A. Alruban, "User profiling based on application-level using network metadata," in *2019 7th International Symposium on Digital Forensics and Security (ISDFS)*, 2019, pp. 1–8.

[14] B. Sharma, P. Pokharel, and B. Joshi, "User Behavior Analytics for Anomaly Detection Using LSTM Autoencoder-Insider Threat Detection," in *Proceedings of the 11th International Conference on Advances in Information Technology*, 2020, pp. 1–9.

[15] M. Shashanka, M.-Y. Shen, and J. Wang, "User and entity behavior analytics for enterprise security," in *2016 IEEE International Conference on Big Data (Big Data)*. IEEE, 2016, pp. 1867–1874.

[16] F. Shoeleh, M. Erfani, S. S. Hasanabadi, D.-P. Le, A. H. Lashkari, and A. Ghorbani, "User Profiling on Universal Data Insights tool on IBM Cloud Pak for Security," in *Proceedings of the 18th International Conference on Privacy, Security and Trust (PST2021)*, 2021.

[17] M. Singh, B. M. Mehtre, and S. Sangeetha, "User behavior profiling using ensemble approach for insider threat detection," in *2019 IEEE 5th International Conference on Identity, Security, and Behavior Analysis (ISBA)*. IEEE, 2019, pp. 1–8.

[18] Sklearn, "Scikit-Learn: Machine Learning in Python," 2021, https://scikit-learn.org/stable/, Accessed on 2021-08-18.

[19] K. Sugiyama, K. Hatano, and M. Yoshikawa, "Adaptive web search based on user profile constructed without any effort from users," in *Proceedings of the 13th international conference on World Wide Web*, 2004, pp. 675–684.

[20] I. I. A. Sulayman and A. Ouda, "Data analytics methods for anomaly detection: Evolution and recommendations," in *2018 International Conference on Signal Processing and Information Security (ICSPIS)*. IEEE, 2018, pp. 1–4.

[21] ——, "User modeling via anomaly detection techniques for user authentication," in *2019 IEEE 10th Annual Information Technology, Electronics and Mobile Communication Conference (IEMCON)*. IEEE, 2019, pp. 0169–0176.

[22] ——, "Designing security user profiles via anomaly detection for user authentication," in *2020 International Symposium on Networks, Computers and Communications (ISNCC)*. IEEE, 2020, pp. 1–6.

[23] B. Veloso, B. Malheiro, J. C. Burguillo, J. Foss, and J. Gama, "Personalised dynamic viewer profiling for streamed data," in *World Conference on Information Systems and Technologies*. Springer, 2018, pp. 501–510.

[24] J. Yu, F. Liu, and H. Zhao, "Building user profile based on concept and relation for web personalized services," in *International Conference on Innovation and Information Management*. Citeseer, 2012.

[25] Z. Zamanian, A. Feizollah, N. B. Anuar, L. B. M. Kiah, K. Srikanth, and S. Kumar, "User profiling in anomaly detection of authorization logs," in *Computational Science and Technology*. Springer, 2019, pp. 59–65.

# Modeling Damage Paths and Repairing Objects in Critical Infrastructure Systems

Justin Burns, Brajendra Panda, and Thanh Bui
Computer Science and Computer Engineering Department
University of Arkansas
Fayetteville, AR 72701 USA
email: {jdb083, bpanda, tbui}@uark.edu

*Abstract*—**Recently, critical infrastructure systems have become increasingly vulnerable to attacks on their data systems. If an attacker is successful in breaching a system's defenses, it is imperative that operations are restored to the system as quickly as possible. This research focuses on damage assessment and recovery following an attack. We review work done in both database protection and critical infrastructure protection. Then, we propose a model using a graph construction to show the cascading affects within a system after an attack. We also present an algorithm that uses our graph to compute an optimal recovery plan that prioritizes the most important damaged components first so that the vital modules of the system become functional as soon as possible. This allows for the most critical operations of a system to resume while recovery for less important components is still being performed.**

***Keywords-critical infrastructure; damage assessment; recovery.***

## I. INTRODUCTION

Critical infrastructure systems are those that are considered extremely critical to the functioning of a government or a country. As described in [1], critical infrastructures are like the vital organs of a body that need to perform their own roles for the human body to function efficiently and painlessly. The US Department of Homeland Security [2] declares that such systems are "so vital to the United States that their incapacity or destruction would have a debilitating impact on our physical or economic security or public health or safety." Therefore, the protection and smooth functioning of our nation's critical infrastructures are indispensable and cannot be ignored.

These systems are becoming prime targets of attackers – primarily state actors – and a major attack on one can cripple the economy of the victim nation. These systems are also more likely to be connected to the internet now to provide benefits like cost reduction (where large systems can be remotely managed over the public network), increased capability (by providing sufficient computing resources for infrastructure hardware with less capability power), and improved efficiency and transaction speed. This connectivity unfortunately makes it easier for attackers to hack into these systems. Consider the New York Times report about the attack on Colonial Pipeline [3]. While the details of the attack are not yet disclosed, a group of cybercriminals were able to compromise data systems using the internet, which resulted in Colonial Pipeline shutting down their pipeline. This outage affected mass transit and other industries across the entire U.S. East Coast and exposed a lack of preparation for such a crisis. This illustrates how an external system can have a relationship with a critical infrastructure system and how such relationships can be exploited to carry out an attack.

It is clear from past incidents and recent reports ([4]-[7]), to cite just a few) that attacks on critical infrastructures are occurring frequently, which indicates that prevention mechanisms are not enough to stop them. Thus, it is of utmost importance to aggressively prepare for post attack activities, which include damage assessment and recovery mechanisms that are critical to making the affected systems available at full functioning mode as soon as possible. This research aims at meeting this important goal.

We propose a framework that models damage spread within a set of data objects based on object dependencies and prioritizes making repairs to the most critical objects first. The framework is based on some of the models explored in critical infrastructure protection and uses a version of previously proposed repair methods that is modified to focus on meeting specific goals when determining the order in which repairs are made.

The rest of the paper is organized as follows. Section 2 offers some work performed in this area. Section 3 defines the problem that we aim to build our model for. We provide details on our model in section 4, which includes three subsections to explain our definitions, model description, and algorithm. Section 5 concludes our work.

## II. RELATED WORKS

This paper aims to examine methods and frameworks used for database and critical infrastructure protection and apply it towards protecting a set of data objects. This section describes some of the publications that are relevant to our proposed framework. One of the major works on damage assessment and recovery within a database uses data dependency to find data affected by an attack to optimize recovery [8]. While this method relies on the direct relationships between data items, an alternate model to recover data from an attack instead uses the transaction log for assessment [9].

Kotzanikolaou et. al describe a model in [10] that assists in risk assessment for possible scenarios that can result in cascading failures within a CI system. For critical infrastructures with data-rich operations, the use of Cyber-Physical Systems can cause new vulnerabilities as described in [11]. Their model analyzes threats that can appear due to these vulnerabilities and analyzes the potential cascading damage they can cause. System dynamics modeling can also be used to analyze disruptive events to characterize such disruptions to critical infrastructure by risk assessment and various impact factors as shown in [12].

Rehak et. al [13] model an infrastructure system as elements and linkages with different types of relationships establishing dependencies and interdependencies. They note that these elements can have varying criticality, causing some elements to cascade more damage into the system than others in the event of a failure. This work is important because by establishing criticality, they quantify damage within a system. We use this concept of criticality later in this paper to direct the optimal repair path of data objects.

We also consider models that assist with recovery during an attack. In [14], an algorithm is proposed to restore damaged element paths by recursively breaking down demand flows into simpler problems. They use a centrality metric to rank damaged nodes and determine which ones should be repaired first and expand on the use of centrality to make repair decisions in further work [15]. We use the concept of centrality to rank data objects in a case where two or more are equally critical. In our algorithm, we also utilize their method of simplifying damage paths to find the fastest route to restoring intermediate data objects. However, the novelty of our approach is twofold: we must repair all components within the system because data objects cannot have computations rerouted, unlike the network components in the work we have reviewed, and we aim to restore the most important components first so that their functions can be restored while repairs to the system are still ongoing.

## III. Problem Definitions

In the occasion when an adversary information attack succeeds, the victim must have the capability to degrade gracefully and recover damaged data and/or services in real-time if it is to survive. It is necessary to immediately carry out damage assessment and recovery process in order to bring the systems to working states. Otherwise, the damage would spread to other unaffected systems that are interconnected. This happens when a valid user or an unaffected system module reads a damaged object during its computation and updates another object based on the compromised value, causing the latter damaged as well. As time goes on, more and more objects become affected in this manner causing the spread of damage to fan out through the system quickly.

For damage assessment and recovery purpose, information about all processes that have been executed must be stored in the log (more on this presented later). This will help in determining the relationships among the processes, thus helping in establishing the damage trail. Moreover, during recovery, the operations of processes that have spread the damage have to be undone and then redone in order to produce correct states of affected objects. The problems with existing systems are: (1) They do not store process execution information in the log, and they purge the log periodically, (2) Their recovery mechanisms are not designed to undo the effects of executed processes, (3) The size of the log, as it must not be purged, will make it almost impossible to continue the recovery process in real-time, and (4) During the damage assessment and recovery process, the system remains unavailable to users. This delay induces a denial-of-service attack, which is highly undesirable in time-critical applications that the critical infrastructures are designed to provide. Due to massive amount of data in the log that needs to be processed, the problem becomes even worse.

The goal of this research is to develop fast, accurate, and efficient damage assessment and recovery techniques so that critical information systems not only survive the attacks gracefully but will continue to operate providing as many vital services and functions as possible even before the system is fully recovered. In the next section, we explain how our model can accomplish this.

## IV. The Model

In this section, we describe our model in detail. The first subsection defines important graphs and metrics that we use for our model. In the next subsection, we describe how the model is built and is used to determine an optimal recovery plan. Finally, we describe the algorithm we use to implement our model.

### A. Definitions

We first define the concept of information flow in a system. This also defines dependencies among various objects in the system and is used in our graph-based model.

**Definition 1:** Given two objects $O_i$ and $O_j$ in a system, if the value of $O_j$ is calculated using the value of $O_i$, we say that there is information flow from $O_i$ to $O_j$. Thus, $O_j$ is said to be dependent on $O_i$ and is denoted as $O_i \rightarrow O_j$.

The above definition helps in determining the spread of damage in the system. That is, if an object is damaged, then all its dependent objects will be considered damaged. During recovery, the parent (pre-cursor) object must be recovered before any of its dependent objects can be recovered.

Next, we define a graph containing the set of objects and all possible paths among them. We call it Possible Paths graph and it spans the entire system of objects and all dependency paths among them. An example of this graph is shown by Figure 1(a).

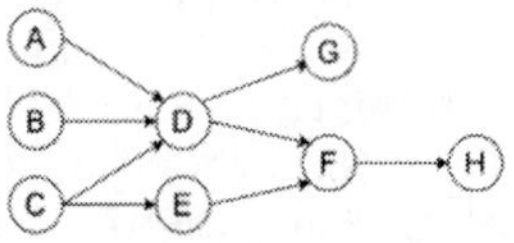


**Definition 2:** Consider a system containing the set of objects $O$. The ***Possible Paths Graph*** (*PPG*) is built by having a node $N_i$ for each object in $O$. There exists an edge $E_{ij}$ from $N_i$ to $N_j$ in the PPG if there is a possibility that information may flow from $N_i$ to $N_j$, that is, $N_j$ may be modified based on the value of $N_i$.

The purpose of building a PPG is that it will help during the damage assessment preparation phase. By assuming the point of attack one can identify the set of items that may be affected consequently. Thus, security officers can be prepared for different types of eventuality.

The second set of objects contains the actual paths that were used to make changes in the system within a specified time span, which for the purposes of the third graph that will be defined, is usually the time passed since an object has been damaged. This set is represented by the Active Paths Graph (APG), and all objects and dependencies in this set exist in the PPG. This graph will help in determining the damage flow in case of an attack. Given an initial attack point (an object), one can determine which objects in the system may be affected by the attack and which ones will not be. Therefore, the ability of the system to carry out its intended functions can be calculated. That is, during the recovery process, the set of damaged objects will be made unavailable while the rest can be made accessible. Knowing which objects will remain unaffected, one will be able to identify what services the system will be able to offer while the recovery continues.

**Definition 3:** The ***Active Paths Graph*** (*APG*) contains nodes $N$ and edges $E$ such that for every $N_i \in N$ and every $E_{ij} \in$ E, both $N_i$ and $E_{ij}$ are also present in PPG, and $E_{ij}$ illustrates an actual information flow; that is $N_j$ was updated based on the value of $N_i$.

Figure 1b. The Active Paths Graph (APG)

Figure 1(b) provides an example of an Active Paths Graph and as can be seen it is a sub-graph of Figure 1(a). As discussed before, once an initial attack point is determined, the APG will help in accurately determining the damage flow and the set of objects affected by the attack. As discussed before, as time goes on, more and more objects will be affected as new objects will be updated based on the value of an affected object. Thus, to stop the spread of damage, all affected objects must be quickly identified and taken offline as soon as possible. This can be achieved by doing a flow assessment using the APG. This leads to the concept of actual damage spread path showing exactly which objects were affected by an attack. If a system is damaged, we represent the spread of damage as a third set of objects, the Damage Spread Graph (DSG). The set of objects and dependencies in this graph must exist within the APG, as damage spread occurs when objects make changes based on their dependencies. Like how the APG is a subsection of the PPG, the DSG is a subsection of the APG. Figure 1(c) is an example of what a damage path may look like. It is important to note that over time, a damaged object will always cascade its damage down to dependent nodes included in the APG. Definition 4 formally defines the DSG.

**Definition 4:** A ***Damage Spread Graph*** (DSG) contains nodes $N$ and edges $E$ such that for every $N_i \in N$ and every $E_{ij} \in$ E, both $N_i$ and $E_{ij}$ are also present in APG and every node in $N$ is damaged through an attack on the system.
Moreover, an edge $E_{ij}$ depicts that $N_i$ was damaged first and then $N_j$ was damaged through the flow of information from $N_i$ to $N_j$.

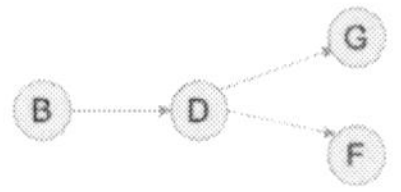


Figure 1c: The Damage Spread Graph (DSG)

Note that the edges between two objects may be bidirectional or recursive. For example, if an object $O_j$ can have a dependency on object $O_j$ and vice versa, then there will be a bidirectional edge between $O_j$ and $O_j$. Similarly, if an object can be dependent on itself, it will result in a recursive graph. To clarify, let us consider an object "salary". When an employee receives an increment that is based on a percentage of the current salary of the employee, it causes the new salary to be dependent on the old salary and is depicted by using an edge from salary to salary itself. However, it must be noted that, for simplicity, we use neither bidirectional nor recursive edges in APG or DSG. Rather, when an object is modified, we note that as a new version of the object, thus creating a new node for the object with the version number.

To minimize the time needed to restore the most important objects within a system of object dependencies, we also define criteria used to determine the order in which repairs are made:

**Definition 5:** The ***criticality*** of a node $N$ is its predetermined level of importance to the system's functions. This must be predetermined for the flexibility of the model to fit various systems and align the model with the goals of each specific system. For example, one system may need to prioritize certain components that other systems do not. The criticality of a component can be measured by various characteristics such as the intensity or scope of an impact caused by its failure as described in [13].

We assign a positive whole number to each node $N$ to represent criticality. A lower assigned value indicates higher criticality. For example, a node $N_i$ with a criticality of 2 would be considered more important than a node $N_j$ with a criticality of 4. It is important to note that criticality values are not unique, meaning multiple nodes can have the same criticality value. When that happens, we use the following metric in the next definition to serve as a first "tiebreaker".

**Definition 6:** Objects that have more damaged dependencies take longer to repair. Therefore, the ***repair time*** of a node $N$ is defined as how many inward-flowing edges $E^i$ it is receiving damage from.

When two or more objects are assigned the same importance, we choose to first repair the one that has a lower repair time. For example, consider two nodes $N_i$ and $N_j$ that are equally critical. If $N_i$ needs 5 other nodes repaired to repair it, and $N_j$ needs 3 other nodes to repair it, then we will repair $N_j$ first, because its operation can be restored more quickly than that of $N_i$.

Figure 2a. A parent node with high centrality

Figure 2b. A parent node with low centrality

**Definition 7:** The ***centrality*** of a node $N$ is the number of outward-flowing edges $E^o$ it has.

We use the above metric to decide the next object to repair when two or more are equal in both criticality and repair time. An object with a higher number of $E^o$ will have higher centrality. Figure 2a and Figure 2b show two subsections of a DSG that highlights centrality. As shown in Figure 2a, $N_4$ has three nodes that are dependent on it: $N_1$, $N_2$, and $N_3$, while as Figure 2b depicts, $N_6$ only has a single node $N_5$ dependent on it. Assume that the repair algorithm has repaired the parent node(s) of $N_4$ and that of $N_6$. To clarify the situation, $N_4$ and $N_6$ need not have the same parents; it is just that both are in line to be repaired next. In this scenario, repairing $N_4$ before $N_6$ reduces the repair time for the three dependent nodes of $N_4$ instead of only one of $N_6$, which can make future repairs be performed faster. Therefore, $N_4$ is considered to have a higher centrality than $N_6$.

## B. Model Description

The model uses the three graphs defined in the previous section to construct a representation of a given system and its sustained damage from the time of the initial attack. The PPG is a preprocessed map of all components and dependency paths within a system. We assume that we know how much time has passed since the initial attack and build the APG by including components and dependency paths that were used in a transaction log in that period. By knowing the component where the initial attack occurred, we build the DSG by tracing the damage through the transaction log. For damage to spread from one component to the next, it must follow two criteria: 1) there is a damaged node $N_i$ that has an edge $E_{ij}$ flowing from it to node $N_j$ and 2) $E_{ij}$ is used for a transaction while $N_i$ is damaged. For the DSG to exist, the initial attack must occur within the APG, otherwise there is no cascading damage.

The goal of the model is to find the optimal sequence of repairs to restore the most important operations of a system as quickly as possible. We use the metrics defined in the previous section to decide which components should be repaired first. The first metric is criticality – the most critical components must be restored first to resume important operations. However, these components may also be dependent on other components that are damaged. These components must be repaired first before the base component can be repaired. At this point, the same problem is applied to the dependency components, and the most critical one is chosen first. If there is a tie, then components with a lower repair time are picked first. For example, a component that has two damaged parent components will be prioritized over a component with three or more damaged parent components if both components are equally critical.

Figure 3. Recovery sequence decision

To clarify, let us consider the graph presented in Figure 3. As shown in the figure, nodes $N_1$, $N_2$, and $N_3$ are dependent on $N_4$. Assume that the damage assessment method identified $N_4$ as damaged; thus, nodes $N_1$, $N_2$, and $N_3$ are also identified as damaged. During the recovery process, $N_4$ was recovered before the other three nodes. However, since it has three dependents all of which are damaged, the question is, which one should be repaired first. As our goal is to have the vital functions of the system to be made available before the other operations, our algorithm would choose the node among $N_1$, $N_2$, and $N_3$ having the most criticality.

## C. The Algorithm

First, we discuss the primary objective of our work. Let us consider the notations used in the following table:

TABLE I. NOTATIONS

| Notations | Descriptions |
|---|---|
| $P = (V, E)$ | Possible Path Graph |
| $A = (V_A, E_A)$ | Active Path Graph ( $V_A \subseteq V, E_A \subseteq E$) |
| $D = (V_D, E_D)$ | Damage Spread Graph ( $V_D \subseteq V_A, E_D \subseteq E_A$) |
| $D = (V_C, E_C)$ | Critical Node Graph ( $V_C \subseteq V_D, E_C \subseteq E_D$) |
| $\delta_{ij}$ | Decision to fix edge $i$ to $j$ |
| $\delta_i$ | Decision to fix node $i$ |
| $t_i$ | Time to fix node $i$ |
| $c_i$ | Centrality of node $i$ |
| $P_{ij}$ | Dependency indicator of node $i$ and $j$ |

Our objective is to find $\min \sum_{i \in V_D} t_i \delta_i$ subject to

$$\delta_i \sum_{j \in V_C} P_{ij} \le \sum_{j \in V_C} P_{ij} \delta_j \quad \forall i, j \in V_C \tag{1}$$

$$\delta_i c_i \ge \sum_{(i,j) \in E_C} \delta_{ij} \quad \forall i \in V_C \tag{2}$$

$$P_{ij} \in \{0,1\} \quad \forall i, j \in V_C \tag{3}$$

$$\delta_i, \delta_{ij} \in \{0,1\} \quad \forall i \in V_C, (i,j) \in E_C \tag{4}$$

That is, the goal is to minimize the time required to fix all critical nodes subjected to conditional constraints of the system. To make sure that each preceding nodes of $i$ are fixed before node $i$ being processed, condition (1) is used. For example, if there is a node $j$ connecting to $i$ but in a prequel order, the sum product of all nodes $j$ status and dependency indicator $P_{ij}$ should be greater or equal than the product of sum of all dependency indicator $P_{ij}$ with node $i$. To make sure that there would not be more out-going flows than the given capability of node $i$, equation (2) is imposed to make sure the total out-going edge would not surpass the centrality of node $i$. Conditions (3) and (4) were built to impose the binary attribute of the dependency indicator $P_{ij}$, the decision whether to fix node $i$ or edge from node $i$ to node $j$.

The algorithms provided in this section use the model described in the previous section to compute the optimal order of repairs to restore the most important functions of a system first. When an attack occurs, we expect an Intrusion Detection System (IDS) to identify the attack and provide the initial point of damage. The working principles of IDSs are not within the scope of this work and so, not described here.

After receiving notification from an IDS, a precise damage assessment is performed. If the damage assessment process is unable to make accurate assessment, i.e., in case a damaged node is not correctly identified, it and its dependent nodes, which are also damaged, will remain unrecovered. This will result in valid users or procedures reading them and spreading damage by updating other objects, as discussed earlier. For a detailed discussion on damage assessment, one may review [8] and [9], which were developed particularly for database systems. However, the methods are still applicable to critical infrastructure systems. Below we provide a basic mechanism to carry out the assessment.

Damage assessment begins with the APG, which shows the actual dependency relationships among the objects in the system (Note that the APG can be built as transactions are executed and dependencies are established among various nodes of the PPG). Given the initial attack point, the corresponding node is then marked as damaged. This is the starting node of the DSG. Then by scanning the log from the corresponding location of the attack point, transactions that read the marked node are identified. Any objects written by those transactions are then marked as damaged in the APG. This process continues until the end of the log. Finally, all unmarked nodes and the edges showing their dependencies are removed. The resulting graph is the completed DSG.

Once damage assessment is carried out, recovery procedure must begin immediately in order to make the system operational quickly. We use Algorithm 1 as the main procedure to initialize an object set for repairs. The algorithm starts by initializing the set of damaged objects $O$. Each node $N$ within $O$ consists of a system component and its relationships with other nodes in $O$. As mentioned previously under Definition 4, some system components may have recursive or bidirectional dependencies between each other. Therefore, system components can have repeat nodes within $O$ to represent their different versions. Each node is assigned values for criticality, repair time, and centrality. Using those metrics, the algorithm determines an initial target node $N_0$ based on criticality. If there are two or more nodes with the highest criticality, then the node with the lower repair time is selected. In the event of another tie, the node with higher centrality is selected. Further ties are broken by random selection. $N_0$, along with $O$ and the repair queue $Q$, are used to make the first call to the recursive function Algorithm 1.1 at step 4.5. Algorithm 1 proceeds until $O$ is completely empty, and then the repair queue is finalized, and $Q$ is printed.

As previously discussed, a node must have its parent nodes repaired before it can be considered eligible for repairs. Algorithm 1.1 ensures that nodes are scheduled for repairs in the proper order while still adhering to the rules set for determining priority. It does this by using a while loop to check the currently selected node $N$ for repair eligibility. If $N$ is eligible for repairs, then it is removed from $O$ and $Q$ is updated, then returned. If $N$ is not eligible, then $O'$, a subsection of $O$ made up of all dependency paths above the currently selected node is created and used to find the next highest priority node $N'$ within $O'$. Algorithm 1.1 is recursively called using $N'$ and $O'$, which can either result in the node's repair or another node being selected for repair again. The recursive nature of this algorithm ensures that each time a decision needs to be made on which node needs to be repaired next, it will prioritize criticality and efficiency among all the nodes that can be repaired at any given step. In this way, the bulk of the work done by the algorithm is choosing the next object for repair within each iteration. Each function call will result in one object being repaired and $n - 1$ additional function calls, where $n$ is the number of nodes within the set of nodes being passed. Since repaired objects need to be removed from the DSG, function calls will need to update and return the global DSG and $Q$.

**Algorithm 1: Initialization for object set repair**
**Result:** Queue of objects ordered by repair priority
1 Initialize set of damaged objects $O$
2 Preprocess object priority using criticality, repair time, and centrality
3 Initialize repair queue $Q$
4 while *$O$ has damaged nodes remaining*
  4.1 Select the highest critical node(s) $N$ within $O$
  4.2 if *Two or more nodes are tied for highest criticality*
    4.2.1 Select the node(s) $N$ with the lowest repair time $R$ within $O$
  4.3 if *Two or more nodes are tied for lowest repair time*
    4.3.1 Select the node(s) $N$ with the highest centrality within $O$
  4.4 if *Two or mode nodes are tied for highest centrality*
    4.4.1 Select a single node at random from those still tied
  4.5 Update repair queue($N_0$, $O$, $Q$) → $Q$
5 Print $Q$

**Algorithm 1.1: Recursive repair function**
**Result:** Schedules a node $N$ for repairs and returns the updated repair queue $Q$
1 Update repair queue(*Selected node N, object set O, repair queue Q*):
2 while *Current object has unrepaired dependencies*:
  2.1 Create subset of damaged nodes $O'$ of all nodes $N'$ and edges $E'$ that $N$ is dependent on
  2.2 Select the highest critical node(s) $N'$ within $O'$
  2.3 if *Two or more nodes are tied for highest criticality*
    2.3.1 Select the node(s) $N'$ with the lowest

repair time *R* within *O*
2.4 if *Two or more nodes are tied for lowest repair time*
2.4.1 Select the node(s) $N'$ with the highest centrality within *O*
2.5 if *Two or mode nodes are tied for highest centrality*
2.5.1 Select a single node at random from those still tied
2.6 Update repair queue($N'_0$, $O'$, $Q$) $\rightarrow Q$
2.7 Remove the most recent object in repair queue from *O*
3 Repair *N*
4 Add *N* to *Q*
5 Return *Q*

The algorithm produces a list of system nodes in the order in which they should be repaired. Recovery procedure then continues to the next step to begin repairs on the system. It is important to note that while repairs are simulated by the algorithm, the process for repairing the actual components of the system is not within the scope of this work.

## V. CONCLUSION

In this research, we have presented a method to repair data objects that prioritizes quick recovery for the most important components of a system. This allows for the partial restoration of functions during the recovery process with an emphasis on restoring service to the most necessary functions. This was first done by building out three graphs to represent the entire system, what changes the system made after an attack, and the cascading damage as a result of those changes. Next, we developed an algorithm to optimally schedule repairs by using those graphs to find damage paths that affect the most critical nodes of a system and calculate the fastest repair order to fully restore those nodes. Our work is most applicable to protecting critical infrastructure systems where services need to be restored as quickly as possible to avoid economic or societal disruptions.

Further work includes considering the frequency at which an object is used to update its dependencies. Objects that are updated at a higher frequency would be prioritized as more important. A method to select the order of repairs for non-critical objects after all critical objects have been repaired is also needed. Finally, a performance analysis of this model is required to be carried out to evaluate the model under various conditions.

## ACKNOWLEDGEMENT

This work has been supported in part by grant H98230-20-1-0419 issued by the National Security Agency as part of the National Centers of Academic Excellence in Cybersecurity's mission to expand cybersecurity research and education for the Nation.

## REFERENCES

[1] E. Viganò, M. Loi. and E. Yaghmaei, "Cybersecurity of Critical Infrastructure", In Christen M., Gordijn B., Loi M. (eds), The Ethics of Cybersecurity, The International Library of Ethics, Law and Technology, vol 21, Springer

[2] *Critical Infrastructure Security*: https://www.dhs.gov/topic/critical-infrastructure-security. [retrieved: October 2021]

[3] D. E. Sanger and N. Perlroth, (2021, May 14). "Pipeline Attack Yields Urgent Lessons About U.S. Cybersecurity", https://www.nytimes.com/2021/05/14/us/politics/pipeline-hack.html. [retrieved: October 2021]

[4] A. Anastasios, "Is the Electric Grid Ready to Respond to Increased Cyber Threats?", https://www.tripwire.com/state-of-security/ics-security/electric-grid-ready-increased-cyber-threats/. [retrieved: October 2021]

[5] B. Barrett, "An Unprecedented Cyberattack Hit US Power Utilities", https://www.wired.com/story/power-grid-cyberattack-facebook-phone-numbers-security-news/. [retrieved: October 2021]

[6] K. O'Flaherty, "U.S. Government Issues Powerful Cyberattack Warning As Gas Pipeline Forced Into Two Day Shut Down https://www.forbes.com/sites/kateoflahertyuk/2020/02/19/us-government-issues-powerful-cyberattack-warning-as-gas-pipeline-forced-into-two-day-shut-down/#5f3061645a95. [retrieved: October 2021]

[7] M. Lewis, "Cyberattack Forces Gas Pipeline Shutdown", https://www.jdsupra.com/legalnews/cyberattack-forces-gas-pipeline-shutdown-76217/ [retrieved: October 2021]

[8] B. Panda and J. Giordano, (1999) Reconstructing the Database After Electronic Attacks. In: Jajodia S. (eds) Database Security XII. IFIP — The International Federation for Information Processing, vol 14. Springer, Boston, MA.

[9] S. Patnaik and B. Panda, (2003). Transaction-Relationship Oriented Log Division for Data Recovery from Information Attacks. Journal of Database Management, 14(2), pp. 27-41.

[10] P. Kotzanikolaou, M. Theoharidou, and D. Gritzalis, (2013) Cascading Effects of Common-Cause Failures in Critical Infrastructures. In: J. Butts and S. Shenoi (eds) Critical Infrastructure Protection VII. ICCIP 2013. IFIP Advances in Information and Communication Technology, vol 417. Springer, Berlin, Heidelberg.

[11] J. Ding, Y. Atif, S. Andler, B. Lindström, and M. Jeusfeld, (2017). CPS-based Threat Modeling for Critical Infrastructure Protection. ACM SIGMETRICS Performance Evaluation Review. 45. pp. 129-132. 10.1145/3152042.3152080.

[12] E. Canzani, H. Kaufmann, and U. Lechner, (2016). Characterising Disruptive Events to Model Cascade Failures in Critical Infrastructures. 10.14236/ewic/ICS2016.11.

[13] D. Rehak, J. Markuci, M. Hromada, and K. Barcova, "Quantitative evaluation of the synergistic effects of failures in a critical infrastructure system", International Journal of Critical Infrastructure Protection, Volume 14, 2016, pp. 3-17, ISSN 1874-5482

[14] N. Bartolini, S. Ciavarella, T. F. La Porta, and S. Silvestri, "Network Recovery After Massive Failures," 2016 46th Annual IEEE/IFIP International Conference on Dependable Systems and Networks (DSN), 2016, pp. 97-108

[15] S. Ciavarella, N. Bartolini, H. Khamfroush, and T. Porta, (2017). "Progressive damage assessment and network recovery after massive failures," IEEE INFOCOM 2017 - IEEE Conference on Computer Communications, 2017, pp. 1-9.